Toward a New
Jewish Paradigm

Toward a New Jewish Paradigm

Amos Mokadi

gefen גפן
publishing house בית הוצאה לאור
JERUSALEM ◆ NEW YORK

Typesetting: Marzel A.S. – Jerusalem
Cover Design: Studio Paz, Jerusalem
Cover Photo: Tomer Ganihar

1 3 5 7 9 8 6 4 2

Gefen Publishing House
POB 36004, Jerusalem 91360, Israel
972-2-538-0247 • orders@gefenpublishing.com

Gefen Books
12 New Street Hewlett, NY 11557, USA
516-295-2805 • gefenbooks@compuserve.com

www.israelbooks.com

Printed in Israel

Send for our free catalogue

ISBN 965-229-253-2 (alk. paper)

Library of Congress Cataloging-in-Publication Data:
Mokadi, Amos [Etgar. English]
Toward a new jewish paradigm / Amos Mokadi

1. Judaism—Essence, genius, nature. 2. Jews—Identity. 3. Bible, O.T—Criticism,
interpretation, etc. 4. Judaism—Social aspects. 5. Orthodox Judaism—
Controversial literature. 6. Human ecology—Religious aspects—Judaism.
7. Judaism—20th century. I. Title.
BM565.M58413 2001 • 296—dc21 • CIP Number: 2001033705

Contents

To my father of the second Aliyah,
To my children and to all those
who stay young

"Where were you when I laid the
foundation of the earth, tell me."

Job, 38,4

Deep ecological awareness is
spiritual in its very essence.

Capra, Uncommon Wisdom

Foreword

One may question the validity of the term "Jewish paradigm" — a paradigm being an enlargement on a certain set of disciplines, as in the case of science. No one speaks of national paradigms anyway; and, since Jews nowadays claim to be a normal nation (never mind a Diaspora greater than the entire population of Israel), how can it be that the Jewish nation should possess what other nations do not? Yet, most Jews, wherever they are, even the most forsworn atheists, do insist on being different from, if not better than, all other ethnic groups. This indicates an awareness of some deep-seated traits, even principles, which are believed to be the hallmarks of Judaism since time immemorial. What lies at the heart of this at least partly conscious difference? It is, indeed, an evasive yet all-encompassing matrix, which I propose to explore in this book.

The term "Jewish" refers to two distinct entities: religion and (what I will designate here as) nationhood.

If one regards the Jewish *religion* as constituting a millennia-long paradigm, the claim to the existence of a Jewish paradigm becomes more acceptable. Various religions claim to constitute a paradigm. In recent years, in conjunction with the evolution of a new scientific paradigm, there have evolved new theological paradigms as well — the most relevant to our subject is the new breakthrough in Christian thinking, as presented in "Belonging to the Universe" by Fritjof Capra and David Steindl-Rast (Harper, San Francisco, 1991). The book contains a five-year-long dialogue conducted by the sub-atomic physicist and his counterpart, the Benedictine monk. Their discourse embraces the latest scientific, spiritual and sociological departures, springing up in all fields of research in recent years. Such a parallel *could* be drawn between science and religion, because Christianity, for one, has always constituted a philosophical discipline as well as a faith. The parallels in the dialogue draw, among others, on the new scientific discoveries, proving that, for billions of years, the main life force has been symbiosis — *not* conflict. If such were the case, the old concept of conflict being the major force in all life — as omnipresent between genders, empires, religions and races — loses its grip. In this vein, in the United States, Jewish religious thinkers have recently expounded on new Jewish paradigmatic departures. (See Reb Zalman Schachter Shalomi's "Paradigm Shift," Jason Aronson Inc., Northvale, New Jersey, 1993.)

So much for religious (or theological) paradigms. But the Jews also constitute a nation — with the State of Israel at its center. The founders of that state were pioneers who divested themselves of the old Jewish religious traditions in order to become "new Jews." Is it possible, though, that their transformation, however deep, may not have been deep *enough?* The present ominous swing in Israel toward old religious straitjacketing indicates that this indeed has been the case.

The old Jewish paradigm permeates all walks of life in Israel A parallel development with the world's new thinking, referred to above — following deep ecological and spiritual guidelines — has hardly occurred in Israel. In this book I intend to demonstrate how, despite Israel's outstanding achievements in other fields, the Israeli Jew is held back by the old Jewish paradigm from opening up to global breakthroughs, on which the future of this planet and all life on it depends.

One can query this by arguing that this cannot be so, since most Israeli Jews are not religious. Yet, our old, dominant traits have survived. The Jews' most distinct feature — in their own eyes as well as in the eyes of others — has always been an insistence on being different from all others. Consequently, when the nation of Israel has succeeded in settling within its territorial boundaries — albeit for short periods — it has always maintained a deep resistance to "normal" national attributes. This, in turn, spawned acrid fanaticism of a unique Jewish brand, which inevitably brought ruin on the heads and on the land of the Jews. This fanaticism is somewhat difficult to comprehend when considering the Jewish flair for social justice, love of wisdom and even acumen for compromise. This inexorable process, of turning fanatic when settled in our own land, is clearly manifest in Israel today and threatens to become the dominant force in our life.

Are we Jews doomed, then, to thrive forever in exile, at the same time suffering one disaster after another? My search for a new Jewish paradigm stems from the belief that the new paradigm has within it the power to overturn more than one well-entrenched truism.

Israel today seems to be the most severely physically threatened Jewish community in the world. But the threat is not only for Israel or the Jews. Mosaic Judaism was bred on strife; it is one of the world's oldest "wisdoms" practiced today. It affects emotions and ideas far beyond Israel's borders. African Americans sing of the tumbling down of the walls of Jericho, satiating their own thirst for freedom; Christians in far-away Japan regard Armageddon as the site of the Apocalypse; millions of Muslims, Jews and Christians regard Jerusalem as their own. The fragile peace in the Middle East almost daily springs at us from the front page of the New York Times.

Interestingly, the modern State of Israel has never been able to survive without massive foreign aid. My plea is that a better under-standing of Israel's deep-seated dilemmas could turn into the best kind of aid — by urging mindful Israelis out of our spiritual stagnation, and, also, by helping to solve some of the world's oldest dilemmas concerning war and peace.

Despite the growing tendency among liberal-minded non-Israelis to turn away from what concerns Israel, the world has become too small a place to believe that what happens here can fail to affect life (including Jewish life) elsewhere. The search for new-paradigm Judaism is a necessity far beyond Israel's borders.

The challenge is great. Let this book be a small but a first step along a long and arduous road.

Amos Mokadi,
Jerusalem, 2001

Chapter 1

A Proposed Mode of Inquiry

All Jews are said to share some common features, emanating from our nation's long history. We are invariably told that we have descended from the Hebrews who, thousands of years ago, crossed the Red Sea in their Exodus from slavery and, in more recent times, have, after long generations in exile, turned a scattered ethnic minority into a normal nation, established a national state, revived a dead language and made the desert bloom.

"The righteous shall fall and rise seven times," we often quote the Bible, referring to our ancient nation's ability to recover as one and rejuvenate itself. However, when we look at ourselves regardless of historical context, we soon realize that, nowadays, we have little in common with the rest of our people; that in many matters large numbers of the Jewish people are completely different from each other — be it in appearance, in general outlook on life and, most importantly, in their particular brand of Jewishness. The dividing line becomes most apparent when it comes to synagogue attendance. In Israel, secular Jews hardly ever attend, while in the Diaspora many of our secular brethren have a deep need to keep up that habit — whether for the sake of communal life or as a means of upholding their Jewishness in the only way available to them.

Faced with this persisting dilemma, Israel's parliament — most of whose members consider themselves as representatives of the most tightly knit Jewish body world-wide, i.e., the Jewish State — has never been able to come to an agreement on *who is a Jew*, despite repeated attempts in over fifty years of the Knesset's existence.

The first challenge facing us is coming to grips with an entity which clearly defies definition. What I propose, therefore, is not to seek strict definitions, but, rather, to try and reach the essence of Judaism — as a *dynamism*, not a determinate, rigid structure.

Indeed, what we will discover to be the hallmark of the contemporary paradigm, in the sense of a fresh, comprehensive mental framework, is not a set of strict definitions (although it includes part-definitions or, rather, attributes). The new scientific paradigm goes even a step further: it is fully satisfied with an *approximation* of the truth, excluding the possibility of ever attaining the *whole* truth. (In Chapter 14, I shall expand on the characteristics of the new scientific paradigm.)

There are several partisan answers to the question, *who is a Jew*. The polar opposites are the Orthodox ruling that one's mother determines one's Jewishness and, conversely, the out-and-out liberal view claiming that anyone can call him- or herself a Jew, if they so desire. Divisions over the issue of who is or is not a Jew have persisted in Judaism for thousands of years — at times to the point of exclusion of opponents.

On the whole, being a Jew indicated an affiliation to a Jewish collective. Yet some of the early Zionist pioneers went *privately* to Palestine, as a matter of pure personal choice — at the same time breaking off the yoke of the "Mitzvot" (traditional religious rulings). Did this make them any less Jewish than those who stayed behind, keeping up the Jewish religion? Obviously not. Nowadays, more than half a world away, in the United States, separate Jewish "congregations," sometimes five-to-ten strong, also follow their own brand of Judaism. My main effort, however, will center on what *unites* those who consider themselves Jewish, rather than that which *divides* them.

I have taken on this task because I felt convinced that without a comprehensive reappraisal of Judaism, we, Jews, as a living and developing human body, are in danger of becoming an appendage — not only in the eyes of the world, but, ultimately, in our own eyes as well. I do this in loving memory of my father, who, in the beginning of the last century, at the age of eighteen, cut off his side locks, emigrated privately from the distant recesses of the Austro-Hungarian Empire to the even farther recesses of Ottoman Palestine, where he literally dug beneath the stones of the barren fields for milk and honey, as was promised in the religious studies he had just rejected!

My main intent is to explore the Jew's attitude towards himself in a world whose problems become ever more intertwined at a rate unknown in the past. Not only does a rise in the price of wheat in Chicago's Corn Exchange cause hunger in Pakistan, but, also, when a million African-American Muslims gather in front of the White House in Washington, a Jew in France fears to go out to the synagogue. Pressing a button somewhere in Russia, or in Dimonah (Israel's little-spoken-of nuclear center) for that matter, could destroy extensive areas of the planet. Carbon monoxide and other gases discharged into the air by our cars and discarded air conditioners overheat the atmosphere, threatening all life on the planet. Present-day research must evaluate all phenomena in the light of this ubiquitous *interconnectedness* and, ultimately, lead one to a new way of perceiving not only a Jew, but also every human, anywhere, relating to the world around us.

Such an investigation should lend a fresh meaning (among other things) to being a Jew. We shall refrain from following the widely accepted trend of searching for the meaning of Judaism within the Jewish *religion*, although we will examine a great many of its tenets for the purpose of our investigation. Nor shall we try to arbitrarily fit the Jewish nation into the accepted criteria of a *national entity*. We have already touched on the reason for avoiding these two separate tracks: there are many Jews who are not religious, while there are many for whom their nationality is a mere derivation of their religion. But, nevertheless, they are all Jews, whether in their own eyes or in the eyes of others. We must, therefore, attain a unifying core in Judaism, either incorporating religion and nationhood or, perhaps, overriding both.

Such a "loose" inquiry has become universal today. Americans seek their roots in the Native American not because they wish to adopt his religion or nationality, but for a totally different reason. The way the American Indian relates to the universe is based on values which differ from those which prompted Europeans to conquer the American continent, exploit it ruthlessly over the centuries, and then continue to plunder natural and human resources all over the world to maintain their so-called American standard of living. Today it is becoming increasingly clear that there is much to learn from the way our forebears related to the earth — a way of *reciprocity*, of a deep grasp (however "primitive") of the fact that air and water are precious resources that must be respected and of awareness that we must not recklessly exploit and abuse them.

This understanding is a basic tenet of the new paradigm, and is of necessity, the foundation of this study as well.

The existing old paradigm, not only the Jewish old paradigm, views its own group-ego as opposed to all others. The fact that such a view has become politically incorrect gives one hope; but economic thinking still allows many of us to regard the earth and most of life on it as something to be exploited — as articulated both in the Book of Genesis and in the writings of the European philosophers of the sixteenth and seventeenth centuries. It is not long since the stranger, too, was mostly one to compete with, fight against, and even annihilate. And while, by the end of the last millennium, many political systems did not openly abide by such tenets, the residuals of the old paradigm still reign. Proponents of the new thinking insist that it must become clear and paramount to all that the entire universe and the life in it are a *totality*, within which each element is in partnership with, and responsible for, the others.

Native Israelis — normally so quick on the uptake — are, in this case, curiously slow in joining this new thinking. This slowness constitutes an enigma, which we are out to unravel (see Chapter 13). But there is one exonerating factor that should be mentioned at this early stage.

Despite having created universal values for itself and the world, the Jewish nation has remained a small minority, whose history has been shadowed by the threat of annihilation. Even today, the Jewish State is not free from threats to its existence. In other words, our constant state of fear, whatever its causes, has not yet been alleviated. Most Israelis have not had a genuine chance, nor been accorded the sense of *liberty*, necessary to devote their attention to the welfare of the planet.

Yet, at this moment in history, the survival instinct must be integrated with the new perspective, otherwise, we may bring disaster upon ourselves and become accomplices in the destruction of life on earth. This concept is not simply *worthwhile*; rather, it derives from a profound sense of the relationship between the material and the spiritual, heralding a core change in humankind's perception of itself.

Today's sciences develop and adopt theories unimaginable a mere fifty years ago, and at a much faster rate. The Gaia (earth goddess in Greek mythology) Hypothesis was introduced by James Lovelock just over twenty years ago; yet many of us already accept, or at least sense, the planet as an organic whole — even those who have never heard the term *Gaia*. One of the most striking features in the new sciences is a growing affinity between what used to be considered purely scientific and what is obviously intuitive knowledge. The demarcation line between the scientific and the spiritual is also blurred. By and large, the new thinking refrains from an indiscriminate uprooting of old beliefs, opinions and cultures; instead, it labors to find in them profound tenets which, rejuvenated, may contribute to a deeper understanding of human and planetary problems. Yet, as said, there exists a strong resistance bordering on fear among most Jews towards a fresh examination of their Judaism. I suspect that the fear of extermination is the major, hidden cause of that resistance.

Indeed, the overall Jewish anomaly is reflected in our perception of ourselves as being eternally persecuted. It is usually tied with having to move endlessly from one country to another. This connection is not as straightforward as it may seem. Today, it may feel to the Israeli-born that we have prospered as a nation only when living within our territorial boundaries — as was the case, for instance, in the Second Temple era. Yet the opposite has been the case! Jews have enjoyed their most protracted periods of prosperity when sojourning away from their homeland — in Babylon, Spain, America and even Egypt. In other words, we often *chose* to be "in exile" — not a very normal national attribute, one might say.

There are no available well tried short-cuts or magic formulas that can safely lead us through the intricacies of this inquiry. What might aid us is to find out what best represents a *whole* in Judaism, from which to diverge and reach down to its parts — as, indeed, the new sciences recommend us to do. Such a whole in most of Jewish history has been the *Torah* — or more precisely, the entire *Old Testament* (henceforth, "the Bible"). The Torah is sometimes called *"The Law"* or *"The Five Books of Moses"* and constitutes the first of three parts of the Bible.

To address this Jewish *core text* should be the most natural and logical step to take. But, surprisingly, to many Jews such a straight-forward approach would constitute an affront, if not sheer sacrilege. This phenomenon requires careful examination, without which we are liable to flounder at many unexpected turns.

Readers may be familiar with the expression *Oral Torah*, which refers to the huge corpus containing all of the exegesis of the Bible, predominantly the Talmud. This hermeneutic corpus is regarded by religious Jews as the chief — often, the sole — authority which determines their Jewishness. In it, it is bluntly stated that reading the uninterpreted Bible is sinful; that it would be far better not to read it at all than to try and understand its *Peshat* (simplicity) i.e., to draw "simply" on the Biblical original text. When I suggest we look closely at the Bible — i.e., its *Masoretic* (traditional) text, "sealed" in 102 C.E. — I am taking the liberty of looking at it freshly, with little regard for its canonized interpretations. I simply believe the source to be more wholesome than its derivations, and that we should inspect all phenomena, at least to start with, as closely as possible to their origin.

Does this indicate that I think Judaism draws predominantly on religion? No! Admittedly, it is difficult to find a people aside from the Jews for whom during a period of thousands of years its religion was also its nationality. Consequently, even to this day, a Jew who converts to another religion has a hard time calling himself a Jew. The Greeks remained Greek in their own eyes even after they abandoned their idols; the Egyptians remained Egyptians despite their departure from their Pharaonic faith: they became Hellenized, and then left their idols for the religion of Islam. The Jew's adherence to the *Torah* ("written" and "oral") as the sole definition of his Judaism remained unaltered for over two thousand years — until fairly recent times when people began discarding religious beliefs altogether. It is certainly ironic, that one of the pioneers of this "discarding" process was himself a Jew — the philosopher Baruch Spinoza — who was the first to part with all religious establishments, and was consequently ostracized by Christians and excommunicated by the Jewish authorities of his time. But we now live in an era in which a substantial group, which has not existed in most of human history, has come into being, viz. a considerable number of people who do not believe in any divinity. And it is clear that a non-believer like myself is not obliged to interpret ancient as well as modern history from a religious point of view any more than an anthropologist needs to accept the worldview of those he studies.

And yet, in order to familiarize ourselves with the Jewish nation, we *will* start by examining its ancient texts and ancient history. In doing so, we must be aware that throughout most of its history all of the disputes within the nation (and the rifts among large sections of it) had to do with the "right way" of interpreting the "Holy Writ." For our part, we will explore the Bible fearlessly, without preconceived beliefs or disbelief. We will check out its historical basis, taste its flavor, listen to the words of the prophets, peruse the books of ethics, stir to its mighty hymns and, in so doing, acquaint ourselves with the *paradigm* embedded in this gigantic work, written, compiled and edited over a period of a thousand years.

As said, for many practicing Jews (though not all), it may be difficult to accept this approach, which will be closer to that of Spinoza, who paved the way of observing humanity as relating not to one's *own* God, but to a *universal* deity.

I do not suggest, however, we necessarily study the Bible devoid of emotions. Often, I "get into it" myself with a child-like curiosity and a deep sense of affinity. Regarding all matters, I will draw on various sources, Jewish as well as non-Jewish. Only seldom will I cite chapter and verse. My reason for doing so is to encourage the reader to formulate his or her own views, freely examining, whenever possible, *all* available sources. I believe that in quoting specific sources there lies a danger of relying on them out of a more general context. To avoid this danger, I propose that we should, first and foremost, regard the *whole* — as broadly, freshly and in as leisurely a manner as possible — rather than being satisfied with a single quote, often chosen at random and under some sort of pressure.

Chapter 2

Ancient Times

L et us browse through the Bible and attempt to discover the attributes — or some of them — which characterize the existing (or "old") Jewish paradigm. We must bear in mind that many values upheld in the Bible have been adopted by non-Jews (such as a single God); at the same time, some Jewish values were developed only after the Bible was sealed, so to speak. Thus, in examining the Bible, in particular its early layers, we will look out for, amidst universally adopted values, those, which have remained (for better or worse) specifically or exclusively Jewish. (I shall enlist the attributes, which will have emerged in this chapter at its conclusion.)

Also, we will have a first chance of testing the mode of inquiry suggested in Chapter 1. This testing process will continue throughout the book.

Thousands of years ago, we are told, there lived a man, named Avram, who left his home to journey to a land that God would show him. At that time he was not yet a father — let alone an *Av Ram*, i.e., a Great Father — and many years would go by before he sired an offspring. When it eventually happened, he had a son by an Egyptian maidservant, not his wife, Sarah. Then Sarah, who had initiated the liaison, changed her mind and abused her maid in a manner so harsh that it would enrage any decent person today. Avram readily agreed to drive the young mother out of his tent into the wilderness, but despite this cruel act, he suffers no disgrace — certainly not from the quill of the Biblical author — and the children of Israel are taught to this day to venerate him, and call him lovingly "Our Father."

Perhaps there was such a man called Avram, later called Avraham (the spelling "Abraham," which I will use henceforth, is due to the Greek transliteration), and perhaps he did indeed travel from Haran to Canaan in the manner described in the Book of Genesis. But we frequently find that a Biblical author names a person to suit the role that person will fulfill. At the same time, the way a Biblical story is told — remembering that documentation in the modern sense did not exist then — is to give events the seal of unquestionable truth; moreover, to endow it with an aura of moral superiority. We may discover different versions of the same story — the Bible is full of contradictions — but, over the millennia, Jewish scholars have worked wonders in reconciling those, to them insignificant, disparities. We are always expected to accept the written texts as representing a true whole, no matter how contradictory and problematic they obviously are. After all, as the saying goes: "It's written in the Bible!" In every name and in every deed, the Bible's editors are quick to find and convey some sign of a grander, divine purpose, allowing little option for interpreting the behavior of a Biblical hero in a different way, no matter what he or she has done. Foolish and treacherous acts are condoned, as long as they are committed by "one of us," and as part of the divine plan.

Going along for a time with the Biblical narrative may clarify the premises of the Bible's authors and editors; but this should not deter us from raising challenging questions, as is customary in unbiased Biblical criticism. Yet, since innumerable scholars and conflicting interpretations exist, I suggest that one first reads a passage without questioning it, makes some notes and then goes on. Strangely, such an easy-going approach may reveal a lot of sense, subtlety, wisdom and even humor, virtually dispelling the constricting coat of morality mentioned earlier. It is a good book, after all. It won't be possible for us here to comb the entire Bible that way, of course. Instead, we will concentrate on some of its seminal situations and fundamental tenets — in the main, those that have become central to our traditions.

When we consider our nation's progenitor and his initial encounter with the Promised Land, we can discover no "good reason" for his trek to Canaan, of all places, apart from his father, Terah, the idol worshipper, having intended to go there in the first place. All we know is that God's purpose was to make a "great nation" issue from him there, and that Abraham's principal virtue became his unconditional loyalty to the God, Who had chosen him for that task. As emerging from the text, Abraham was a peace-loving person, who did not arrive in Canaan as a conqueror, claiming rights; rather, he felt himself an outsider, a temporary resident. When famine ravaged Canaan, he readily "descended" to Egypt, as his grandson Jacob did later, following his sons. The Children of Israel — "Israel" being Jacob's second name — were then quite happy to stay in Egypt for centuries, having no inclination to "ascend" back to Canaan. It is clear then that for them, living in the Promised Land was not yet considered to be any great privilege or obligation.

On his return from Egypt, Abraham bought a plot of land in which to bury his wife — the sole land purchase he made in Canaan. But, after two generations, Jacob did not consider this important enough to inter his beloved wife, Rachel, in that family tomb, known as the Cave of Machpela, though she died but a short distance from it. Living on and being buried in the soil of the Promised Land, gained significance much later. For our forefathers, human life and family ties were manifestly rated much higher than was the land they stood to inherit.

In his advanced years, the great miracle finally came to pass: Abraham's ninety-year-old wife gave birth to their son, Isaac. In Hebrew, the word "Isaac" is derived from a root that means "laughter." Indeed, it appears that the persona of our forefather,

Isaac, is closely linked to laughter — firstly, when Sarah, whose faith in God was apparently less than that of her husband's, burst into laughter when she heard the prophecy of her imminent pregnancy; and then when Abimelech, King of Gerar, espied Isaac in the act of "sporting with his wife." (The Hebrew root "tz-h-k" [laughter] is used here for "sporting.") Perhaps Isaac's name also hints at the ease with which his son, Jacob, tricked him over the matter of his first-born, Esau's, birthright. Isaac's life is described as rather uneventful, compared with both his father's and his son's exploits. He was a pleasant-mannered fellow — perhaps more so than his father — never once straying outside the Promised Land, busying himself with the digging of wells.

And now we come to the most complex of the three forefathers: Jacob. As his Hebrew name suggests, Jacob bypasses, cheats, and is a perpetrator of interminable schemes. Patently, he is his mother's pet, at whose promptings he steals for himself and his offspring the right to the land from Esau, his older brother. The latter then goes on to father the nation of Edom, which for future generations, among all of the ancient nations, has come to symbolize the deadliest of our foes. The problems connected with the misfortunes of the father of Edom are so far-reaching that they require we give them some space.

Accounts of betrayal and deceit are at the core of many ancient tales, but there is a marked characteristic that differentiates the Biblical accounts from most other national epics (some of which were found on clay tablets buried in the earth for thousands of years). The Bible had undergone long centuries of careful, judgmental editing prior to its final canonization. Obviously, Biblical stories had many versions (stories were passed from one generation to the next by word of mouth and thus altered in the process), and it is hard to conceive why the Bible's editors were so especially drawn to accounts of villainy in the lives of the forefathers and other great figures, like David. Nowadays, there are two contradictory explanations. According to the version popular within Israel's ultra-Orthodox strongholds, Esau being cheated of his birthright by his younger sibling served him right. It was based on their contrasting lifestyles, viz. that while Jacob diligently studied the holy Torah in the *Beit-Midrash* (House of Learning), the wastrel, half-wild Esau frittered his time away in roaming the fields and hunting, just like an uncircumcised boor — and naturally did not deserve a birthright. The other explanation is offered by secular academics, who keep trying to prove that the enduring power of the Bible resides precisely in that it does not seek to cosmeticize the nature of its heroes. This secular interpretation, however, ignores the high moral tone of the Biblical narrative; it also endows the ancients with our own, present-day literary criteria. The question persists: Why does the Bible expose so much of the dark side of our forefathers' character? There are times when one cannot but suspect that the editors deliberately elected to reveal their heroes' flaws so as to imply that no one can possibly adhere unfailingly to strict measures of justice, and that, in order to survive, both mortals and nations must sometimes transgress.

In his more benevolent moments, Abraham displayed greatness, too. His argument with God about the fate of the inhabitants of the sinful cities of the plain, Sodom and Gomorrah, is particularly memorable. The hundred-year-old patriarch negotiated an agreement with God to the effect that if ten righteous people could be found in them, the evil cities would be spared. But that magnanimous mood is at odds with Abraham's unconditional readiness to slaughter his only legitimate son — an attitude far more characteristic of the old Jewish paradigm than a willingness to act on behalf of some *strangers*. While it is not plausible to assume that a present-day *Hassid* (extremely observant Jew) would slaughter his son on his rabbi's order, there are many Jews who will go to tremendous lengths for their Judaism. An overall sentiment of pride and *loyalty to the nation*, for better or worse, can be taken to be the first characteristic of the old Jewish paradigm. In Biblical times, this loyalty mostly took the form of loyalty to Israel's God; but this trait has persisted among many Jews up to present times, regardless of religious faith. Enough to mention the inexplicable courage of the Warsaw Ghetto fighters — mostly secular Jews: having no chance of being victorious in their uprising against the Nazis, able to escape in the tunnels they had dug and thus save their own lives, they chose to die fighting, for the sole purpose of displaying, for all to see, the undying Jewish spirit. Their feat is a sure sign of the immense power of the above-mentioned trait. Needless to add here that this attribute — as well as others we will come to later — does not apply to every Jew at all times. It is, however, significant for our purpose in having its roots in the ancient lore and surviving through unimaginable trials and tribulations.

Let us return to the story of Jacob and Esau and learn its overall import. Cheating a first-born brother out of his birthright cannot be rated as something in which to take pride. There was no divine command whatsoever for Jacob to steal the birthright; it was plainly a stratagem of an astute Jewish mother who adored her favorite, younger son. The way the devout often justify Jacob's act is that, if Rebecca hadn't succeeded with her plot, all of us Jews would be the descendants of Esau, God forbid!

Jacob is overwhelmingly a survivor — a sense of justice being as far from his heart as East from West. We might very well describe him as the first anti-hero, had it not been for the fact that from time immemorial we have been taught to regard him as the righteous forefather who turned a family into a nation and perpetuated it through the exploits of his brilliant son, Joseph. Israel is Jacob's second name, given him by God himself for his feat of prevailing over God's angel. Now, for Israel to deceive his biological father in so grave a matter as inheritance blatantly flouts the Commandment to honor one's parents. The religious explain this transgression by simply reminding us that in the time of the theft, the Torah —

which contained this and the other Commandments — had not yet been given to us (forgetting that, a while ago, they claimed Jacob was studying the Torah day and night). It is not, of course, a simple issue, since the idealized images of the forefathers persists throughout the entire Bible, and in Judaism as a whole. Be that as it may, the indiscriminate veneration of the forefathers, based on what we read about them in the Bible, highlights the attribute of *unity at all costs* in Judaism — the second of the old Jewish paradigmatic traits.

The way the tale of Jacob and Esau is treated in the Bible sheds light on an important historical and historical-philosophical problem. The Bible's never-yielding hostility towards the Edomites stems not only from their country's geographical proximity to the Land of Israel, but from an inextricable bond typical of closely related rivals. In later generations, it was the Edomites who cried against the fallen Jerusalem: *"Raze it, raze it to its very foundation!"* and in revenge the Psalmist roared back: *"Happy is he who seizes your infants and dashes them against the rock!"* Such words make one's hair stand on end, bringing to mind the worst horrors our own people has suffered. While many will claim that the tales in the Book of Genesis are not meant to constitute practical directives based on historical fact, those who espouse the old paradigm — certainly the extremists, who are so vocal in their declarations — insist that the Bible is absolute truth and constitutes an infallible moral guide. We are required, therefore, to separate the various elements in the Bible and extract those which encourage and make it possible for a son of the "Nation of the Book" to fall in with the rest of humanity. To this end, it is useful, indeed necessary, to discover varying opinions among the Bible's authors themselves. The following is an example of diametrically opposed views within the Torah itself, both of which relate to the very same event:

Edom is mentioned in the Torah twice in connection with Israel's crossing that nation's frontier on its way from the Sinai desert to the Promised Land. The first time is in the Book of Numbers; the second, in the Book of Deuteronomy — the greater part of which is believed to have been written long after Israel had settled in its own land. In the earlier report, we learn how Moses *implored* the King of Edom to allow Israel to pass through his country, promising not to harm it in any way, to pay for drinking water etc., and how the King of Edom bluntly refused the request and positioned a heavily armed force in Israel's path. The moral is obvious: Edom is a sworn enemy of Israel, and, hence, *"Happy is he who seizes your infants and dashes them against the rock!"*

In the Book of Deuteronomy, the details change, though Israel's route and other circumstances appear to be identical. In this second account, God *warns* Moses *in advance* not to enter that kingdom and not to cause it any harm, for, He reminds Moses, Edom is "your brother." We have two stories, then, about the same event, yet differing from each other and, more to the point, containing totally opposing morals. (Further on in Deuteronomy, we find a specific directive pertaining to Edom: *"Do not abhor the Edomite, for he is your brother."*) Assuming that the author of Deuteronomy was also familiar with varying versions of the forefathers' stories, and being in league with Israel's new revolutionary prophets, it is not hard to imagine how, while compiling or even just copying the Book of Genesis, he *deliberately* chose to retain the shameful tale of Jacob stealing the birthright. He thus made a strong case for acting compassionately towards other nations, especially those close to us, whom we have wronged.

As we have shown, the Bible is a collection of many documents, which in numerous instances present different concepts, some of which are contradictory. The overall commandment that one should scrupulously follow the entire Torah, adhering to every jot and title of it, poses a knotty problem. But for those not bound to keep intractable ancient commandments, a third core element in the Bible (and Judaism as a whole, perhaps) presents itself: *contra-*

diction — even though a common denominator linking contradiction with unity might be, at first glance, hard to conceive.

This problem becomes even more complex when we consider opposing concepts of justice — the same strict, divine justice that so many believe was imparted to the world through the Torah and the People of Israel. A popular song sung in Jewish homes can serve as a good example of the absurdities deriving from faith in the Torah as a just, divine and immutable whole. Its lyrics tell how, through the ages, the Torah has sustained Judaism: "In every generation, our enemies sought to destroy us / But the Holy One, blessed be He, saved us from their designs / Through the Torah!" The Torah is said here to have protected the People of Israel from annihilation. But how can this even be considered, regarding a corpus so filled with contradiction?

We raise the question not only of whether the Torah contains undeniable instruction about one's moral behavior — this is quite easy to refute — but also how precisely the Torah "sustained" us through generations of dispersion and persecution: a concept not as easy to deny. Perhaps, in searching for a foundation in Judaism that is *parallel* to the Torah, we may discover that the Torah's very contradictions have sustained it — and us! Everyone, including Jesus of Nazareth, could interpret the Torah in a different way, because of its contradictions. What emerges here is that contradiction, which is ingrained in the world, in nature, and in mankind, is at the heart of the Torah. But contradiction cannot be termed "instruction." Is it possible that covert recognition of contradiction, as being inherent in every phenomenon, has made our early teachers insist on strict observation of all the Mitzvot — most of which are so difficult to keep and so contrary to logic — as the only way of perpetuating Israel through thick and thin? Without doubt, following all of the commandments is the most vital element running through the Jewish religion. *Obeying the Mitzvot*, then, emerges as the fourth precept, perhaps the most dominant one, of the old Jewish paradigm. (Please note: The word mitzvot — sometimes spelled mitzvoth — indicates both those appearing in the Torah and those added later, purporting to be an interpretation of the earlier ones. In English, however, the word "commandment," when written with "C" — i.e., upper case — refers to one of the Ten Commandments; when written with a lower case "c" refers to any of the Jewish Mitzvot.)

I have elected to highlight the subject of contradiction within the Torah by citing the "naive" tales of the forefathers. I've used them as a prelude to the most central chapter in Jewish history: the Exodus from Egypt. In a book by a preeminent Black neighborhood activist, Jim Wallis of Washington, D.C., entitled The Soul of Politics, the story of the Exodus is held up as the greatest of all the accounts of struggle for freedom in history. Perhaps his claim is correct, but a thorough examination of the story yields not only jarring discrepancies and amoral concepts, but it may also indicate a "moral" code under which people are instructed to enslave all foreigners, if not worse.

After the People of Israel had lived in Egypt for many generations, enjoying the best the land had to offer, we are told of a new Pharaoh "who knew not Joseph," who decided for his own reasons to enslave and then eliminate the Hebrews, by issuing an edict to slay all their new-born male babies. From that point on, the Bible gives us a highly dramatic description of the birth of a nation, a narrative that reaches its climax with the events at Mount Sinai. Initially, twelve Hebrew families journeyed to Egypt; six hundred thousand males, aged twenty to sixty, are purported to have departed from it, as well as the elderly, the women and the children. All in all, some two million Hebrews would have gathered at the foot of Mount Sinai.

How at the ripe old age of eighty, having been raised as a nobleman in Pharaoh's palace, Moses managed to lead the Hebrew slave masses is a feat that only divine intervention can explain.

Outside the Bible there is precious little in ancient documents to support the existence of the man. Some third-party reports (Artaphanus, third century B.C.E., as quoted by Eusebius and Clement) intimate, in a legendary style, that Moses was a brilliant commander in the wars waged by Pharaoh Khenefres against Ethiopian invaders, as well as a superb administrator who earned great acclaim. Eventually, Moses' popularity engendered Pharaoh's jealousy, and he had to flee Egypt for his life. Freud (though not usually considered a historian) pointed to a possible link between Moses and Akhnaton, the revolutionary Pharaoh who, prior to the Exodus, tried to change the Egyptian religion from polytheism to monotheism. Other than that, we have to rely on the Biblical account.

It all started when Joseph, Jacob's son, elevated himself from a classless Hebrew slave to the position of Pharaoh's top administrator, re-organizing the vast Egyptian economy so that its people were spared seven years of famine. No wonder, then, that the Israelites were happy to settle there, until the Egyptians' attitude towards them changed. Just at that moment, so it is written, God suddenly *remembered* His promise to the forefathers and decided to rescue their descendants from Pharaoh's scourge. We have no hint that the Israelites on their part remembered their ancient God, though it appears they had retained their Semitic vernacular. On the contrary: what we are told is that had it not been for their terrible misery, they would not have welcomed His reappearance. God then chose to harden Pharaoh's heart to the point at which only horrendous plagues would at last compel him to free the Hebrews in a spectacular and unforgettable manner.

Was all of this God's plan? An early statement in the Book of Genesis tells us that in some way it was. Yet later, in the Book of Exodus, after He suddenly "remembered" us, what follows makes little bones about His motives, i.e., that in the same way He one day decided to create the universe, He simply waited for the right moment in which to reveal Himself in all His glory once again.

We should consider the context in which the Sinai Revelation — which has had such a tremendous impact not only on Judaism but on all of Western civilization — and how it must have seemed to those who put it down in writing. First and foremost, it was a reaction to the Egyptian experience. Even nowadays, the briefest of trips to Egypt presents the visitor with a picture of an incomparable civilization; it is hard to comprehend, both regarding its beginnings and then its fall from grace. From time immemorial, that great nation has worshipped a myriad of deities. Yet all of that culture — including its impressive temples made of stone which had to be transported from thousands of kilometers away, its magnificent tombs with their hundreds of chambers quarried deep into the earth, its wonderful art and richly-textured everyday life — was destined to serve only one purpose: assuring the smooth passage of Pharaoh, the divine balancer of fertility and desert, from the realm of life to the realm of death. The collective wisdom of Egypt's priests, military commanders, engineers, artists and poets devoted itself to that single end: Pharaoh's safe journey from world to world. The Egyptian religious practice was a closely guarded secret, knowledge of which was restricted to the priests alone, who interminably elevated Pharaoh's divine status. This was the Egyptian reality throughout nearly two thousand years prior to the purported time of the Exodus.

We have noted the appearance of a monotheistic religion in Egypt for a brief period prior to the Exodus. (Recent research by Egyptologist, David M. Rohl, sets Akhnaton's reign in a period *following* the heretofore-estimated time of Israel's conquest of the Promised Land.) Scholars and poets have been fascinated by Akhnaton's character no less than they have been with Moses'. The main difference in our knowledge of the two lies, however, in the fact that, while Akhnaton is a historical figure (i.e., there is objective archeological evidence concerning him), there is no contemporary evidence regarding Moses' life. What we "know" of Moses is found almost exclusively in the Bible and was set down many centuries after the events connected with him are said to have occurred. (The other historians I've cited post-date Moses by a thousand years.) Nevertheless, we are aware of two monumental figures in that period, both of whom postulated monotheism. How they differed from each other should give us more than a clue to Moses' specific contribution.

We know now — as the Biblical authors must have been generally aware of then — that Akhnaton had inherited from his father a vast kingdom, a sprawling empire that spread far beyond the Nile basin; its boundaries reached far into the western desert, into present-day Turkey and into modern Iraq. The symbol of Akhnaton's monotheistic deity was the sun, from whose disc ray-shaped arms, each with a human hand at its extremity, streamed down to earth. For the first time in written or illustrated history, the divinity is portrayed as reaching out to *all* human beings, wherever they may be. Other of his qualities were also rare for the time, e.g., his relationship with his wife and family, who for the first time in Egyptian art are pictured as living persons. However, despite his universalistic philosophy, Akhnaton was still a Pharaoh: only he was permitted to interpret, and to be in close touch with, the new divinity. As interesting as his life-style may be for us, we are here primarily concerned with the way his monotheism differed from that of Moses.

Every single Hebrew who came out of bondage is said to have witnessed the events at Mount Sinai; everyone "*saw* the voices" (as is written), not just the priests. For the first time in history, everyone experienced the presence of the invisible, single God, albeit with the necessary restrictions: even Moses glimpsed His figure only from behind. But it is neither the number of people nor what they witnessed that is so significant. Of prime importance here is the fact that people who but scant weeks before had been slaves, without any status whatsoever, were instantly transformed into a "nation of priests"!

As mentioned earlier, until now, no independent historical evidence about the Exodus has come to light; and while one need not necessarily accept the Hebrew Biblical Encyclopedia's assertion (third volume, p. 754) that this unique phenomenon — that of a nation regarding itself as originating from slaves — is ipso facto sufficient to validate the Exodus, the Jews' view of themselves as ex-slaves is dominant in the Jewish self-image. The Ten Commandments begin with a powerful reminder that, "*I am the Lord your God who brought you out of Egypt, out of the house of bondage.*" The Exodus experience is quintessential to our national image.

The account of the Exodus is, indeed, spectacular. Gone were the animal-headed gods with wings, who vied with each other for supremacy, each employing his or her own particular power (fertility, thunder, deep of the sea, thickets of the earth); gods before whom human beings were nothing — unless they were kings or their descendants. Instead, here were hosts of mankind without distinction of class, who had suddenly become privileged, each and every one of them, to experience in person the presence of their own single God, the God of Justice.

Under the circumstances, it was in no way possible to confer the benevolence of the revealed God on all human beings. Pharaoh had been defeated and left behind to lick his wounds, not having the privilege of being a liberated slave. Neither was it conferred on the other nations, including the Canaanites, who dwelled under their vines and fig trees, who never harmed Israel nor had any inkling of the divine plot to wipe them from the face of the earth.

The annals of history are rife with examples of liberators and liberated turned nation-wreckers and enslavers. Does Yehoshua bin-Nun rate as one of them? In other words, in what way does the

Sinai experience itself prescribe — in part, at least — the commandment to annihilate the dwellers of Canaan? It was certainly Moses' order, which his loyal servant, Joshua, implemented to the best of his ability. While the notion of superiority of one's own group over all others may very well have been the way of the world and not a Hebrew attribute alone, the concept of a sanctified Chosen People — chosen to carry out God's will — has become the unshakeable cornerstone of the Jewish religion, persisting for thousands of years.

The most conspicuous attribute of the old Jewish paradigm is that of the *Chosen People*. And it all started at Sinai. The Ten Commandments — the foremost constitutional document of Judaism — were given there, and, as I intend to show in the next chapter, they already harbor the separatist seed. In fact, all the events building up to the "giving" of the Commandments lead to it.

Just envision the scene! Several thousand people gathered at the foot of the smoking mountain (the figure of two million must be attributed to Middle Eastern exaggeration: so many humans could not possibly have survived in the Sinai desert), led by an aged stuttering *outsider* who somehow had managed to supply food and water in the harsh conditions of the wilderness. Merely a few weeks had gone by since that tongue-tied leader, who kept claiming he was a Hebrew, beat Pharaoh's powerful army and sent it reeling to the bottom of the sea. A month earlier, that same leader, Moses, had, during a terrible thunderstorm, gone up to the mountain peak — alone, without provisions — to "speak with God," and has not returned. Before departing, he had made the promise that he would take us all to a fertile land — but where was that Promised Land? There was nothing but bleak sand and rugged rock in evidence. To keep us in check, he left behind his entourage, who call themselves "Levites" (the root of "Levi" in Hebrew indicates to escort, to accompany), who indeed are top-notch administrators and quick swordsmen. But the fear of being abandoned in the wilderness is more overpowering than the menacing swords of the Levites...

Common people often find unexpected ways of cheering up in grim situations. Perhaps, for the hell of it, someone said, "Let's make a calf-idol, the way the Egyptians do, finish off our remaining food and water, then turn around and go back to Egypt! At least, there we didn't die of hunger." But at that instant — before or after the calf was cast — Moses reappeared. No one recalled that he had taken any carving tools with him; yet he bore in his hands two impeccably carved stone tablets onto which words had been engraved. With leonine majesty he raised the tablets aloft; the light of the setting sun burnished his features with a fiery glow. (Through mistranslation, the Latin Bible actually suggests that animal horns appeared on his head.) Flanking him, with drawn swords, stood his escorts, ready to cut down any opposition. Suddenly, it seemed that the invisible, intangible God that Moses had spoken of did after all exist. The memories of the lushness of Egypt became blurred — in particular, when the Levites went on to slaughter all those who had turned to serve the golden calf. The promise of the fertile land that would come into our possession fired the imagination. If we had bested the powerful Egyptians, did it not prove that we were the greatest? And did not Moses, once again, prove he could achieve the impossible, and in plain view of thousands? And, if so, he might as well get us into that land of milk and honey... (The full story is a lot more detailed, and certainly deserves to be re-read.)

It is not difficult to fathom how an episode of such magnitude, or one even remotely like it, set in motion a process singling out the Israelites from all other nations. It sanctified, above all, the Commandments carved on those tablets — which, incidentally, in the Biblical account, were never spied in close quarters by any mortal eye, save, it seems, that of Moses himself. Over the coming centuries, the impact of the Sinai Revelation grew in strength, until, ultimately, it gave birth to Halachic Judaism — the old Jewish paradigm's chief characterizer — that has retained its vitality to this very day.

Before we go on to consider the most sanctified of texts, I should like to emphasize that in no way is one asked to assume that new-paradigm thinking does not exist at all in present-day Judaism. I trust that more than one reader recognizes some of what has been said here as having appeared elsewhere (for instance, in the early Zionist writings), and already accepts many of my ideas as his or her own. Yet, more likely than not, this may not yet constitute a conscious, or wholly conscious, new worldview regarding Judaism. My purpose here is to encourage its maturation through a new kind of awareness. Later on in this inquiry, I will bring up a parallel development in the new Christian school of thought. By so doing, I hope to demonstrate that we Jews are not the only ones in need of a thorough re-examination of our old ideologies.

We have now reached the moment of our nation's birth, the time when, according to the Biblical account, the Jewish people took upon itself the yoke of the Mitzvot and at the same time were instructed to conquer and appropriate the Promised Land. Interestingly enough, the injunction to settle in the Land of Israel does not appear in the Ten Commandments. We will return to this particular commandment after giving our attention to what the Ten Commandments *do* contain.

The five old-Jewish-paradigm attributes, in the order they have emerged so far, are:
1. Loyalty to the nation;
2. Unity at all costs;
3. Contradiction;
4. Obeying all of God's commandments;
5. Chosen People (i.e., chosen by God).

Once again: what we are trying to reach here is a sense of an inter-connected *whole* in Judaism. Having itemized some of Judaism's Biblical attributes, and touched on their genesis, still, the *way* those attributes have emerged is more relevant to our research than their sheer, separate itemization.

Chapter 3

The Ten Commandments
Law and Justice as a National Attribute

We are accustomed to regard the Ten Commandments as transcending religion and race. They herald the era of social justice and its ongoing slow implementation. For the religious, however, the Commandments hold yet another — for them, higher — principle: the one God. And to most Jews they represent the core document of our nationhood. Still, despite their threefold nature — embodying social justice, fundamental religious principles and the birth of a nation — we normally regard the Commandments as one whole. We seldom inquire into their specific content and, in particular, into their varying elements, which, on examination, reveal a fairly fragile structure, reached at through a long process preceding their final formulation.

It seems that, very early on, in order to bar a person from doubting the Biblical account of how the Commandments were "given," and what they actually contain, an injunction was created, prohibiting any mortal from ever, I repeat: ever, seeing the famed tablets. Even a mere and accidental touching of the Ark of the Covenant, in which they were allegedly housed, resulted in a terrible death.

Another, less-remembered fact has to do with their disappearance. When Solomon's Temple (i.e., the First Temple) was destroyed by the Babylonians in 586 B.C.E., no mention of the tablets was made — contrary to all the other Temple paraphernalia which the Bible describes in minute detail. No hint of their whereabouts was ever given, as if they had never existed. Neither did the returnees to Zion, fifty years later, dig in the rubble to salvage a shard of evidence proving the existence of the most precious of divinely-created articles. Again, we have no choice but to study them from the only source available to us — the Bible. My only trepidation in doing so stems from my belief that most readers will find it, at first, hard to accept what is about to be revealed.

The complete text of the Ten Commandments appears twice — first, in the Book of Exodus and, next, in the Book of Deuteronomy. Following the first version — i.e., in Exodus — the most ancient detailed legal statutes of our nation appear. This section is generally referred to as the Book of the Covenant. Together with the Commandments, these laws, appearing in Exodus, constitute the nation's earliest ethical and legal code. Other than that, the two versions are pretty well identical, apart from some *slight* changes in the wording here and there, and one *significant* change of content which appears halfway through the second version. Important to mention here is that most researchers believe that the latter version is an adaptation of the earlier one, made under the influence of Israel's "late" prophets, i.e., some five hundred years after the purported Exodus.

There are two main homogenous blocks in the Commandments. The first three Commandments expound monotheism, whereas the ultimate block, which contains five short Commandments, deals with moral dictates pertaining to *just* relations between one human and another. The immediate question arising here is whether there exists an intrinsic link between the two innovations — i.e., God being a *single* god, on the one hand, and His preoccupation with social justice, on the other hand. From a purely logical standpoint, the two may appear contradictory — for, after all, being single by definition may render One insensitive to others. However, there is one Commandment in which a fusion between the two blocks is created: the Commandment regarding the Sabbath. It actually "links" the two sections; and it is the one that has been awarded two widely different formulations. This Commandment also indicates most clearly the long process of evolution. Coming between the two main blocks, the Sabbath acquires a central position in early Judaism's moral achievement.

In regard to the setting down of the Commandments in writing, one should bear in mind that regular use of Hebrew writing began several hundred years after Israel's assumed desert wanderings. The story of Joseph, for instance, if written close to the time of the events described in it, was written in Egyptian hieroglyphics, and the version which reached us, is, at best, a Hebrew translation. But the Ten Commandments, as well as the Book of the Covenant, are of the kind known verbatim by every judge; and, since the memorizing of entire texts (legal as well as poetic) was common to all pre-literate civilizations, the Ten Commandments show every sign of having been known by the People of Israel long before they were finally written down.

Let us examine, then, the first, monotheistic section. In the introduction, which is regarded as a separate Commandment, God announces Himself by His chief attribute, that of being single — an "I" — being all gods turned into one. "*Eltohecha*" literally means "your gods." He then goes on directly to cite His chief act on behalf of His people, as the One "...*who brought you out of the Land of Egypt, out of the house of bondage.*" In a sense, the connection, however implicit, between God and His acumen for social justice is introduced at the very start.

The two Commandments that follow proceed to lay down the rudimentary requirements of monotheism. Thus, in the second Commandment (some divide it into two separate Commandments; altogether, the division of the Commandments into *ten* is arbitrary and must have been introduced later, as a matter of convenience) God's command is that the people abandon all other gods forthwith — most certainly, though by implication, those they had known in

Egypt. He forbids them to make statues and masks, and adds, *"Thou shalt not bow down to them, nor serve them."* Here, the first threat appears, namely, that he who disobeys this prohibition is an enemy of God and will not be forgiven, nor will his son, his grandson and great-grandson go unpunished. Also, those who will obey it, "God's lovers," will be "given benevolence." This injunction has caused idolatry to be regarded as the most heinous of sins. Also here, by means of simple cross-reference, the first discrepancy appears in regard to other facts mentioned extensively in the Bible.

Israel continued to make statues for centuries to come after the Exodus. The Book of Kings describes cherubs (in the shape of winged calves) and lion figures adorning Solomon's Temple in full view. For a long time, these could not have been considered sinful by the religious authorities. One may argue that the people did not necessarily "bow down" to them. But, then, Moses' *copper serpent* adorned the Temple, too! In this case, it is reported explicitly that the people of Judea had venerated it with the burning of incense — an absolute equivalent to bowing down. Are we then to understand that Moses himself erred, or is this an editorial message reinforcing the idea that though he may have done so, we, each of us, must take on the burden of never repeating his error? Be that as it may, this discrepancy supports our understanding that the Commandments, at least in part, reached their final format in a long process that may have *started* in the desert.

Another important point which is made clear here is that, however inconsistent, the God of Sinai appears as zealous and vengeful towards anyone who chooses to differ with whatever His edict may be at any given moment.

The next Commandment continues to deal with the relationship between man and God. It also ends with a threat towards the transgressor, though the threat is more general than the previous one: *"Thou shalt not take the name of the Lord in vain, for the Lord will not hold him guiltless that taketh His name in vain."* It is not clear whether this refers to a false oath — as it may be taken to mean today — or that the name of God should not be invoked in everyday matters, i.e., "in vain." Some believe it refers to witchcraft, so abhorred by the first monotheists. The language of the Commandment is ambiguous, however powerful.

The first religious block of the Ten Commandments is fundamental. While the Halachic term for idolatry, *avodah zarah*, never appears in the Bible, there is no doubt that the absolute prohibition of idol worship was finally accepted and remained the chief theological injunction separating us from the rest of humanity. The rejection of idolatry caused an early, total distinction from the way in which all peoples had, until then, perceived themselves and the world around them.

So far, the *universal* message in the Commandments is far from explicit, while separatism is deeply rooted in the experience of the Exodus. For instance, the term *holy* is referred to in the Book of Genesis only *once* (concerning the sanctity of God's rest on the seventh day). Nor can we find any other word in Genesis that even derives from the Hebrew root for "holy" (k.d.sh.). Yet the idea of holiness practically fills the Book of Exodus, the second Book of the Bible.

The concept of the *holiness* of the Hebrew nation, and the holiness of its God, appears for the first time when God revealed Himself to Moses in the Sinai desert at the burning bush. The same befalls the concept of *impurity* — having to do with anything not pertaining either to the God of Israel or His people and its Land, which follows immediately after the introduction of holiness. Herein may well lie the greatest of all paradoxes in Judaism: that, concurrently with establishing equality among all members of the one group, there also springs the barrier that separates it from all others. If a new concept of Judaism is at all possible, an addressing of this paradox will have to be thoroughly undergone, leading up to its total resolution.

Additional to the Sabbath, and flanking it, there is another Commandment in which God is nominally involved, though the content of that other Commandment pertains to inter-human relationships, viz., to honor one's parents. Both are complex and we shall give them special care. Following them, appear the fairly short, straightforward, inter-human injunctions, to be found in the written or unwritten law of almost all peoples, old and new. They are:

- *Thou shalt not murder;*
- *Thou shalt not commit adultery;*
- *Thou shalt not steal;*
- *Thou shalt not bear false witness against thy neighbor;*
- *Thou shalt not covet thy neighbor's house; thou shalt not covet thy neighbor's wife, nor his slave, nor his maid, nor his ox, nor his ass, nor anything that is thy neighbor's.*

Let us spend a little time over these. The first thing that springs to mind is that none of the Commandments prohibit plain lying — perhaps for the simple reason that no community or individual can ever hope to uphold such an injunction. However, there is a specific injunction against telling a lie at a trial — at which one is required to bear witness. This is true homage paid by the Hebrews with regard to justice, a realm to which our inquiry will lead us many times yet.

"*Thou shalt not covet*" takes us elsewhere, to the domain of the heart. But God, who created us in His own image, should have realized how unreasonable it would be to expect a person not to desire something his heart desires. No present-day psychologist — let alone logician — would countenance such a ruling. But the science of psychology did not exist then, and it is clear the ancient lawgiver believed that this divine edict should — and, indeed, could — overrule human nature. This Commandment also lumps together the value of woman, house and donkey — not too surprising in a patriarchal society — and overlooks the fact that the Israelites could not have owned houses in the desert — which fits well with our understanding of the Commandments as having developed over a long period.

The most widely quoted of the "short" Commandments is, *"Thou shalt not kill."* The Hebrew text reads, *"Thou shalt not murder,"* which is, of course, what is meant. But it still leaves us with the question, "Murder whom?" Immanuel Kant regarded this injunction as the strongest imperative appearing in the Commandments. Yet, according to the Biblical account, Joshua, who later carried out the annihilation of Canaan's inhabitants, stood there at Moses' side at Mount Sinai! We cannot but infer that, at the time, the Commandment did not forbid murdering the members of other peoples — so long as such was done as part of God-ordained national aspirations. Since this context excludes from the injunction *"Thou shalt not murder"* the butchering of other peoples, quoting this Commandment must, therefore, always be followed by a clear reservation, clarifying that its original meaning, as derived from its Biblical context, diametrically opposes what we would nowadays mean by, *"Thou shalt not murder!"* — i.e., not to murder *any* human.

Let us now turn to the intermediate Commandments, which speak of the Sabbath and of the honoring of one's parents. Both bind together divinity and human relations. The Sabbath was originally regarded as embodying a holy tenet and therefore was placed in close proximity with the opening, monotheistic Commandments; the latter could be said to contain matters of intra-human relationships and was therefore positioned to flank *those* matters. Yet this order could have been easily reversed — i.e., placing the Sabbath well within the humanistic arena. For those who may feel that this is not the way to regard Holy Scriptures, a little patience will prove how central the question of the *humanity* of the Sabbath was for the scribes who wrote the later version of the fourth Commandment in the Book of Deuteronomy. Either way, I would like to leave dealing with the Sabbath — which seems to me to be the uncrowned queen of all the Commandments — to the very last.

The fifth Commandment, which follows the one regarding the Sabbath, reads: *"Honor thy father and thy mother that thy days may be long in the land which the Lord thy God gives thee."*

At first glance, this injunction seems to suggest neither a religious nor moral imperative. And yet, besides God's promise (made in the religious Commandments, to reward His followers benevolently or punish them according to their behavior), this is the only case in which there is a promise of tangible reward for obeying a Commandment: days can be counted and land can be measured. In some way, it sounds as if God is offering an exchange here, a fair deal, as it were. But what are the exact wares that are here reckoned with? Why should honoring one's parents ensure one's land, and from God's hand?

No one could possibly object to honoring one's parents, neither the righteous, nor the thief nor the murderer. In general, the Bible has endless injunctions to honor and respect all fellow human beings, e.g., *"Honor the face of an old man,"* and *"Children's children are the crown of old men."* (We moderns would have it that children, not elders, come first.) There is also the general directive: *"Love thy fellow human as thyself."* (Some medieval Jewish interpreters ruled that the term "fellow human" applied to Jews only; but the wording is quite clear: it refers to *all* fellow humans.) Now, since all human relationships are covered, why then is there such a special emphasis on honoring one's father and mother in particular? And what happens if a righteous person's father is a notorious culprit? Is the son nevertheless expected to honor his sinful father? The answer is to be found at the tail end of the Commandment, which initially did not seem to add up: the connection to the land.

In Biblical times, owning land was the chief, if not the only means of a respectable livelihood. While it is true that in the desert the Hebrews did not yet have their own land, we know that the Commandments address issues of central importance to a normal nation. Even to this day, a murderer does not lose his rights to his property, and so it was in those times. The injunction to honor one's parents was reinforced by — if not based on — the fundamental ties to one's landed inheritance. A person who did not honor his parents would have forfeited his claim to his land.

The introduction of God into this particular aspect of human affairs is subtle and has more than one facet. Not only is the conquest of the Promised Land thus hinted at, but, also, a kind of identity is established between our Father in Heaven and our earthly begetter. In other words, God is involved in our closest blood relationships — let alone our claim to our parents' property.

This "cold" analysis may arouse objection. For why should we tamper with such noble guidance, which, after all, touches on the intimate matter of filial/parental relationship? But, unlike endless other lofty injunctions, which the Bible puts up at every given chance, which direct one to be overwhelmingly caring for the truly needy (such as the orphan and the widow), this is the only one which has found its way into the Ten Commandments! One cannot escape the conclusion that it has to do with the very backbone of the social structure of those days. Personally, I find that this ancient injunction also projects into the far-off future. In our era, it is accepted that orphans and widows should become the responsibility of the state's social services, while the aged, however "cared" for, are often ignored and cast away by their very offspring. Even if the Biblical lawgiver did not consider this social angle, it renders him prophetic.

In the main, we have so far dealt, on the one hand, with the injunctions pertaining to the absolute adherence to our benevolent God, who may, in certain circumstances, direct us to decimate another people; and, on the other hand, with those which contain the mandatory laws of being just and respectful to others. Now we reach the fourth Commandment, which aims at an exalted fusion between these two overtly disconnected entities. It represents the height of legislation, which our nation created for itself and for others. It should shine forth in flawless splendor. It is the Sabbath, which allows — nay, commands — every living creature full rest every seventh day.

The Sabbath has a special status for observant Jews. Only when it comes to matters of life and death is a Jew allowed to break it without "violating" it. And that should hold sway for the non-Jew as well. On that day, it says: "... *thou shalt not do any work, nor thy son nor thy daughter nor thy servant nor thy maidservant nor any stranger that is within thy gates.*" Obviously, the master can choose to rest at any time: not so his servants. Rest for the slave, the worker and the beast — status-less and defenseless — expresses the deep humanistic essence of this Commandment. (There were, of course, no gates in the desert; nor is it likely that our ancestors, just freed from slavery, had so soon acquired slaves and maidservants of their own, but the inconsistency of the Commandments regarding the time they are said to have been handed down has already been discussed.) So, what is it that made us so fortunate, we and our slaves and our donkeys and the strangers within our gates, slaves as well as free men, outsiders as well as Hebrews (wives are not mentioned, but let it be put down to oversight) fortunate enough to receive this wondrous gift of perfect rest, for an entire day every week, in such hard times of constant strife and toil? As it is written: "*For in six days the Lord made heaven and earth, the sea and all that is in them, and rested on the seventh day; therefore the Lord blessed the Sabbath day and hallowed it.*" How splendid! When He rests, let all rest! There exists a profound affinity between God and all His creatures.

But something troubles me here. I recall childhood stories

which describe the "Sabbath goy," i.e., the *gentile*, who works for a Jew on the Sabbath, cleaning, pumping water, kindling the cooking fire and so on. And I ask myself, if that matter of giving a day of rest to the slave and the stranger was ever taken seriously. I open the Book of Deuteronomy, turn to Chapter 5 and read the familiar words, *"nor the stranger that is within thy gates,"* and to my surprise I find no period there. A moment ago, i.e., in the Book of Exodus, it was there, and now it has vanished! The sentence in Deuteronomy continues thus: *"...that thy manservant and thy maidservant may rest as well as thou."* How hadn't I noticed? Now, I expect to find the familiar explanation here, viz. that *"for in six days the Lord made heaven and earth,"* etc., but it's not there either. Instead, something quite different appears: *"For thou shalt remember that thou wast a slave in the land of Egypt, and that the Lord thy God brought thee out from there with a mighty hand and an outstretched arm; therefore the Lord thy God commanded thee to keep the Sabbath day. Honor Thy..."* but I've already run into the next Commandment. So I turn back to the Book of Exodus and discover that there is no mention whatsoever of either the reason appearing in Deuteronomy, i.e., *"that thy manservant and thy maidservant may rest as well as thou"* nor the forceful reminder spurring one to stick to that reasoning through high water and hellfire, i.e., that *"thou shalt remember that thou wast a slave in the land of Egypt!"*

What can possibly explain this remarkable amendment in the holiest of texts?

Those who haven't read the above mentioned Biblical chapters recently (and I don't blame anyone, remembering how they are rammed down our throats at school) might have forgotten what preceded the handing down of the Ten Commandments. The Bible gives us an amazing description, telling us how God descended on the mountaintop in a tremendous cloud of smoke and what happened thereafter. The religious author who wrote the first scroll of Deuteronomy was not likely to doubt that the description was true, that events occurred precisely in that fashion, and that the moment was the most awesome any human would ever experience. And yet, that same author, as he copied down the Ten Commandments from the Book of Exodus and reached the paragraph about the Sabbath, *changed* it, eliminating what he found and inserting a completely different one in its place. What was the author thinking at that moment? After all, it cannot be that God said that which was written in the Book of Exodus and that which was written in Deuteronomy at one and the same time. Or perhaps, in the author's mind, God could very well say two different things at once, and he, the scribe, somehow received the second version — which differed from the first — five hundred years later. One is asked to believe that the handing down of the Ten Commandments really took place — but which text was spoken to Moses and engraved on the tablets? The first or second? We cannot avoid the question; clever explanations and circumlocutions will not help. The Commandment to keep (or to remember) the Sabbath, moreover, the profound reason for its fulfillment, is explained *differently* in the two Biblical books, each version representing a *different point of view* — or, in our terms, a paradigmatic shift in emphasis.

A paradigm is a set of premises. According to the first explanation, the gift of the Sabbath is conferred on those who obey God and follow His radiant example. No other reason is given. According to the second explanation, man is a conscious partner to the giving of this gift, drawing on his own experience, having himself been a slave. It is his morality and understanding that should guide his conscious decisions towards others. The first view is God-centered; the second puts the onus on man himself, albeit as commanded by God. As we will discover later, these diverse approaches will have caused many divisions throughout Judaism, culminating in the great ethical prophets, who always elevated personal responsibility by each member of society for his and her own acts over blind adherence. In a wider sense, for the first time in history, a human should be totally responsible for his and her moral conduct. A paradigm shift.

Though the two approaches are found in the Hebrew Bible, I believe that the Bible has become holy to other nations as well because of the second, universalistic viewpoint. At the foundation of the universalistic approach lies the tenet that justice is proffered not only to the Jews. But for a very long time the new religion of the Hebrews, who had exited from Egypt, was for them alone: for only they had been privileged to receive the divine revelation. Accordingly, God — our god — rewarded us and commanded us in ways that did not and could not apply to other peoples. Furthermore, we were instructed to eliminate any outsider who stood between the divine promise and us. According to that view, the outsider had no rights; and even those given to him were peripheral and open to varying interpretations.

The new paradigm cannot in any form condone the idea of one human being inferior to others. "White" and other forms of slavery still exist in the world. But, for the readers of this book, these heinous practices constitute a part of an obsolete philosophy, which must be rejected. At times, the Bible directed that the fate of slaves be less harsh than that suffered under foreign legal codes. Nevertheless, there appeared definite discrimination between Hebrew and non-Hebrew slaves. In the Book of the Covenant, it is specified that, after six years of slavery, the Hebrew slave would be eligible for freedom; if somehow he wished to remain a slave, the text criticizes him severely. But the outsider, who was not present at Mount Sinai, deserved in some instances a fate worse than that of a donkey — unless and until the reigning view was amended, so as to clarify, beyond any shadow of doubt, that the same justice we regard as our own right was given by us to others as well, as indeed was achieved through the amendment to the fourth Commandment.

It should be noted that the new version never replaced the old one: both live in the Bible side by side. Consequently, the humanistic version is sometimes regarded as an afterthought, something that Moses just remembered to slip in prior to his departure from the world of the living. Yet the Book of Deuteronomy is by no means an afterthought. Like in the case of Edom, discussed in the last chapter, it introduces totally new ideas, meant to enlarge on — sometimes to replace — the old, constricting ones. Thus, the future reader of the Bible was left with the *choice*, whether to adhere to the sectarian views attributed to the old God or to let himself, herself, open up to the rest of humanity, regardless of religious or other denominations.

The amendment in the Commandment concerning the Sabbath is a supreme example of how, even in time of stress, a man of conscience will never tire from probing the rudiments of accepted views, questioning the justness of his own deeds. He or she will keep doing it, in order to make us humans deserve the claim of having been created in the image of God — for a religious person, the highest accolade — and will follow this deeply humanistic call at whatever personal cost it may incur.

Chapter 4

From Tribalism to Monarchy
The Circumstances Leading to the Birth of the Universal Perspective

Reaching the middle of the three volumes which constitute the Hebrew Bible, entitled "Prophets," the first thing to note is its accepted division into two main sub-sections: "First Prophets" and "Last Prophets." The former is to convey historical events: the latter, the words of Israel's great prophets. Yet, as we shall soon see, the historical authenticity of the latter exceeds that of the former by far.

Let us stop once again and ask ourselves: What is there of such great value in looking for that which is historically true in the Bible?

In historical research, there usually pertains the common ruling by which past events are divided into *pre*-historic and historic categories, wherein only study of the latter — based on (a) archeological findings, (b) authentic written evidence and/or (c) that which can be corroborated by alternative sources — provides us with a reliable picture of the past. Yet, to many, doubting the veracity of the events described in the Bible appears totally irrelevant. What counts for them is that those events were *accepted* as true for thousands of years. "What difference does it make," they will argue, "if such a person as Abraham actually existed, when everyone for hundreds of generations believed that he did? And what difference does it make if what occurred at Mount Sinai really took place, while we cannot ignore the enduring impact of Sinai on all of Western civilization?" In other words, when reading the Bible, not the *facts* should concern us, but something else.

But what if some facts are verifiable and others are not? Should that make no difference at all? With all humility, I think it should, and here is why.

Not for a moment do I doubt the power of Biblical stories. However, after years of close proximity, I have come to regard a true account in a way other than I value a story whose authenticity cannot be substantiated. It happens that I relate to the words of an honest person in a way other than I do to the words of someone who uses a shred of fact to make a lie appear like truth. The reason for this insistence is exactly the amazing power of those stories, turned in the hands of the Orthodox into the only true account of the past, the interpretation of which is exclusively in their hands. This, in turn, becomes an awesome political power, driving out of court, as it were, any other possible interpretation.

"Last Prophets" is comprised of fifteen books containing the words of as many prophets (Isaiah, Jeremiah, etc.), to whom the creation of an ethical, universal worldview is attributed. Their appearance is halfway through the period of the monarchy, hundreds of years after what purportedly took place at Mount Sinai. Yet, unlike the Five Books of Moses, and a great deal which appears in First Prophets, the words of the Last Prophets are considered, with little exception, to be their actual utterances. It is important to point out that the Last Prophets were active at a time when Hebrew writing had already come into widespread use. It served as a powerful tool in their hands. This is why they are also referred to as the Scriptural Prophets. In contradistinction, the words of Buddha, Jesus and Mohammed — and Moses, too — were set down in writing many years after their time. The same is true regarding a great deal of which appears in First Prophets. However, since the first kings of Israel, in about 1000 B.C.E., royal annals were kept and our written history got under way.

If it is true that the words of the Late Prophets were written down by them or by their immediate contemporaries, in their Masters' presence, as it were, Hebrew readers are privileged to study the utterances of Amos, Isaiah, Micah, Jeremiah and other prophets practically in their "original." The texts cannot be taken to comprise the "whole truth," of course, for the circumstances in which they were written, inevitable omissions as well as many facts which are not mentioned in the writings, require some elucidation and interpolation, in order to be understood by us today. All the same, it is a unique experience to read them, as if one were actually there at the time, hearing them fall from the speakers' lips. They are singularly authentic. People of the utmost integrity spoke them. They were held to be most sacred, so they have been almost unaltered. And, thus, they represent some of the most valuable records of antiquity. I am quite ready to admit that, because of their unique authenticity, their spiritual impact is greater on me than, say, the story of Adam and Eve, however beautifully the latter is told, representing human nature. The prophets, too, were human, and I believe it is due to them that humanistic Judaism has survived, more than the beauty of Genesis.

The following survey is made, by and large, on the strength of comments dispersed through some less historically-reliable Biblical texts, describing what largely preceded the Late Prophets: the Books of Joshua, Judges, I & II Samuel and I & II Kings. These Books are called "First Prophets," since "non-Scriptural" prophets were active then, and some of their most remembered exhortations are dispersed throughout those Books. Most of the events in that earlier section cannot be corroborated — yet there is little reason to doubt the overall processes they trace.

There is no doubt, for instance, that in the several hundred years following the conquest of the Land of Israel, new systems of governing and organizing evolved, moving from tribal structures to monarchy, from regional to central government. The Bible does not discuss many fundamental issues, which must have faced the new settlers. For example, how did the desert nomads acquire the skills necessary for sedentary agricultural living? But here and there we find some clues. The Book of Joshua relates that the military leader ordered his people to clear mountainous forestland, a lengthy process requiring training and skill. Independent research confirms that most of the land was indeed wooded. Predatory beasts, unknown in the desert, roamed everywhere. In the Book of Exodus, we find a "reason," endowed with visionary foresight, for not expelling all the native dwellers of Canaan *"in one year — lest the beast of the field multiply against thee!"* It turns out that the Israelites, however divinely motivated, did not drive out the local valley dwellers immediately, or "in one year," as is written, for they simply could not, discovering that the local inhabitants had had *"chariots of iron."*

This brings us to a basic question of the "conquest": How long did it take to complete and what were its methods? The above references already negate the Biblical claim of it all happening in one fell swoop. Learned opinions — like that of Prof. S. Yeivin of the Hebrew University — suggest a lengthy process lasting some one hundred and fifty years, bringing to mind Abraham's gentle methods rather than Joshua's slam-bang ones. No end of digs have ever substantiated the tale of the walls of Jericho tumbling down within two generations following the Biblical Exodus, though a similar fate seems to have befallen the city at some other, altogether different period.

Since the Bible dwells mostly on religious adherence, it supplies us with some relevant information regarding the adherence of the Israelites — or, in Biblical terminology, their "return" — to the one God. All through the period in which the Hebrews consolidated their hold on the land, they kept the memory of their parochial God, who had taken them out of Egypt. But, at the same time, they certainly seized every opportunity to "commit adultery" with the more amenable local deities, the gods of rain and fertility. As is shown in the Book of Judges, Moses' Levites controlled all Jehovah-oriented religious practices, preferably from the center in Shiloh, but also in the cities and villages throughout the land. How dominant was the desert faith? It fluctuated, to say the least, influenced by many religious and "non-religious" factors, such as external wars and trading relations.

On occasion, various tribal "judges" emerged to come to the rescue. However, our judges' faith in the God of Israel was far from exemplary. Going by his name, one of the earlier judges, Shamgar Ben-Anat, was not a Hebrew, but a Canaanite. And how observant a Hebrew does rowdy Samson look to us? Not very. Deborah, on the other hand, spoke out clearly in the name of Israel's desert God — Whom, for some reason, she described as coming out of Edom — yet she failed to unite, under His name, a good number of Israel's tribes in the would-be national war she captained. Gideon, too, was a champion of a jealous Jehovah, but then, in his later years, he shamelessly erected an idol in his native city of Ophrah, and the people "whored with it." On the whole, the People of Israel went on consorting with other gods. It was only when a war for survival erupted that they returned, in some degree, to their "own" God.

Throughout that period, Israel is portrayed as a community of farmers. Samson roams the fields, Gideon threshes grain, and Deborah sits beneath a date palm. The chief attribute of the God of Israel is His being the God of the offspring of slaves-turned-farmers, the God of the weak confronting the powerful.

This formative era came to an end with the advent of Samuel, to whom the Bible devotes two entire Books. These books already bear the marks of contemporary literacy. They look as if they were written by a historian, probably, a court historian, whose aim was the establishing of an overall view as to how the monarchy should be conducted. Samuel appears as judge, priest and prophet all in one, a statesman rivaled by few in our history. He crowned the first two kings of Israel — Saul and David — despite the warnings about the evils of monarchy attributed to him. The pressure of the Philistines on the tribes of Israel, as well as other circumstances, necessitated a centralized government, and Samuel was the right man at the right place and at the right time.

In creating the monarchy, did Samuel effect a deep change on Israel's religion as well? The answer is, yes! It is clearly stated. Yet, this historical comment, relating to the most important and far-reaching religious upheaval in that period, although written down, is hardly ever heeded. It has in it too much to negate later claims in the would-be historical books in the Bible, that all the laws in the Bible originated from Moses.

In the first chapters of I Samuel, we learn that the Levites will no longer control the priesthood: *"I will cut off thine arm and the arm of thy father's house,"* God tells the aging Eli, the last of the Levite priests, referring to the House of Amram, i.e., Moses' father, *"and every one that is left in thy house...shall say, 'Put me, I pray thee, into one of the priests' offices, that I may eat a morsel of bread!'"* The Levites were unceremoniously demoted to a lower class, often ranking with the orphan, the widow and the "stranger that is within thy gates." The priesthood became the sole province of the loyal supporters of the new monarchs.

Now the Bible turns to describe the exploits of Israel's first kings, which it does with great subtlety and verve. In contrast to the armor of truth that protects the works of the Late Prophets, the Biblical writers took great liberties with accounts of the first kings, particularly with those establishing the House of David — i.e., David himself and his son, Solomon.

On the one hand, the text leads us to believe that these two rulers totally lacked morality, stopped at nothing to gain and maintain power, holding eternal grudges against all who opposed them (the House of Saul, for one). On the other hand, they are described as noble, devout and richly endowed with sublime artistic talents. In the midst of deadly wars — during the period when for the first time King David forged the querulous tribes of Israel into one centralized kingdom — we are also asked to believe that he worked day and night to compose most of the one hundred and fifty Psalms, reflecting the puniness of mankind and the greatness of God. He is also described as being loyal to his predecessor, the "messiah of God," King Saul, even when offering to fight with the Philistines against the rejected king in the battle in which Saul met his death. Moreover, after Saul's fall, David continued to fight against Saul's sons in a "long war" (sic).

David's son Solomon, was born to a woman of doubtful virtue. He rose to power through a series of bloody intrigues and ruled over the vast kingdom he had inherited by exploiting his subjects in a ruthless fashion. Yet he, too, is painted throughout as sagacious — a sensitive poet and dispenser of refined justice.

Both these kings were loyal to God, except when their loyalty conflicted with their earthly interests. But the Bible's various writers and editors gave in to the call of duty when presenting the creators of the Kingdom of Israel also as symbols of faith in God, endowed with virtues that they, the writers, regarded as befitting both God and His nation. Despite all their efforts, however, they ultimately portrayed the God of David and Solomon as no more than *our* God, Who conveniently looked the other way when it suited His more or less loyal subjects.

In no way can one find universal attributes in David's faith in God. Based on its own internal reference, the Book of Joshua was written in the time of David. It reflects the attitudes of our first great kings toward conquered neighboring nations, whose fate was to be annihilated or totally subjugated. Nor is Solomon, who finally built the House of God, so righteous. He is known as much for his wisdom as for his thousand foreign wives and concubines and his stores of silver and gold, the latter being exactly those that Samuel warned against, but which the Biblical author still describes with unadulterated praise. Toward the end of his life, Solomon comes in for some rebuke, when, according to the Bible, his faith deteriorated under the influence of his foreign wives. Then, this wisest of men went on to erect "high places" for foreign idols all over Jerusalem, including an altar for Moloch in the Valley of Hinom, where humans were sacrificed by common people and Jewish royalty alike for generations.

His womanizing and his idolatry, though on an international scale, indicate anything but universal attitudes. They are, rather, Solomon's method of increasing his power at justice's expense. In a like manner, Solomon's marriage to Pharaoh's daughter demonstrates diplomatic opportunism, not forgiveness toward the Egyptians. After Solomon died, his son, emerging from the text as one of the biggest fools that ever lived, totally succumbed to his lust for power. He caused the larger part of the kingdom to rebel and split away from under Judean rule, creating the separate northern Kingdom of Israel, also known as the "ten tribes." Incredible as it may sound, that same kingdom will always be portrayed as sinning against God, for reasons I will touch on later.

How, during this period of the monarchy (in the circumstances and with the personalities described) did the prophets of Israel rise to create a doctrine of universal, ethical Justice? I hardly believe that anyone can actually explain this unique phenomenon. Yet, in the same way many of us would like to know what goes on in today's world, hoping it would give us some guidance as to our choice and beliefs, a fair knowledge of the past may furnish us with the sense of contemporary, parallel developments. In other words, how are we to regard the spiritual phenomenon of the ethical prophecy in relation to both the past *and* our present time? It is in order to launch such a quest that it is highly necessary to try to envision the actual circumstances prevailing then, rather than follow the ornate tales engulfing David and Solomon.

All this may sound straightforward enough. What is not so self-evident is how the utterances of the prophets (which, contrary to pious protestations, hardly ever became the ideology of any ruling class, religion or nation) are notwithstanding the basis of most ethics in our present-day world. In order to answer this question, we should look for the kernel of the Prophets' universalism.

In those days, it was commonly held by all peoples that their "national" deity ruled the whole world. It was not unique to our nation. What makes the late prophets so outstanding (even if not all of them and not to the same degree) is their credo that all human beings and nations share equally in the divine gift. But since God has known only Israel from all the nations, we, therefore, are more obliged than anyone else to show justice to others. In fact, we have been given more obligations than privileges!

We have observed that the faith in a just God, the God of the desert who looked after the weak and the oppressed, permeated our national consciousness during the epoch of the Judges. But once we became a strong nation, members of two great kingdoms, God increasingly neglected to fend for the helpless and the victims. According to the Bible, of course, it was the people of Israel who turned their backs on God. Through the Holy Temple in Jerusalem and other temples in the northern kingdom (referred to in the Book of Amos as "kings' temples"), a system of centralized religion evolved. But its priests proved no less venal and corrupt than the secular King's servants. *"The priests thereof teach for hire,"* in the words of the prophet, Micah. *"I hate and despise your feasts"* [in the temples], declared Amos.

A great deal has been said about the prophets' contribution to the establishment of the rule of justice as an ideal in our people's consciousness. I have also shown that this view had existed in us as a *leaning* for generations, creating the breeding ground for that ideal to flourish. Little, however, has been said about the legal system and law enforcement mechanisms, which also must have existed at the time of the monarchy.

This obvious lack is partly due to the prophets' unbridled attacks on the system, whenever it had failed to carry out what they considered to be God's commands. Also, the preoccupation of the later editors of the Bible with idolatry did not motivate them to deal with the law enforcement mechanism, which had developed in Judea and Israel. The main bulk of "Moses' statutes" in the Torah originated in the Second Temple era and, therefore, cannot give us much of a picture of the legal system that constituted the fiber of daily life during the First Temple era.

Reading through the two Books of Kings — our main historical source for the First Temple era — is not much help. This is because every king is branded above anything else as one who did *"that which was evil in the sight of the Lord,"* or *"that which was right in the sight of the Lord"* — as the case may have been regarding his attitude toward idol worship. But many outstanding legal reforms did occur, as can be gleaned from stray remarks referring to this or that king's exploits. These reforms had no mean share in nurturing the prophetic vision, aiding it to take root in the hearts of the people. Let me cite one out of many examples, seldom given their appropriate weight.

During Amos' childhood, in the first half of the eighth century B.C.E. and half-way thorough the period of the Judean monarchy, King Amaziah captured and sentenced to death two of his "servants" (i.e., king's men) who had murdered his father, King Joash. The Biblical account adds here that he did not, however, put to death the murderers' sons, and that this concurred with "Moses' law," found in Deuteronomy, which reads: *"The fathers shall not be put to death for the children, nor the children be put to death for the fathers; but every man shall be put to death for his own sin."* From this, and other episodes, it can be clearly inferred that this had not been the practice up to that time. Only from then on did it become legally

binding that every man be solely responsible for his own deeds —
which, incidentally, went contrary to all other legal systems in the
region. This legal innovation soon became a fundamental tenet in
the teachings of Israel's prophets.

Altogether, it seems that the monarchy was never *felt* to be
appropriate for Israel. This inappropriateness begins with the
warning attributed to Samuel and, then, with Elijah, the half-
legendary prophet, who predated the Scriptural Prophets by a
hundred years and confronted the powerful King Ahav with the
words, *"Hast thou murdered and also inherited?"* Throughout the
centuries, prophets in Israel rebuked their monarchs in far stronger
a manner than did their counterparts in other nations. On many
occasions, we find that a king requires a "covenant with the people"
in order to rule (as in the case of King Jehoash's coronation, some
two generations prior to the first Scriptural Prophecy). This clearly
indicates that, even in those far-off days, our monarchs depended
not so much on absolute rights as on the support of their people,
who, somehow, had an ingrained "democratic" flair.

From the time of David and Solomon, a new socio-political
factor came into play. For the first time since they had thrived in
Egypt, the Children of Israel could view themselves as a part of the
rest of humanity. Solomon traded widely. Through marriage, he
formed alliances all over the civilized world. He did not affect it all
by himself, of course. Officials, intellectuals as well as merchants
spoke foreign languages. *"Speak, I pray thee, to thy servants in the
Aramean language, for we understand it; and speak not with us in the
Jewish language, in the ears of the [common] people that are on the wall,"*
requested Hezekiah's, the Judean King's officers of Sennacherib,
the Assyrian king's representatives.

The ubiquity of writing was yet another factor in opening up to
the world. After all, "out there," writing had been in use for
thousands of years, while, with the exception of a number of words
here and there (in main part to identify ownership over some item),

there is no archeological evidence of Hebrew writing before the period of the monarchy. Moses' Levites may have been able to read and write while in Sinai; they kept their Egyptian names until the time of Samuel. But there is no evidence that they remembered any of the Egyptian language or its script after having settled in Canaan. The first complete archeological document written in the Hebrew language — the Gezer calendar — dates from approximately 1000 B.C.E., the time of King David's reign.

With their conquest of the Land of Israel, the Israelites encountered the rich culture of Ugarith, a small kingdom to our north, preserved for us in writing on clay tablets. For the first time in history, our northern neighbors set down poetry and law in a purely alphabetical script, and in a language most similar to Hebrew! Still, the process of writing original Hebrew material seems to have developed slowly, as the people of Ugarith were pagan, and a lot of adaptation and circumvention was needed by Israel's religious leaders to accept what those neighbors had to offer. But, with the establishment of a central authority, i.e., from the era of David and Solomon, writing became essential and came into use in everyday communication. (By that time, Ugarith had long been destroyed, but there is plenty of evidence that its literature was well known to the Prophets as well as to the authors of some of the Psalms.) The Hebrews were then quick to learn. They were obviously most gifted storytellers and documentarists. Indeed, the power of the Bible derives in part from the extraordinary literary skills of its authors. According to Martin Buber, Biblical poetic works express more historical truth than official documents. The poetic linguistic ability of the prophets was supreme, affecting the hearers' hearts as well as their minds. In short, it seems that writing came to serve diverse categories, civil, literary, and not least the ideas of the new visionaries in that period.

Ironically, most of the Scriptural Prophets did not rely on written laws, but on their deep trust in natural justice that could be visible to all "at the gate." Still, their teachings have come down to us *by means* of written texts, and, from then onwards, the art of literacy gathered momentum to reach heretofore-unknown depth and dimension. New books, whose authors strove to imitate the prophets' style, followed, though their contents often digressed from the prophets' principles. When there were thirty-nine of these books, the collection was given the overall title of "Holy Books," and then sealed.

We should always remember to look for the message of Israel's prophets in their own words. This is not so crucial in the other Biblical books — most of which were written later and then undergone editing for hundreds of years prior to being canonized, while the early written prophecy remained mostly unchanged.

My aim in this inquiry is to explore the broadest essence of Judaism, in the face of life's new demands, as well as to examine Judaic principles with the potential for a new perspective. What Israel's Prophets thought and believed has inspired thinkers for many generations to come. I propose that their elevated teaching is applicable to our own age as well.

In concluding this chapter, let us review the discussion to this point.

We have recognized the difficulty in pinning down the essence of the Jewish people, while accepting that such an essence exists. We have observed that the world's problems have become increasingly intertwined, and that it is now critical for Jews to develop a new perspective to be able to form a new, overall perception (paradigm). We have indicated a number of that paradigm's attributes. We have viewed what is traditionally accepted as our nation's ancient history, despite the troubling contradictions and discrepancies in the Bible. What has emerged from our historical survey is, first and foremost, that the oppressed Hebrews were among the first of all peoples to view their God as an intimate deity of the entire nation, and that social justice became an inextricable component of the faith in that one God.

During that formative epoch, the People of Israel developed a sense of being fundamentally different from the other nations. Although universal elements can be traced in the Ten Commandments, they are minor as compared with the perception of the Jews as a "chosen people."

Finally, we looked at how the Children of Israel settled in Canaan and moved from tribalism to monarchy. We discovered that a keen awareness of their origins in slavery persisted in the national consciousness, coming into conflict with both the monarchy and the priesthood. We thus came to grips with the circumstances, which became the nursing ground of the ethical prophecy.

And all that time, we are intrigued by the linguistic power of expression of that small nation.

Chapter 5

The Scriptural Prophets
All the Way to Universalism and Back

For humanity to see itself as an integral *conscious* part of the universe can be regarded as the zenith of human attainment. As it happened, while the universalist pronouncement was first made glorious by our Prophets, it was not given to us, their people, to propagate it for long. In this chapter I will demonstrate how within two, at most, three hundred years after the first expression of ethical universalism, our spiritual teachers reverted back to our non-universalist outlook.

We have already discussed the development of the *social* justice impulse. With our great Prophets it reached its peak; it became the *style* — to run down slavery. Yet slavery continued to exist. A few lines from a seemingly independent Biblical passage may give us a taste of that dual standard. They appear in the Book of Deuteronomy, as a part of an epic poem ascribed to Moses shortly before his death, known as "Ha'azinu" ("O, hear ye"). In it, the one hundred and twenty-year-old leader *predicts* the destruction of his people, brought on their heads as punishment for sins they are destined to commit: "...*And Yeshurun* [meaning, the straight-looking one, i.e., Israel] *waxed fat and kicked out.*" This is followed by the damning reproach, "*Thou didst wax fat! Thou didst grow thick! Thou didst become gross!*" The meaning of these images cannot be mistaken: the People of Israel betrayed and/or will betray God by putting on weight, i.e., accumulating immense earthly riches at the expense of higher, spiritual values.

Though the poem does not specify our having been slaves (in the writer's words, God found Israel in the desert) nor does it damn social injustices as such, it invokes the image of an idyllic, poor and humble desert society in bygone days, contrasting it with a sedentary society, living on its land, which, by growing gross with affluence, repudiates the values of chaste living. This picture fully supports the morals of the Late Prophets. Other internal evidence also points to the Prophets' authorship of Ha'azinu. For instance: our Prophets normally castigated the *whole* people, which the poet does here; it was always clear that the chief transgressors in the eyes of the Prophets were those who "put on weight," i.e., the rich, and so is the case here.

The rejection of slavery created a deep suspicion toward the monarchy. This sentiment was attributed even to Samuel, the king-maker himself. His warning reads: *"...he* [the king] *will take your sons, and appoint them unto him, for his chariots, and to be his horsemen.... And he will appoint them...to plow his ground, and reap his harvest.... And he will take your daughters to be perfumers, and to be cooks.... And he will take your fields and...your vineyards, and give to his officers... And he will take your goodliest young men, and your asses, and put them to his work... And ye shall be his servants."* The abominable term "slaves," which is used here in the Hebrew text, was somehow reduced to "servants" in the English version. In Hebrew it does say "slaves," and no mistake.

The kingmaker's warning became an everyday reality when the King and his officers increasingly exercised their new powers by appropriating the land, which belonged to the poorer members of their communities, in lieu of unpaid debts and other misfortunes. Furthermore, when the price of the land was not sufficient recompense, the one-time landowner himself was sold into slavery to make up the debt. In Amos' powerful words, *"they sell the righteous for silver, and the needy for a pair of shoes!"* Thus, the general repudiation of slavery as a *memory* turned into a painful *reality* when the most abhorrent form of social injustice was directed against the major section of society.

And then, borne on the struggle for social justice, for a relatively short period, the idea of a universal, higher justice dawned on the horizons of human consciousness. It first appeared halfway through the monarchy, about mid-eighth century B.C.E., while its last great expression is found in "Deuto"-Isaiah, in Babylon, some two hundred years later. It was to become the inspiration of many spiritual leaders and liberation movements throughout the ages. In today's *interconnectedness*, one cannot but hope that both planetary conditions and human consciousness may have evolved sufficiently to join together again and bring about universalism's most complete and enduring revival.

In giving an account of the Prophets of Israel, we should stop to comment on a basic dilemma they had to cope with vis-à-vis Israel's enemies. Propagating the new universal concept, i.e., that not only all persons, but also all nations are basically equal, did not tally with the idea of Israel being a *chosen people*. Furthermore, it would be wrong to assume that our Prophets felt that we, Israel, had not been chosen for *some* task. But, then, due to the new idea of our God being the god of all peoples, a particular task in the divine plan was to be allotted to the other nations as well, viz. that even when ill-treating God's chosen people, they, the other nations, did so by God's command! Thus, when Israel was beaten, conquered and driven into exile, according to both Ha'azinu and most of the prophetic exhortations, those *strangers* fulfilled God's wishes. They were, in fact, God's tools.

Although placed as sixth in the Biblical section of the "Last Prophets," Amos, according to references to the kings in whose reign he prophesied, was the first of our Scriptural Prophets and, as such, the first outspoken proponent of the universalist perspective.

Let us first look at a number of his utterances to discover how he went about introducing this new idea.

In his opening exhortation on Israel, following the existing "style" of castigating the rich in defense of the poor, Amos immediately went further in bestowing the title *Tzadik* (righteous man) *exclusively* on the poor. The reference here applies to *all* the poor, of course, but it relates to a specific case, when a man was sold into slavery for an unpaid debt — a pair of shoes. Since many of his listeners *were* poor, it was easy for them to accept the title of *Tzadik* being conferred on them. But, then, when repeating the same exhortation, Amos *changed* the title. Instead of "*Tzadik*," he now spoke of "*dalim*" (i.e., the poor), indicating that the reference applied to *all* the poor, not only the Israelites. This teaching was repeated seven hundred fifty years later by another: Jesus of Nazareth.

I invite the reader to delve into Amos' work: it is full of magnificent, subtle stratagems, all serving the new worldview he initiated — sometimes modifying ancient rules and, at other times, totally negating them. The *utter* repudiation of slavery, it should be noted, went contrary to *allowing* slavery in the earlier edicts, appearing in the Book of the Covenant.

The evolvement of social justice into universal justice could not help but negate some old beliefs. Amos concluded one of his last prophecies, with an unheard-of rhetorical question: "*Are you not as much mine as the children of the Kushiyim?* [The term for African Blacks] he proclaimed, "*O, Children of Israel, says the Lord. Have I not brought up Israel out of the Land of Egypt, and the Philistines from Kaphtor, and Aram from Kir?*" His audience knew well, from hard experience, that the Philistines and the Arameans had been Israel's deadliest enemies for ages. Yet here, a man of God went as far as equating them with Israel, calling to his aid the most momentous act of God towards His people — the Exodus. All along, Amos told his amazed listeners that their very own God wished them primarily to set a moral example for the rest of hummankind. When saying, *"Only you have I known of all the families of the earth; therefore I will punish you for all your iniquities!"* the implication is that having been *known* by God gave Israel no privileges, only moral responsibility toward the surrounding nations.

Later in this chapter, we will discover how Amos' universal vision got modified even by his immediate followers, with the result that a Hebrew could eventually go back to praising the smashing of enemy infants on the rocks, and to the blood-curdling curse, repeated annually round the Passover table, *"Pour out Thy wrath on the nations that do not call Thy name!"* How did all this happen?

I am not sure one can actually *know* what gave Amos his inspiration. What can be detected with certainty are the ebbing fortunes of his universal message, as appearing in the visions of three members of practically the same generation as his. The difference in the attitudes of the first Scriptural Prophets cannot be taken to be a matter of sheer nuance. On one occasion — in the case of the *End of Days* vision *("Nation shall not lift up sword against nation; neither shall they learn war anymore...")* — one Prophet actually *appropriated* the words of his colleague, in order to prove the opposite point made by the latter!

Other than that, the texts in the four Prophetic Books leave little doubt as to their authorship. This statement is based on textual and historical cross-references and, also, on their varying *personal* styles. Once again, while there is no doubt regarding the major events referred to in them, what we are looking for are the Prophets' varying *views* regarding those events.

We will follow the *chronological* order of their prophecies, as distinct from the haywire order in which they appear in the Bible. It is hard to tell why the Biblical editors chose to place Isaiah as first of the Late Prophets; one criterion may have been *size*: The Book of Isaiah is three to four times longer than the extant work of each of his three predecessors. All four started prophesying in mid- to late-eighth century B.C.E. They were:

(1) Amos, who hailed from Judea and prophesied in the northern Kingdom of Israel;

(2) Hosea, Amos' close contemporary, who also prophesied in Israel, his native land;

(3) Isaiah of Jerusalem, Judea's capital, who prophesied in his city at about the same time as Hosea did in Samaria, Israel's capital;

(4) Micah, Isaiah's contemporary, who was born in the provincial town of Maresha in the lower plains of Judea.

Let us examine the four in some detail.

(1) Amos, a shepherd from Tekoa, a village east of Bethlehem bordering on the Judean Desert, left his home for Samaria, the bustling capital of Israel in the north. At that time, Israel's great King, Jeroboam ("The Second"), son of Jehoash, expanded the conquests of his father both to the north and the east, at the expense of mighty Aram, the latter being locked in a struggle for survival with the rising Assyrian power to its east. The new realm of Israel extended beyond King David's "divinely promised" borders. Amos makes no mention of Assyria, which may be due, in part, to the overwhelming confidence in Israel's power. The Assyrian threat seemed, at best, a long way off. Amos' main preoccupation was with what happened internally, though in relation to the world at large.

Compared with all of Israel's other prophets, it is quite surprising to discover that Amos never preached against *foreign idols* (with the exception of one contemptuous remark). His arrows were directed predominantly at social oppression that was exercised concurrently with the false, pompous Jehovah worship in the temples. For him, those venal practices could never be God's demands; in fact, they contradicted them.

Not less revealing is the realization that, in his own fashion, the great King Jeroboam was exceptionally faithful to Israel's God. This supports Amos' new teaching, viz. that Israel and its fortunes were far from being God's only concern. The popular slogan in Israel during Amos' time was *"Lord God's Day! Jehovah's day!"* — i.e., a day of great festivities, a day that would usher in a yet better era for Israel's kingdom. Amos ridiculed this slogan, saying: *"The day of the Lord will be darkness, not light; of gloom, not of brightness!"* And he went on: *"Take thou away from Me the noise of thy songs; and let Me not hear the melody of thy psalteries. But let justice well up as waters, and righteousness as a mighty stream!"* By now, it is clear that by "justice" Amos means *universal* justice, not necessarily justice for Israel alone.

Rejecting false piety, Amos prophesied Israel's fall, the destruction of Jeroboam's House *"by the sword"* — a proclamation which brought on him the charge of conspiracy against the king — and the total destruction that would befall Israel. The greatest punishment of all would be exile, although Amos, as mentioned (and as far as we know), did not specify the enemy who would effect it.

A close reading of Amos shows, however, that he fully recognized the global historical powers at work. But his main concern was to avert the practices of Israel's ruling circles, which weakened the nation's social fabric so recklessly that they would eventually make it impossible for the kingdom to stave off external attack.

He is best loved and known for his passionate stand for the impoverished and, accordingly, his scathing attacks on the rich. *"Hear this word, you cows of Bashan, who are in the mountains of Samaria, who oppress the poor, who crush the needy, who say to their husbands, 'Bring, that we may drink!' The Lord God has sworn by his holiness that, behold, the days are coming upon you, when they shall take you away with hooks..."* And, similarly, *"Woe to those who lie upon beds of ivory...because you trample upon the poor...* [you] *shall be the first to go into exile!"* But Amos' most momentous and original contribution — never to be underrated — was to elevate the God of Israel to the God of all peoples, while propounding that justice is fundamental to any living, healthy, social, political and spiritual structure anywhere, and that espousing this idea was at the very heart of faith.

(2) After Amos was driven out of Israel, his prophecies of wrath materialized. The enormous gap between the realities of life as described by him and those which come to light in the prophesies of Hosea, his probable disciple, opens up the question of what was the nature of the sudden change in the political and social climate before Israel's fall, and what had become of the reigning faith, however misguided, in the God of Israel.

It seems that the royally inspired popular faith in the Lord God had gone by the board. A mere six months after the coronation of Jeroboam's son, the young king was murdered. Robbery, violence and assassinations were rampant in the chaotic kingdom, whose dissolution had already begun during the last years of Jeroboam's reign. Amos' expulsion could not have gone unnoticed. It coincided with a general abandonment of faith in the God of Israel, a faith that had disappointed the nation. In its place, people slid back into worshipping the gods of fertility, into openly practicing ceremonial prostitution in the temples and to a vicious dog-eat-dog way of life.

Hosea was an Israelite who loved his people with a passion bordering on pain. He witnessed the collapse of the spiritual edifice that his teacher had erected, and prophesied Israel's imminent defeat at the hands of Assyria. He declared that the coming downfall was solely the result of the betrayal of God by His people, which he likened to the betrayal of a husband by his wife, drawing on his own marital crisis. The Book of Hosea is based on his knowledge that God had *commanded* his own wife's unfaithfulness, in order that he, God's messenger, would bitterly experience what it was like to be betrayed.

Hosea did not lay much stress the questions of social justice, as though the need to reinstall it hardly had to be mentioned. He still referred to it throughout when saying, for instance: *"Oppressed is Ephraim [Israel], crushed in trial, for he willingly strayed from justice."* But, first and foremost, he assailed idolatry: *"My people inquire of a thing of wood, and their staff gives them oracles... they have left their God to play the harlot!"*

Hosea knew that only utter devastation would bring his God to forgive His people. And only then, after the calamity — addressing the future, repentant people in the feminine gender — He would say to them: *"Yea, I will betroth thee unto Me in righteousness, and in justice, and in loving kindness, and in compassion; and I will betroth thee unto Me in faithfulness, and thou shalt know the Lord."*

Hosea's great contribution is in introducing the idea of *charity*, which in comparison seems lacking in his teacher's exhortations. A just society can be the one in which love would bind together all elements. But, in order to reach that ideal, idolatry must first be obliterated; then the charitable state would reign forever. God would again say to Israel, *"Thou art My people,"* and the people will reply, *"Thou art my God."*

In Hosea, we find almost no trace of God belonging to all nations: in the wretched land, facing cruel occupation, the Prophet's immediate and only concern is his people's return to God.

The Book of Hosea demonstrates a relentless self-search as well as a detailed knowledge of Israel's history. His language is on a high plane, compounding intricate literary skills. Like those of Amos before him, Hosea's prophecies were clearly composed during a period and in an environment in which literacy had become an integral fact of life.

(3) This literary feat continued, reaching far-away Jerusalem; one

cannot speak of Isaiah ("The First") without realizing his linguistic ability raising his faith and vision to the summit of human expression.

Isaiah prophesied during the reign of four kings: Uzziah, Yotham, Ahaz and Hezekiah. Covering this period, his prophecies fill thirty-nine chapters. Consequently, and uncharacteristically, in comparison with most other Late Prophets, with Isaiah it is not always possible to relate his utterances to specific events, though he was personally involved in the king's court and his opinion on pressing political and military issues was often sought. We do know, however, that during his lifetime Judea fought two major wars and sustained terrible wounds — this being probably the background for his persistent claim that Judea had been incessantly the innocent victim before cruel foreign powers, heralding a new national trait: *self-pity*.

Regarding the rulers in Jerusalem, their behavior did not differ from that of the rulers in Samaria. The first chapters in Isaiah testify how deeply influenced he was initially by Amos's prophecies and their import, causing him to strike out relentlessly at Jerusalem's leaders, *"the rebellious companions of thieves who thrive on bribery and chase after rewards; they judge not the fatherless* [with equity], *nor does the cause of the widow touch them."* Likewise, he ridiculed the rituals and sacrifices in the Temple, which, he claimed, contravened the course of justice. Like his contemporary, Hosea, Isaiah vehemently condemned idolatry. But eventually, the external blows that rocked the kingdom shaped an entirely new vision in him.

Several years before Samaria's fall to the Assyrians, the still undefeated Israel allied itself with Aram. Together they waged an all-out war against their southern neighbor, Judea. Isaiah was outraged. He described Israel as, *"The crown of pride of the drunkards of Ephraim."* His feverish attacks on the neighboring sister kingdom were by no means less fierce than his assaults on the perpetrators of social injustice at home. Still, for a while, concurrently with his castigation of Samaria, he kept up his caustic remarks about Jerusalem's leaders: *"Scornful men that rule this people,"* so arrogant in their behavior that it had made them believe they had *"forged a covenant with death."*

Yet, when the great capital of Israel did finally go down and Judea remained the only place where the words of the Lord God could be freely spoken, Isaiah began to see Jerusalem as the only and ultimate venue for the expounding of divine justice, even though that idyllic situation would come to pass only at the *End of Days*.

Soon, his incipient belief in the central position allotted to his city in the divine scheme received further sound confirmation. Twenty years after the destruction of Samaria, an event of even greater magnitude came to pass. Following Judea's rebellion against Assyria, which Isaiah had enthusiastically supported, the army of King Sennacherib overran Judea and captured all its fortified cities except for Jerusalem. Isaiah's faith in the city's strength remained firm and he advised Hezekiah, his King, not to surrender, despite assurances from the conquering Assyrians that they would treat the inhabitants of Jerusalem well. Then, suddenly and inexplicably, the invincible Assyrian army backed off. No independent, extra-Biblical explanation for the Assyrian withdrawal has ever come to light. Some surmise that a lethal plague swept through the besieging army; others connect it to a revolt back in Assyria which made the army rush home. But since the time of that incredible occurrence, Jerusalem's name and status soared to majestic heights, and David's City overnight became the core symbol of the holiness, strength and endurance of the whole of Israel. *"And it shall come to pass in the end of days that the mountain of the Lord's house shall be set on the top of the mountains, and shall be raised high above the hills, and the nations shall stream unto it…. For out of Zion shall go forth Torah and the word of God from Jerusalem…. And He shall judge among the nations and shall magistrate among many peoples, and they shall beat their swords into plowshares, and their spears into pruning hooks. Nation shall not lift up sword against nation; neither shall they learn war any more. O, house of Jacob, come and let us walk in the light of the Lord!"*

Isaiah's later vision of the "End of Days" — the one which Christianity holds to contain the first hint of the coming of a Messiah — is as magnificent as is his first. *"And a branch shall grow out of the stock of Jesse* [King David's father] *and a shoot shall spring from its roots.... With righteousness he shall judge the poor and decide with equity for the meek of the earth. And he shall strike the earth with the rod of his mouth, and with the breath of his lips he shall slay the wicked.... And the wolf shall dwell with the lamb and the leopard shall lie down with the kid.... They shall not hurt or destroy in all My holy mountain, for the earth shall be full of the knowledge of God as the waters cover the sea."*

No other nation is mentioned here by name — except for Ephraim (Israel), which will finally unite with Judea. Then, quite suddenly, the picture changes: The two of them, Judea and Israel, *"together shall spoil the tribes of the east; Edom and Moab will be in their clutches!"*

After the bitter wounds his country has received, Isaiah, like Hosea but to a greater degree, proclaims the unqualified superiority of his God and of his nation. Commensurate with these beliefs, he demands the punishment and devastation of other nations. There is no escaping the fact that the surrounding countries had inflicted injury on Judea; but Judean kings, starting with David, had attacked those countries too, wreaking havoc and destruction in their own stead. However, such fine distinctions failed to mar Isaiah's vision any longer.

From that moment on, wherever we look, Amos' universalism is on a downhill course. This did not happen in one stroke. When Isaiah envisioned the ascent of all the nations to Mount Zion, he did not necessarily place Jerusalem *above* them in any temporal sense, nor did he seek to detach Jerusalem from the rest of humankind. On the contrary, he bestowed justice on the whole world, as *emanating from Mount Zion*. One should not blame this loftiest of visionaries because his brand of universalism has become a scourge in the hands of today's black-gowned fanatics: rather, one should attempt to find out how it all came about.

As stated, it began with Isaiah himself. But then within a few hundred years, Joel, one of the last Prophets — a resident of the Holy City after it had been restored to eminence by Ezra and Nehemiah — completely twisted Isaiah's epiphany by calling for his fellow-residents to expel all foreigners, thus: *"Beat your plowshares into swords and your pruning-hooks into spears!"* he harangued. *"The weak shall say, 'powerful am I!' Then Jerusalem shall be holy."* And for what purpose? So that *"no strangers will pass through her any more!"* What a blood-curdling vision and how reminiscent of those racial declarations one hears today, regarding the Holy City of David!

(4) We will now leave Jerusalem, which has just been spared destruction, and move on to the desolate provincial cities. Micah's Book, though the smallest of the four, is no less powerful than the three that precede it chronologically. Being a native of Judea, the issue of Jerusalem is close to his heart, but he observes her without Isaiah's involvement and elevated aspirations. Micah accepted the Assyrian conquest as divinely ordained, including the overrunning of his own hometown, Maresha. However bitterly felt, he regarded it as a fair punishment for His people's sins. Consequently, Micah's attacks on the sinful, oppressive rich do not abate with the Assyrian withdrawal. Most fierce is his condemnation of the now-complacent rulers of Jerusalem, *"who build Zion with bloodshed and Jerusalem with iniquity…. Therefore, because of you, Zion will become a plowed field, Jerusalem a heap of ruins, and the Temple Mount rough moorland!"*

From here, Micah proceeds to his altered version of the End of

Days, starting with a faithful repetition of what we have just read in Isaiah. He then adds a prophecy of his own which ends with a seemingly bland remark, thus: "...*they shall sit every man under his vine and under his fig tree; And none shall make them afraid; For the mouth of the Lord of hosts has spoken,*" and then he concludes: "*For let all the peoples walk each one in the name of its god, but we will walk in the name of the Lord our God for ever and ever!*"

Manifestly, having just invited all nations to go up to Jerusalem to learn just ways from our God, he sends them away to live in peace with their own gods elsewhere. He is more realistic than Isaiah, being content for God's word to prevail, first and foremost, in his own land. Micah is a humble person. "...*What does the Lord require of thee? Only to do justice, and to love mercy, and to walk humbly with thy God.*"

Another important principle in Micah is that our nation will wage war on others *only* if they invade us — unless that invasion is under God's instruction, of course, as in the case of the war that Judea has just fought. Micah makes a clear point of justifying wars of self-defense only. His teachings are much like those of Amos: under no circumstance will he view his nation as superior to others; humbly, he does not strive to glorify Jerusalem: all he seeks is justice for all.

The centrality of Jerusalem and its holiness, which Isaiah so pointedly espoused, became the religious foundation of the Jewish nation for thousands of years to come. Those who hold to the old paradigm still keep sacrosanct Jerusalem at the heart of their national aspirations. To me it appears that the new paradigm has more in common with Micah, who wanted to worship his God with humility, than with the elevated and erudite member of the king's court in Jerusalem, Isaiah.

Before concluding our examination of Jerusalem's centrality, let us for a moment look at the matter from a purely historical viewpoint.

According to Assyria's plans, Jerusalem was to have been destroyed twenty-one years after the destruction of Samaria — not, as actually happened, one hundred and thirty-six years later, at the hands of Babylon. At the time of the Assyrian siege, Jerusalem's sins, as listed by Isaiah and Micah, were no different from those of Samaria, as described by their near-contemporaries, Amos and Hosea. The prophecies of impending disaster are pretty much the same, too. There is no logical reason, nor a divine one for that matter, for Jerusalem to have survived much longer than Samaria. The delay of Jerusalem's downfall was an historical accident, resulting from the fact that Assyria became bogged down in a war with Babylon and could not return to the region. So, it was finally to the Babylonian power — not the Assyrians — before which, over a hundred years later, Jerusalem succumbed. In the prophetic view, however, this tragic event clearly came about because the Judeans had committed the very same old sins as the Samarians did — this time laid bare by the last of the Judean Prophets, Jeremiah. What, in the interim, had enabled Jerusalem to flourish and acquire its central status for thousands of years to come?

Following the abrupt and unexpected retreat of the Assyrian army from the besieged city, Jerusalem prospered. According to archeological findings, within just a few years after Samaria's fall, Jerusalem grew to twice her former size, presumably due to a stream of refugees pouring in from the north, including writers, builders, blacksmiths, artists and artisans of all kinds, who made her their new home. For the Prophets' followers — including the authors of Deuteronomy and many other great works — there was now only one setting in which the partisans of Jehovah could be active: Jerusalem. And all this because of an historical accident!

We cannot be sure, of course, that Assyria and Babylon would have spared Samaria and Jerusalem had their inhabitants piously followed the teachings of the Prophets. Jerusalem was not near the great powers' arterial road — which Samaria dominated — and may therefore have been granted longer breathing space. If not for that predominantly geographical factor and the sudden retreat of the Assyrians, we may well assume that the name of David would have been mentioned far less than that of Jeroboam ("The First"), son of Nevat, the great liberator of Israel from the tyrannical reign of King Solomon's son. After all, even according to the Bible, God's prophet, Achiah Ha'Shiloni, guided Jeroboam in his revolt!

Given that scenario, perhaps Samaria (where great prophets such as Elijah, Elisha, Jonah, as well as Amos and Hosea had lived and taught for generations), would have been crowned the eternal city of the People of Israel, rather than Jerusalem, where prophecy developed much later. But who can argue with success — even when unfair, and born of sheer chance?

Chapter 6

Destruction and Exile
Leading to Normative Judaism

We now come to the emergence of Judaism.

This statement may surprise the reader, for we have been dealing with Judaism ever since the days of Abraham, have we not? No, we haven't. The term "Jewish" did not come into existence until the destruction of the First Temple, in 586 B.C.E. (unless one is referring to the Hebrew dialect spoken in Judea). Before then, all Hebrews saw themselves as Children of Israel, citizens of one of the two sister kingdoms, and also belonging to one of the Twelve Tribes. Judah, being a large tribe, formed its own Kingdom of Judea. (The two terms, "Judah" and "Judea," are identical in Hebrew.)

It was for the first time in Babylon that the exiles from Judea, living there in separate quarters and needing to support each other while mourning their lot, felt and thought of themselves as *Jewish* ("Jewish" means "Judean" — both being adjectives derived from "Judah"). They probably also wished to distinguish themselves from the interspersed descendents of the exiles from Israel, who may have retained some distant memory of their origins after nearly one hundred and fifty years away from their land. The Israelites must have looked on the newcomers — their one-time neighbors and enemies — with mixed feelings of delight and apprehension. Although, after the destruction of Samaria, the position of Jerusalem became central in the spiritual life of the nation, a *Jewish* consciousness came into being only in Babylon.

It is time to turn to the two personalities who are by far the most influential in creating this new national-religious entity — the prophets Jeremiah and Ezekiel. Both were active at the time of the fall of Jerusalem: Jeremiah, for quite some time before the event and for a number of years following it; Ezekiel, for a brief period prior to the tragedy, but mainly after it had come to pass. Both were *kohanim* (i.e., priests) and had well-formed ideas as to how their religion should be practiced. As for Jerusalem, Jeremiah had little doubt about her destruction but prophesied the exiles' return to their land. Ezekiel, having been banished to Babylon before Jerusalem fell (together with a few thousand leaders and highly-prized artisans), warned of the approaching catastrophe from afar, and then concentrated his efforts on *specific* ways for his people, now in exile, to fortify themselves in preparation for their return to Zion. Some call Ezekiel "the founder of Judaism." However, Jeremiah played no small part in forging his stiff-necked people into a "holy people."

Reading the Book of Jeremiah is not an easy task. While being rich with biographical details, the sense of total dedication to God renders it, at times, above human grasp. Ever since he was a child, in his small hometown of Anatot to the north of Jerusalem, Jeremiah knew that he was destined to be a prophet. He must have studied all those who had preceded him and, like Amos, saw in simple objects divine omens — an almond tree representing God's constant wakefulness, and a pot, hanging over a fire, the coming of the Chaldeans (the Babylonians). At that time, during King Manasseh's fifty-two-year-long reign, religious practices in Judea were predominantly — perhaps altogether — pagan (at least as can be inferred from the young prophet's protracted, denigrating admonitions).

Jeremiah is the first prophet whose writings touch only marginally on the abject material state of his people. Instead, he laments endlessly their sinful behavior in deserting their god.

During that period, other "true" prophets — along with a plethora of "false" ones — were active; but Jeremiah saw himself as a *loner*, taunted and persecuted by all, "*a man of strife and contention to all the land*," the sole defender of Jehovah. He never married or had children, for he was certain that they would die a terrible death. Only his faith mattered and prodded him to denounce idolatry endlessly.

But, as said, Jeremiah was not the only champion of the Lord Jehovah in Judea. Five short years after he had begun to prophesy, young King Josiah led a bloody religious reform. He cruelly uprooted all vestiges of idol worship throughout the land, to the extent that archeological excavations find practically no trace of idol worship in that period. For some unknown reason, Jeremiah said *nothing* about this reform in his writings, which, it seems, he edited himself. What possibly could have been the reason for this strange omission?

In the first phase of his prophecy, Jeremiah spoke repeatedly of the coming exile. As we shall soon see, the inescapability of exile developed into a dominant concept in his prophecy. It must have gone contrary to his beliefs to accept that an *external* wiping out of idols was sufficient to effect *internal* transformation. What occurred then was a twenty-year period of utter silence on his part — which may well indicate the turmoil he experienced, facing the blows wreaked on his countrymen by Josiah's cruel reform, simultaneously nurturing his deep distrust of quick and easy changes. And, indeed, as we learn from his later prophecies, the people never fully came round to forsaking their old idol worship. There was now no way open to him other than reverting (this time with greater confidence based on bitter experience) to his firm belief, that only the hardships of exile could serve as the melting pot necessary to instill into his nation a total loyalty to God.

This, to my mind, marks Jeremiah as a true prophet. Not because I particularly savor his ideas, but because he saw to the core of things, and knew well in advance all that was about to happen. God's message was clear: *"I will regard as good the exiles from Judah, whom I have sent away from this place to the land of the Chaldeans. I will set My eyes upon them for good, and I will bring them back to this land. I will build them up, and not tear them down. I will plant them, and not uproot them. I will give them a heart to know that I am the Lord; and they shall be My people and I will be their God, for they shall return to Me with their whole heart."* (The Hebrew text can be interpreted to mean that the prophet went as far as saying that God looked with favor not only upon the exiles, but upon the exile itself!)

And all this time Jeremiah knew well in his heart that his people would repeat other words he had uttered: *"Pour out Thy wrath on the nations that know Thee not, and upon the peoples that call not on Thy name!"* But how, pray, could any "goy" (i.e., a member of the other nations) *"that know Thee not"* — have a chance of getting to know Him, when, at every Passover Seder, God is entreated to pour out His wrath upon his head? Jeremiah could never be bothered with that question. Only his people and their faith in their God concerned him. He was an avowed radical, for whom it mattered little how and where other people lived — and, for that matter, how his own people lived, as long as they were forged through and through to carry out all of God's commandments.

Do these words have a familiar ring? Of course they do. Within the confines of normative Judaism, exclusive loyalty to the God of Israel and to the Torah constitutes the entire meaning of life. Jeremiah seldom bothered himself with most *practical*, everyday aspects of the Torah either. Those matters would be addressed by Ezekiel — and then by Ezra, more than one hundred years after Ezekiel's time. But Jeremiah's prophecies transformed the religion of Israel and endowed it with hitherto unknown cohesive — and exclusive — qualities.

After his prolonged silence, Jeremiah reappeared in the besieged city of Jerusalem. The towns of Judea, including

Jeremiah's own town of Anatot, had been overrun by the Babylonian army, and many of their citizens had fled to find shelter within the walls of the big city. In this setting, Jeremiah emerged as a valiant and resourceful adversary. The prophet, who had hitherto been all but ignored, found in beleaguered Jerusalem fertile field for action. Under siege, he resorted to pleading for social justice, more than he had ever done before. He now demanded that Hebrew slaves be set free in accordance with the Torah, and, for a time, slaveholders did respond to his demands. But as soon as the siege slackened, the masters retrieved their slaves, and Jeremiah lashed out, once again, foretelling the imminent destruction of the city.

He did not shrink from advising Jerusalem's citizens to desert the city and give themselves up to the Babylonian forces, for this would prove to be *"the way of life"* (i.e., to remain alive) for them. He urged the king to capitulate — counsel far different from that offered by Isaiah, some one hundred and fifteen years earlier. Again, we find that Jeremiah had little hope for Jewish revival until *after* the exile took place, until the day when the people learned, through suffering to be unreservedly loyal to God.

I hope I am forgiven for not allowing more space here for this prophet's gigantic work, which is abundant with detail and rich in imagery, always carrying the deepest sense of personal involvement. It is also the second longest of the Biblical Prophetic Books. Jeremiah, like Isaiah, outlived many kings. He personally survived the tragic fall of Jerusalem and chose to join those of his countrymen who immigrated to Egypt, where he hoped to establish a nucleus of the returnees. That nucleus, however, was eventually created in Babylon and became so powerful that, even after the return to Zion, Babylon remained central in Jewish life for thousands of years.

It doesn't feel right to leave this great prophet without paying homage to the deep love he felt for his land and the members of his tribe of Benjamin. *"A voice is heard in Ramah,"* he lamented, *"wailing and bitter weeping. Rachel weeps for her children, refusing to be comforted."* Jeremiah was also a prophet of consolation: *"Stay your voice from weeping and your eyes from tears, for your work shall be rewarded and your children shall return to their land."*

Ezekiel, the Jerusalemite, was very different from Jeremiah, the sensitive small-town dweller who fathomed God's will in the blossoming of the almond tree. Having been a practicing priest who had served in the Temple, he was a man of the world, adept at intrigue and in the nuances of protocol. While Jeremiah foresaw the fall and prepared himself for its coming, Ezekiel was torn away from the vibrant life of the city and could not be consoled for years. When he reached Babylon, the one-time Temple priest could not escape being impressed by its majestic pagan temples. Despite his hatred for his enemy's idols, it feels as if they fired his imagination and ignited his hallucinatory visions.

From his detailed knowledge of the Temple, it is most likely that Ezekiel was present when the priests and the community leaders hounded Jeremiah; but there is no mention of Ezekiel's having protected the harassed prophet, whose words he knew well, as we will soon discover. It took Ezekiel five years in exile to reflect on what his colleagues had brought down upon his people. Then he began to prophesy.

To begin with, it looks as if the exiles believed they would soon return home. After all, the new king in Jerusalem had been appointed by Babylon, and if he only conducted himself properly the rebelliousness of his forebears should have been forgiven. But things did not turn out that way. Despite Jeremiah's strident warnings, Jerusalem's rulers persisted in their rebelliousness. After five long years of exile, Ezekiel, too, understood that all hope was lost and that Jerusalem would be destroyed.

Ezekiel's initial prophecies are invested with a sense of terror: God and devils whirling about in space machines! His own behavior, as well, causes one to shudder. For three hundred and ninety days, bound by rope, he reclined on his left side and subsisted on a mixture of mash and excrement. Then he turned over onto his right side for another three hundred and ninety days. His strength, so he declared, was mightier than that of his people, though they were "*a rebellious house*." He was determined to scourge them in order to save them. Having absorbed all that the prophets before him had said, he was bitterly remorseful over his failure to take action at the Temple when he was in a position to do so. He now conjured up the vile abominations taking place in Jerusalem, where, in the city's last days, the priests worshipped idols, while at the same time trying to hide it from the eyes of God!

Again, it is not possible here to deal with the entire Book of Ezekiel, the longest and most complex in Biblical Prophetic literature. All the same, it is vitally important to point out the prophet's inestimable contribution. The most famous and frequently quoted of Ezekiel's visions is that of the Valley of the Dry Bones, in which the bones symbolize the dead People of Israel, who will live once more; the sinews and flesh will reproduce and divine breath will course through the newly alive people, until, as one, they will rise and return to their homeland. The peoples of Judea and of Israel will knit together and again become one nation.

The revival of his people was Ezekiel's prime mission; and to its achievement he dedicated his life. When, one evening, his wife died, he did not stop to mourn for her, but rose the following morning to continue his preaching.

Ezekiel's most difficult dilemma lay, however, in the total despair of the exiles. Bringing them solace was not enough! He had a major theological problem to cope with, a problem of such magnitude that, in order to surmount it, he had to challenge one of the most sacred tenets of the Jewish faith.

Such radical change as Ezekiel introduced does not occur often. It may happen seldom in the life of an individual and, in a nation, or a religion, once in several centuries. Martin Luther's posting of his theses on the door of Wittenberg Cathedral some five hundred and fifty years ago is such an act. In our own time, Martin Luther King, Jr. comes to mind. The courage that propelled Ezekiel was of the same kind as that displayed by the disciple of the Prophets, who altered the precept pertaining to the Sabbath (discussed in Chapter 3) and of Micah altering Isaiah's *End of Days* vision. This kind of change may cause a historical pendulum to be set in motion, when a new plunge into human consciousness at one and the same time evokes its opposite. In our case, the Jews, seemingly following the Prophets, turned a great deal of what their elevated teachers had taught them into a closely-knit nationalistic code that ultimately allowed for no compromise whatsoever.

Ezekiel must have now risen from his soiled bed to address not only the shaky hearts of his listeners, but also their troubled minds. As everyone knew, in the Ten Commandments, after the prohibition of idol worship, came the corollary warning, *"You shall not bow down to them or serve them, for I the Lord your God am a jealous God, visiting the iniquity of the fathers upon the children to the third and the fourth generation of those who hate Me..."* But this is exactly what seemed to be happening! The people of Judea, having sinned by worshipping idols, were now being punished, and so would their offspring be for generations to come. Why should they now mend their ways, if even their great-grandchildren would never be forgiven? In one sweeping paragraph, the erudite priest-turned-Prophet wiped out the threat of enduring punishment, as set down in the Commandment. He did not challenge it directly, of course, but his meaning was crystal clear. Those who heard his new ruling were dumbfounded. *"Impossible!"* they cried, *"the way of God!"* But Ezekiel lashed back: *"Is it my way which is impossible? It is your ways that are impossible!"*

The way he effected the near-heretical change was cunning. Using the well-known dictum spoken by Jeremiah, which bore the identical scourge contained in the Commandment, viz. that the offspring would be punished for the sins of their fathers, he now said, *"What mean ye when ye use this proverb in the land of Israel, saying: 'The fathers have eaten sour grapes and the children's teeth will be set on edge?' As I live, says the Lord God, you shall not have occasion to use this proverb in Israel any more!"*

Ezekiel's audience must have been sensitive to the difference between his first mention of Israel, referring to living on its land, and the second, when Israel was being deprived of that land, i.e., now in exile. In other words: what applied there, did not apply here any longer. God could change His rulings, when the prevailing conditions demanded it.

From that instant onward, an explicit and powerful injunction of Moses became invalid. Henceforth, each and every individual became responsible for his own deeds and accountable for his own sins only. Ezekiel presented to his people a new way of thinking in which every person was permitted — moreover, directed — to examine his own self and, drawing on his own strength to take full responsibility for his life. Without this radical change of the law, the community of exiles in Babylon would not have found the spiritual wherewithal to survive, and would have — as did so many other exiled minorities — disappeared from history.

Having decreed thus, Ezekiel went on to cite the specific sins, for which a transgressor would be punished unless he desists from his evildoing, then to be pardoned forthwith. They were: idol worship, adultery, sexual relations with a woman during her menstrual period, deceit in matters of debt, theft, withholding bread and shelter from the needy, demanding interest on loans. To these were added prohibitions of a general nature, such as behaving unjustly and disobeying the laws and the commandments of God.

It is essential to note that most of the above-mentioned transgressions are sins against *another person*. Only the first and the third are of an exclusively religious nature, i.e., idol worship and impurity. Here Ezekiel proclaimed man's new path to God. He could not afford, like Jeremiah, to be fatalistic. The most severe punishment — exile — had been meted out; now, in the new situation, it was up to every individual to save himself. It was incumbent upon each one to do it whereas the old, ongoing threat held no more. It is no accident that God addressed Ezekiel not as "Prophet" but rather as "son of man," which in Hebrew means no more, but no less, than simply a human being.

Here, another issue emerges: do the "a-religious" commandments in Ezekiel's list of unpardonable sins apply to *all* human beings or to Israel only? There are clear instructions in the Book of Deuteronomy as to how to treat a son of Israel *differently* from a *goy.* For example, it is permitted for a Jewish moneylender to exact interest from a *stranger* (i.e., anyone who is not a Hebrew) even before the loan has been given (one of the iniquities against which Ezekiel warned). Deuteronomy does not only *permit* such money-lending practice, but when the borrower is a stranger, *encourages* it and, at the same time, forbids it toward a fellow-national. What is behind this specific command that has caused Jews so much abuse through the centuries? Let us examine this discriminatory ruling in its historical context.

In just a brief period after their exile to Babylon, the Jerusalemites attained impressive economic position there. Such quick economic rejuvenation was characteristic of the Jews in exile wherever they went — in part due to laws they developed in order to protect themselves against the Gentile majority. Obviously, exile presented difficult problems of survival. But to what extent did the Jews *choose* to be separate, and to what extent did they become separate because of edicts the local rulers had issued against them?

It is quite possible that, initially, the Jews indeed chose to discriminate against the non-Jew, for the sake of economic advantage (and cast the discrimination in the cloak of religious law). But later they were to suffer harsh measures discriminating against them, resulting from the religious views and sheer economic interests of the people in whose midst they lived. In such a situation, the instruments that had been created to gain advantage were now employed in the defense of life itself. In the course of this inquiry, we will bring up the following pivotal question: Have conditions nowadays altered so radically, that they allow us to cast away, once and for all, the ostensibly religious cloak under which all the oddities that separate us from others keep smoldering?

It is unlikely that Ezekiel was alive to hear, fifty years after the fall of Jerusalem, the proclamation of King Cyrus of Persia (with which the Bible ends), and to witness the return of the first exiles to Zion. But Ezekiel's contribution to the consolidation of his people and to the formation of normative Judaism will always rank high in human physical endurance and spiritual power to rejuvenate.

Chapter 7

The Forging of Ultra-Orthodox Judaism

When I say "normative Judaism," I refer to the overall set of minutely defined dos and don'ts in the life of a religious Jew. They pertain to everything, from everyday affairs to the itemization of the most farfetched religious commands. This Jewish "norm" has known stricter and more amenable interpretations. In today's Judaism, its most astute interpreters are the ultra-Orthodox, known as *haredim*. They, too, are divided into many sub-sections. The most extreme among those are *Natorei Karta* who, while in Israel, will not vote in the general elections, refusing to accept any authority save that of their rabbi's. Visiting their polling station on Election Day resembles a visit to a morgue.

For me, the more I delve into the era of normative Judaism, the more pressing the subject becomes. Instead of soaring on the wings of Prophetic vision, with men who valiantly battled for their beliefs, the few against the many, I suddenly come up against mountainous reefs of *Halachot* (religious statutes). Since the beginning of the Common Era, they have piled up upon each other, ostensibly fathoming the "true" meaning of Torah, until, by dint of their sheer quantity, they formed the Talmud ("the Study"), and then mushroomed even further into what, to the uninitiated, feels like the score of an ungainly, never-ending tune, a complex score, virtually regurgitated for centuries by those privileged to have attained the status of our Bygone Wise Men. And to what end?

Perhaps the answer can be found in the opening of the Book of Proverbs: *"That men may know wisdom and instruction, understand words of insight... That prudence may be given to the simple and discretion to the young...*" To the question, Does this sound ungainly? My answer would be, Well, if it doesn't, the simple reason for it is that the Proverbs are not — and never have been — *Halacha*, but, rather, a kind of poetic instruction.

It rather looks as if two distinct styles developed during the period of the Second Temple, both representing Jewish thought. The one found its way into the Bible, and, like Prophecy itself, ended there. The other, being Biblical interpretation and ramification, kept alive and passed into the pages of unspecified numbers of works written by a variety of *poskim* (rabbinic authorities), all of whom created the "Oral Law," or, rather, the Halacha. This mammoth corpus of intricate statutes became legally binding in the life of every Jew.

In contrast to the grandeur of language and thought of the Bible's Wisdom literature and poetry (such as Psalms, the Proverbs, Job, Ecclesiastes and the Song of Songs — all of which were written in the Second Temple era), whenever I read the writings of our "Wise Men," I am disturbed by their sheer ignorance of both the language and the history of our people. For them, it feels like everything leads up to a sententious motto: "*Law to Moses from Sinai!*" But why "*to* Moses"? Why, pray, use such lame and ungrammatical language? When venturing to put the question to a rabbi, I received the terse answer, "Go and learn!" (This, in Aramaic). Another time, it was intimated to me that, if I went and learned from him, together with other students, untold secrets would open up to me. I suggested dialogue — i.e., that, hearing his interpretations, I would, in front of the same students, suggest other possible interpretations, drawing on other Biblical material. The result was that I never heard from him again. The upshot of both encounters was clear: how could I, an ignoramus, discuss the Torah, i.e., their incontestable interpretation of it, with men who pore over it for days without end? Obviously, I could never win any argument, as far as they were concerned at any rate. Eventually, I turned to a different, lateral way of examining my nation's longest enduring consistent practice — that of the Oral Law — and I invite you to join me in this foray.

But first let us stay for a little longer on a more familiar ground, *this* side of the Bible's exit gate, to consider two Books which shed light, with remarkable accuracy, on the emerging Second Temple era — the Books of Ezra and Nehemiah. They reveal the very soil in which normative Judaism took root. We do this to discover the final tenets out of which extra-Biblical Judaism evolved.

Ezra and Nehemiah are the only historical leaders in the Bible whose standing enabled them to record their life's achievement in the first person. Both grew up in Babylon, some one hundred and fifty years after the fall of Jerusalem, nearly a hundred years after the Chaldeans succumbed to the new Persian power. Both were determined to salvage the new Jewish entity in Judea, the descendants of those who had returned there with the Persian takeover a hundred years before. Both received their authority directly from King Artaxerxes, who had succeeded Ahasverus (the latter, remembered from the Esther Scroll, the *Megilla*). Ezra and Nehemiah's uncontested sway over Jerusalem's Jews derived not only from the considerable financial backing of the Persian King, but also from the right to take the possessions and even the life of anyone disobeying them. The King's letter of authority to Ezra is quoted in full in the Bible, in the Aramaic original, and, hence, little known to most Hebrew readers. It certainly warrants our close attention.

"*Ezra,*" wrote King Artaxerxes, "*according to the wisdom of your God, which you hold in your hand* [most likely, the newly compiled and edited Torah], *appoint you magistrates and judges that they may judge every inhabitant in the Province Beyond the River* [i.e., Judea] — *everyone who has knowledge of the Laws of your God; and those who are ignorant of the Laws, teach them! Whoever will not obey those Laws and the law of the King, sentence will be passed on him without delay —*

whether that sentence be death, exile, confiscation of property or incarceration..."

Never before did a Jewish leader hold such absolute power, conferred by God or man!

It is no wonder then that, whenever I read Ezra, *"the skilled scribe in the Law of Moses,"* I shudder. The greater part of his Book, aside from a list, carefully naming each and every one of the exiles whose families had lived in Jerusalem close on a hundred years, is given over to the demand to expel the non-Jewish *women*, daughters of *"those abominable nations"* (i.e., the non-Jewish, local populace) whom the holy sons of Israel took for wives.

Ezra arrived in Jerusalem bearing the Torah (which, according to most beliefs, he had compiled and edited himself) much as the Conquistadors bore the cross on landing in America. He seemed to have one idea dominating his mind: to rid his people of the bane of mixed marriages. Toward this purpose he had prepared another list, specifying those who had sinned by conjugating with the aforementioned abominable females. Despite the torrential rains, he demanded an immediate ethnic purge. All the foreign women and their children were to be banished forthwith — *"Such must be done, according to God and the haredim and in accordance with God's commandment and the Torah!"*

The punishment to be meted out to sinning Jews who would fail to appear at the site of purification (the ceremony took place before the "House of God") was known in advance: their possessions would be confiscated, and they would be excommunicated. At the ceremony, Ezra did not in fact reveal *all* of the powers that the King had granted him. But it is easy enough to imagine how even such a sentence as confiscation of one's property and physical expulsion from the community into the hands of bitterly hostile, non-Jewish neighbors was a fate no better than death.

On Ezra's arrival in Jerusalem, the city is described as prospering. It is not clear exactly what happened to her afterwards, when thirteen years later, Nehemiah, King Artaxerxes' Jewish cupbearer, was informed that Jerusalem was in a desolate state: *"...her wall is broken, and her gates destroyed by fire."* One must conclude that Ezra's *haredim* excelled neither as builders nor as guardians, having perhaps exhausted themselves in the process of decimating their own community.

After Ezra, the Book of Nehemiah brings relief. Nehemiah emerges as a man of extraordinary ability in mobilizing his people for the rebuilding of Jerusalem. In spirit, he calls to mind the early *halutzim* (last century's Jewish pioneers), the heroes of the *Homa u'Migdal* (Wall and Watchtower). Our own parents, those latter-day returnees to Zion, were deeply moved by Nehemiah's example and repeated, in song and dance, the Psalmist's description of what took place here two and a half millennia ago: *"The stone which the builders* [the original builders of King Solomon's Temple] *rejected, has become a cornerstone!"* — i.e., in their enthusiasm, the masons did not shun any building material available to them, however formerly "rejected," in the process of rebuilding their new-old beloved city.

Still, Nehemiah, the man of action, accepted Ezra's theological leadership. Together they managed to bring about Jerusalem's reconstruction and fortification. However ultra-Orthodox their views may have been, without their far-sightedness and leadership, we probably would not have been able to discuss a Jewish paradigm, or any other aspect of Judaism for that matter. And yet, what a heavy price we are paying for their zeal!

In what way does all this reflect on later Judaism and on our situation today?

The history of mankind is studded with ethnic and religious cleansing. There is scarcely a nation that, at the outset, did not subject elements considered alien to a nefarious screening process. Nor are we the only nation ultimately to suffer severe blows resulting from this practice. Christian refugees, Protestants and

Catholics alike, fleeing persecution, comprised most of the immigrant populations of North America, while in the lands they had left behind their kinsmen continued to fight bloody religious wars for centuries on end. (The Irish keep it up to this day.) Throughout the ages, almost every nation has indulged in religious strife, so why make such a fuss in our case? I guess there is more than one possible answer. The loftiness of Prophetic vision and, in contrast, its failure to materialize; Judaism having demonstrated such astonishing vitality, while showing little ability to forgo its separateness, endlessly claiming its moral superiority over other nations. All this seems to be unchangeable and thus forebodes disaster. Considering this, I am often plunged from great heights of elation to deep despair: I fear that overcoming the negative in our history is near impossible. But then occasionally, I toy with the idea that, perhaps, we *have* been given the task of proving that every player in the human drama is, after all, capable of change...

We must remember that the Prophets were an insignificant minority, often hounded out of court. *"The prophet is a fool; the man of spirit — mad!"* was called after Hosea in the streets of Samaria. Often, when the morality advocated by the Prophets was accepted, it became a tool in the hands of people whose standards were very different. The Prophetic principles were put on a pedestal when they suited those in power, but seldom followed in practice. Yet their ideals have survived.

The Jews were hardly ever in a sovereign position. What may turn out to be relevant to our discussion is the astonishing fact that the Torah-based political and social system which Ezra and Nehemiah created — always within a larger foreign system — was so successful. So far, we have hardly touched on the *practical* statutes contained in the Bible — viz. the legal corpus edited by Ezra, plus sections added later during the era of the Second Temple. These pertained to everything: from personal status to justice, from strict laws concerning purity to laws regarding sacrifice in the

Temple, from *Kashrut* (dietary laws) to *Shemitah* (allowing fields to be fallow for one year in every seven). In short, everything imaginable. Those statutes are often difficult for a modern person to appreciate, for, nowadays, farmers rotate their crops routinely. But that does not decrease the immense importance of the Shemitah before the invention of crop rotation. Presently, the ancient laws of purification are not needed — washing with soap daily is sufficient. But at one time those laws were unique and most beneficial. The "oral" law, ordering the washing of one's hands before eating, later saved entire Jewish communities in Europe from the ravages of the plague — and incidentally brought on Christian accusations that the Jews had poisoned Gentile wells. The "separatist" dietary injunctions helped the Jews gain a thorough-going knowledge of anatomy and contributed to making them the most sought-after physicians in the world. Again, those strict and complicated dietary laws were developed in the Second Temple era: in the whole of the authentic pre-exilic literature there is no mention of them, but they are contained in Ezra's Torah (ascribed to Moses, of course), prohibiting, for instance, the eating of pork. This particular prohibition first appears in the contemporary writings of that period only in the final chapter of Isaiah II, i.e., scarcely one hundred years before Ezra's time. There is nothing particularly holy or wholesome about not eating pork, as compared with other meats; according to some scholars, the prohibition against pork-eating came about in order to differentiate our sacrificial rules from those around us, who ate and sacrificed domestic hogs abundantly.

The crowning virtue of the Torah, however, both Oral and Written, rests on the principle of *equality before the law*. This principle, heretofore unheard-of, applied to Jewish interrelations only; but such a principle did not exist in *any* society worldwide, until the Renaissance in Europe (except the laws applying in societies of slave holders *among themselves* in ancient Greece and

Rome). It is not surprising, therefore, to find so many Jews filling the ranks of Socialist movements. Even though Karl Marx's family had converted from Judaism to Christianity, he is typical of the many Jews who had internalized egalitarian values from ancient times, even up to the pioneers who founded the modern Jewish State who had abandoned the practice of religion.

There seems no need to belabor the point that maintenance of egalitarian values within one's own nation can no longer be regarded as serving overall justice. In the global village situation, we have junked the idea that a colonial power can maintain justice at home while abusing it in its colonies. (The British socialists, for instance, were ready to believe it, as we learned here in the days of the British rule in Palestine under the Labor Government.) Today, there is a principled requirement to extend justice beyond one's national boundaries if one wishes to truly serve humanity, including one's own nation.

And so, while a new Jewish paradigm clearly cannot draw its basic tenets from what the Bible and its offshoots stand for — certainly not exclusively — but, conversely, since it is not possible to understand Judaism without them, it would be a great error to try and discard Jewish values as irrelevant. It would certainly be impossible to envisage a new *Jewish* paradigm without them. They contain troves of wisdom and beauty (apart from historical data) which have become part and parcel of our — and the world's — culture.

With this in mind, before we plunge into the complex fabric of the Halacha, let us take a brief excursion to those places in the Bible which are not connected umbilically to major events in our nation's history or to its legal system, but rather to such treasures which, being a part of our old paradigm, have helped to keep us alive as a nation, at times at odds with all rational explanation.

Chapter 8

The Holy Bible
Stagnation. v. Creativity

The Torah is far more than a compilation of laws, but being presented as *holy* often causes it to be treated with a kind of stuffy veneration that interferes with free access to all its riches. This barrier may affect one's relation to the Bible as a whole. Overcoming this barrier may enable one to freely savor its beautifully told, gem-like stories and discover in the process their relation to everyday basic issues. Let me cite a few examples.

Is there anything regarding *sex*, which has not been discussed of late — from Freud through Alfred Kinsey to Desmond Morris? Today most of us are able to admit that not a day passes without our giving thought to sex; it has not always been like that. Yet, after the creation of the world, the Book of Genesis plunges straight into it — divulging not so much the power of our sexual *drive* as the ubiquity and, indeed, necessity of sexual *inhibition*. Adam and Eve are expelled from Paradise for having attained the "knowledge" of both enjoying sex and the need to hide it. Today, we would probably term these discoveries the earliest form of self-consciousness. However, ever since that "moment," both in Genesis and in our own lives, sexuality has been cast over with guilt. That is how Jewish Orthodoxy and most of Christianity would have us regard it forever: man, by definition, is *guilty*.

And what about *crime* being so constant in our lives? As soon as the first humans are banished from the Garden of Eden and are forced to work by the sweat of their brows in order to live, the worst type of crime is introduced: fratricide. In a way, modern psychology would have us believe that this must be so forever — that man is bound to be jealous of his fellowman. Yet the Biblical story does not mark Cain *forever*; it is intimated that Cain's offspring *"walked with God."*

No wonder some of these stories have become archetypal: on the one hand, they encourage us to consider our natures from many, *diverse* angles; on the other hand, they seem to hint at some *unchangeable* traits, both in our nature and in the nature of the universe. This latter quality gives the Bible its strength; it is also its chief weakness.

Nowadays, we are involved in women's struggle for their rightful place in society. Almost at its start, Genesis presents us with the image of woman as the source of evil, as has been ever so long ingrained and accepted as Heavenly-ordained truth. In passing, she is also called there *"the mother of all life."*

There is no clear moral to all these stories, but they touch on the deepest aspects of life. Morality will come later on.

These subjects inhabit the legends of all peoples, though for the main part they are told as taking place amidst gods and demi-gods. In contrast, the Bible, first and foremost, deals with human beings. Even God has human failings. Strolling about in His garden, where He has placed the creatures He has just created in His own image, His omniscience soon fails Him. Does He indeed not know that Adam will not resist tasting the forbidden fruit? Yet, when Adam succumbs, God takes it hard. This God is no less human than the gods of Greek and other mythologies, except that He is soon to be endowed with unfailing morality. Later, much later, He will admit defeat and escape from earthbound involvement to the distant heavens. But our erstwhile intimacy with Him persists; a natural scientist might say that He is *imprinted* on our collective consciousness.

A female American Green Movement activist, Charlene

Spretnak, once asked me what I thought about the statement in Genesis to the effect that mankind has dominion over the land, the fish in the seas, the birds in the skies and all of the animals on the earth. From the way she spoke, it was clear that such an attitude negated the new ecological worldview, and did not conform to her understanding of *ancient wisdoms,* as she called them. I tried to equivocate by telling her that Genesis tells two *different* stories of Creation, but got myself into more trouble, since it turned out that the alternative version in Genesis was unecological as well! The second story states that as long as Man is not there to till the soil and reap the fruit, plants need not grow. Both versions are *anthropocentric,* placing Man as the sole purpose of Creation; both are opposed to present-day deep ecological consciousness. Arne Naess, the aging Norwegian philosopher who founded the Deep Ecology Movement, maintains that "every living thing has intrinsic value." Naess' view rejects the centrality of Man in the universe.

But the idea of putting man at the center of the universe *was* revolutionary and progressive for its time. The Book of Genesis and Moses' work are permeated with this new understanding, and that is their strength. This tendency does not weaken after Moses' death; it continues through most of the Bible and in Judaism as a whole. The trouble lies in the difficulty of separating various interwoven elements in the Bible: not only man's centrality is confused with the centrality of Israel, but deeper universal insights are also turned to indicate that they, the would-be universal values, "in fact," concern only us, i.e., the Jews. A clear distinction between the two opposing trends that co-exist in the Bible — i.e., the broad, universal approach versus the narrow, nationalistic one — is, alas, too rarely made.

Perhaps this is the moment to touch on the way the Bible is taught in most Israeli secular schools. The method is scandalous. It ventures to reach the Bible's *essence* by pseudo-scientific methods and compulsive analysis, which make the subject alien to the majority of students and is thus considered "a plague" by them. And rightly so. This rationalistic method simply dries up the Bible's living sap and makes it into an object to be, at best, mechanically memorized and to be forgotten as soon as the exams are over. But this is not the whole story. Something *does* remain — a sense of fuzzy veneration, which plays into the hands of those extremists who never tire from saying that they are ready to *die* for their life-giving Torah!

The Bible includes seemingly incompatible opposites. That is its central attribute and what makes its epics and songs such a unique treasure. All attempts to make of it some kind of linear, scientifically explainable phenomenon are doomed to fail.

To add insult to injury, the Bible is taught from early childhood in our schools as *history*, as if every event it recounts really occurred. We have already looked at the story of the Exodus, realizing how loosely we should regard it *historically*, while responding to it *laterally* increases its lucidity. This latter approach, in turn, enables us to consider freely its moral and immoral commandments, which apply both to ancient times as well as our own.

As for the Book of Joshua, most events described in it are overwhelmingly without any verifiable basis — so why teach it at all? In order to teach it, and all the other early Biblical stories with integrity, a creative way should be employed, which deeply (however implicitly) questions the veracity of the events and, more importantly, the views of the Bible's storytellers themselves.

As a whole, the Bible holds that everything is centered on what is good for Israel, and that the events that support this view are bound to be true. The teacher who presents the bellicose Book of Joshua as describing just and true acts, emanating from our God's commandments, is both wrong and misleading; first, he/she teaches them as *history* and then goes on to present them as being above reproach, however heinous they may be. Surely, those who present the Book of Ezra, which is a great deal more historically accurate, in the same light, are equally at fault. In short, the Bible, or at any rate parts of it, should be taught primarily as literature and poetry, not as hard fact. When facts are historically verifiable, they should not be taught as necessarily resulting from, and amounting to, a valid moral code.

All this applies to all documents in the Bible, even to those attributed to the Scriptural Prophets and, to a greater degree, to the quasi-historical books, such as the First and Second Books of Kings. Kings require constant critical evaluation with regard to historical accuracy and, more importantly, to their editors' views, which are set down as divinely inspired.

The Bible is far from being of one piece. Yet for many reasons, also due to its incredible richness, it has become holy, giving out an aura of a whole. Now, a while back I suggested that one should absorb the Bible's *spirit*, which may suggest a spiritual *whole*, and here, not one page afterwards, I seem to revert to recommending careful scrutiny, i.e., a kind of scientific dissection of that living whole. How can that be?

To my mind, nothing can or should be *proven* by what is written. Those who ardently believe a certain script is holy end up by "proving" first, that something else, connected with it, is holy, too — like the Mitzvot — and then implying that all the rest is sinful! If the idea of holiness is valid at all — such as, for instance, the idea of the sanctity of life or of the earth — its roots are *everywhere*, not necessarily in any Holy Writ. As an idea, it can draw, if it wishes, on many different Scriptures, but certainly not on all the commandments set down in any one of them. It is the free, inquisitive spirit that makes us human. No end of analysis can produce or sustain our humanity; it is not something that is in need of a scientific or other kind of proof.

The purpose of the historical survey we are conducting is not to create a new method of Biblical research, nor discover the "true" roots for our perceptions; but, chiefly, to free ourselves from the commonly accepted idea that we *must* do so, i.e., discover the truth. No new concept is bound to rely exclusively on any old lore. Yet, our inquiry is also intended to allow us to look freshly at all which is available to us in our cultural heritage, and discover that which is wholesome in it and, indeed, will probably remain so for all time. Despite our nation's vitality and resilience, the claim that faith in Israel's God (including its derivations, i.e., Christianity and Islam) is supportive of a new worldview is — to go by God's working record to date — still moot.

A good example of what I mean is found in the popular, naive story of Noah, taught at one time or another to all Israel's young. I confess that, until quite recently, the terrible implications of that tale and the profound influence it may have on a child's mind have evaded me. Reading Noah usually evokes great joy, because he succeeds in saving himself and, of course, all those cute animals from the flood waters. Scarcely a thought is given to the monumental catastrophe that, because of the sins of Man, destroys all life on earth. To start with, the young reader is led to accept that there could be one, single *tzadik* in the entire world. In his or her mind, the *tzadik* becomes...me: "*I* am just," feels the eight-year-old, "therefore *I*'ve been justly saved and let the rest perish!" Is it any wonder that the Jew, let alone Western civilization as a whole, is considered arrogant, when raised on this example? No Pharaonic hard heart was ever harder than the divine one reflected in Noah.

The fact that the Bible is taught as history puts the cap on it: it reinforces the notion that, since time immemorial, we have always had the right, if not the duty, to be insensitive to others — including other species. The idea of historical continuity magnifies that moral: we, *tzadikim*, sons of *tzadikim*, are always right and above the rest. The inescapable result is that, more often than not, the indiscriminate embracing of the Bible as a whole numbs one's ability to question the morality of one's own deeds.

The Bible, being an awesome compilation of literature, moral and immoral edicts, the story of the Creation and, of course, historical and pseudo-historical documentation, requires us to address courageously the question of how to teach it. Not surprisingly, poetry, too, is turned to wasteland in our schools. Poetry needs to be *spoken* and, at the same time, internalized; it is nourishment for the soul. If I were asked to teach the Bible, my students would vie with each other in reading sections aloud, telling stories and dramatizing them. "My" Noah, I expect, would be struck down with agony on seeing the earth after the flood, rather than becoming *carnivorous* — as the Bible tells us he did then. He would turn vegetarian for all eternity.

The Bible is above analysis. I do believe, however, that it can become a tool of intimately perceiving a superior moral being (for those who have such a need) and the infinite world He created — as long as it is done responsibly and with a great sense of freedom. One thing is quite certain: approaching the Bible in a stultified, archaic way, as well as in a "post-modern" alienating one, could never encourage new thinking. The reverse is much more likely: both hallowing and dissecting the Bible may ossify our spiritual ducts and cause harm and pain to an even greater degree than our people has known to date.

Chapter 9

The Halacha
"Torah to Moses from Sinai?"

"Halacha" is either a single, traditional legal statute appearing in the Talmud, which reached its final formulation in the sixth century C.E., or the entire Jewish legal codex, including parts which were legislated later. It is fully binding on the life of an Orthodox Jew. It materialized from prolonged discussions flourishing among a variety of Sages for generations, whose aim was to reach the true meaning of Biblical statutes and inferences. Notwithstanding, all Halacha is ascribed in its entirety to Moses, who, according to the Halacha's own testimony, decreed all which it contains thousands of years before its formulation.

Before enlarging on the question of Halachic authority, let us examine a couple of examples pertaining to the manner in which Halacha interpreted and expanded a Biblical injunction.

In the statutes that follow the Ten Commandments in the Book of Exodus, after instructing the Hebrews that they should offer some of the first crops to God, suddenly, at the tail end of a phrase, it is written: *"you shall not boil a kid in its mother's milk."* This injunction has no collateral anywhere else in the Bible, apart from two verbatim repetitions in, more or less, the same context. Otherwise, it does not feature in any pre- or post-exilic Biblical literature. It never seems to be the concern of any of the Prophets. Yet what a meal is made of it in the Halacha!

What the original injunction suggests feels rather like a *humanitarian* sentiment. There is the she-goat suckling her kid! Do not take that kid from her, milk what is left, boil the milk, slaughter the kid and then, boil it in its mother's milk before her very eyes. Nowhere does it say that one should not boil *any* kid in goat's milk, or in any other kind of milk. Neither does it suggest that the two should not be *eaten* at the same time. And what about birds? Should they also be included in the prohibition concerning the mixing of meat with milk? The Halacha claims emphatically that *of course* all this, and more besides, is exactly the intended meaning. It goes on to detail how long the interval separating a chicken drumstick from bread and butter should be. Furthermore, when dairy products are consumed first, the interval may be shorter, since they take less time to digest. What Moses also omitted to mention was that the crockery in which milk was boiled or served should be separately stored from meat utensils, etc., etc.

Sometimes, the views of the different Sages varied from one another. This gave the Talmudists a good chance to argue about them for many centuries to come. For a certain period, there were two Houses of Learning in Jerusalem, working side by side. The most famous of those *pairs*, as they are called, were those of Hillel and Shamai, the former being the less strict in all matters than the latter. Now, the question arose, whether an egg, which was "born" on the Sabbath, could later be consumed, for — that was Shamai's ruling — the poor hen must have *worked* in order to lay that egg. And work, as we all know, is not permitted on that day. I hope I am forgiven for not being sure whether this matter has ever been settled.

As can be gathered from what has already been said, the Halacha, both in theory and in practice, has a deeply alienating effect on most secular Israelis. There are diverse reasons for it. The main one, I expect, is the Halacha's avowed and practiced proverbial intractability. Altogether, since it is not my intention to be drawn into arguing with any Halacha (for reasons on which I will enlarge later) and, conversely, since Halacha is so often equated with

Judaism, it is necessary we allot it its due space here, in order to diminish our need to refer to it endlessly later, when we try to crystallize an altogether *new* conception of Judaism.

The authority of Halacha, as specified in the Talmud and often quoted by the Orthodox, appears in the opening chapter of the "Wisdom of the Fathers." A clear chain is described there, handing down authority from Sinai and Moses, to Joshua, via a variety of Wise Men throughout the ages and, presumably, down to the last present-day rabbi.

It is this, sometimes bland, sometimes ferocious authoritarianism, which causes Halacha to embody a philosophy that goes contrary to everything that I, for one, consider to be the rudiments of a modern, liberal, democratic way of life. Although *in manner* it is not dissimilar to that of present-day legal practice, in that it interprets a written *constitution*, the Halacha's particular "constitution," i.e., the Torah, belongs in the Iron Age.

I confess that I don't say this out of a thorough study of the subject, but rather from hard life's experience in this country. In other words, it is primarily the Halachic *practice*, the way it affects non-observers here, which opens the seemingly unbridgeable gulf between the Mitzvot guardians and the *Hillonim* (i.e., the non-religious). What few people realize is that the word *"hilloni"* derives from the root H.L.L., indicating empty, hollow; yet the way it is spouted by leading rabbis shows that they don't need that piece of information in order to express their contempt for all of us, empty Jews, who do not keep Halacha.

To discuss Halachic matters with one who abides by Halach's rulings feels rather like what a Copernican must have felt when discussing astronomy with a Jesuit in 1534; nay, what a modern would feel *today*, faced with someone who insists that the sun revolves around the earth. But those who believe the Ptolemaic theory to be true don't control modern science, whereas the champions of Halacha show every sign of intending to run all life in Israel.

To lump together all religious Jews, or even all the Orthodox, would be a mistake. I don't believe there is any other organized religion that is subject to so many divisions and sub-divisions as the Jewish one. Even a definition of the overall nature and outer limits of Halacha itself is far from being universally accepted. As distinct from the immutability conferred on it in the aforementioned reference in the "Fathers," the more progressive Orthodox claim that the most distinct feature of the Halacha is its flexibility! (The word "Halacha" is derived from the Hebrew root signifying *walking*; hence the claim that it "walks" perpetually, veering this way and that.) A young Orthodox rabbi once told me that even today Halacha keeps changing. Yet this is far from being the experience in day-to-day life in Israel.

As for its duration, all agree that Halachic practice started around the time of the dawn of the Common Era (drawing on Moses, of course), but then the point at which it reached its final formulation is not agreed upon. The "classical" claim is that it occurred sometime in the sixteenth century, when it was compressed into the *Shulchan Aruch* codex by Joseph Karo and then "sealed." This view is, of course, at odds not only with the claim that it keeps forever ambling, but also, with endless strict Halachic rulings (such as the hassidic garb among many, many others besides) that have sprouted since that time, under the guise of "interpreting" the old codex in diverse, often opposite directions.

But there is one intractable feature which unites all Halachic followers; it is, that only the Halacha has the power to determine who is a Jew. Later in this and the following chapters I intend to show how deeply this, and other Halachic nonsense, is ingrained in the consciousness of the non-religious Israeli as well. But, first, let me address this "unifying" Halachic concept.

As discussed in Chapter 1, prior to the appearance of non-religious Jews, religion was the only available means of defining Judaism. The very fact that I am composing this book (which I originally wrote in Hebrew) is in itself sufficient evidence that this is no longer the case. Judaism outside religion and outside of Halacha does exist. But my assertion goes even further: it diametrically challenges the claim that Halachic Judaism is the only validation of *Mosaic* Judaism.

This assertion requires some elucidation. In Chapter 6, I explained that Judaism came into existence only after the destruction of the First Temple. Yet being Jewish certainly connects with what had preceded that time. In the same way that Jesus was not a Christian; he was a Jew — yet no one can claim that he is not part and parcel of Christianity, in a like manner, the ancient part of our history, even from the days of Abraham, is part and parcel of Judaism, even though it was *called* Jewish only at a later point. That early part of our history was certainly not Halachic: neither the term nor its manner had existed before the first one hundred to one hundred and fifty years of our nation's sojourn in Babylon, viz., the period that separated Ezekiel from Ezra.

In other words, Halacha is patently what a logician would call a *private case* of Judaism (as the Jewish nation as a whole can be considered a private case of the entire human race). Before Halacha became a major factor, our national consciousness had existed — although it was not "Jewish" then either by name or in its normative sense — and, as from the eighteenth century C.E. onward, Judaism diverged and an increasing and vital part of it thrived outside of Halacha. Halacha, as the only identifier of Judaism, is limited to a period of just over a thousand years.

Taking our history as a whole, Halacha, however powerful and long enduring, is *not* the single identifier of Judaism, certainly not nowadays. In the remaining part of this book, I will endeavor to substantiate this view, obtaining to more general and vital elements in Judaism — without an awareness of which a new Jewish paradigm has no ground upon which to stand.

Having disarmed, as it were, Halacha of its exclusive claim on Judaism, I will now proceed to examine other disturbing aspects of Halacha, as emerging on the tumultuous Halachic/secular arena.

How does one experience Halachic power in present-day Israel? Can any of its teaching prove amenable to normal living? It is Arne Naess' advice to always seek those elements in the "other camp" on which you may agree and even unite. But how is it possible to unite, even for discussion's sake, with those who refuse to accept me as a legitimate partner in their Judaism? It is the motto, *"Torah (or Halacha) to Moses from Sinai,"* which pulls the common carpet from under the feet of such a discussion. I will return to that rudimentary carpet-puller, i.e., *"Halacha to Moses from Sinai,"* at the end of this chapter; it may yet prove to be useful ammunition!

The impact of Halacha on life in Israel is horrendous. Recently, a battery of rabbis — donning the title of Halachic, uncontested arbitrators — mustered their obedient followers in their hundreds of thousands to protest against a High Court verdict. The Court had imposed an $8,000 fine on a certain religious organization for not complying with yet another Court ruling. The more extreme among them had previously ostracized the late Prime Minister, Yitzhak Rabin (this, in secret, in their *codes*, whose invidious meaning seeped into the general public consciousness only later). This act rendered Rabin *ben-mavet* (one who should be destroyed). I expect that the readers of this book remember the terrible consequences of that Halachic ruling.

The fashion in which non-religious Israelis uphold their democratic principles against Halachic theory and practice is often quite ludicrous. Yom Kippur, the Day of Atonement, is considered a "double Sabbath": what pertains on the Sabbath should *doubly* pertain on that day. On the Sabbath, the religious had long succeeded in stopping all public transport in Israel. On Yom Kippur

— though no legislation to this effect has ever been passed — no transport whatsoever is seen on Israeli thoroughfares. Yet thousands of young Israelis crowd the streets on bicycles and skateboards on that "double Sabbath." It sometimes looks as if all Israelis have accepted the Halachic ruling that the leisurely driving of a motor vehicle on the Sabbath was forbidden by Moses, who foresaw it all atop Mount Sinai all those ages ago, while, at the same time, he allowed the strenuous practice of skateboarding on that day of rest.

It is not long ago since the ultra-Orthodox chief way of violently interfering with secular life in Israel was restricted to stoning motor vehicles on an "ordinary" Sabbath, and physically obstructing archeological excavations, lest they chance on some Jewish bones, thus making it impossible for that individual Jew's remains to rise and ascend Mount Zion when the Messiah appears. These serene days seem to quickly disappear from public memory. Gone are the days when our secular leaders refused to wear a skullcap on *any* occasion. Nowadays, not a week passes by without Labor leaders, properly capped, are seen on television, rushing to the homes of bearded Halachic arbitrators, with the hope of getting their blessing for one or another of their political moves.

There is not an area where the rabbinical influence is not felt here. Most of their rank and file is poor. They are exempt from most public life, certainly as far as *contributing* is concerned. Recently, the Health Services have gone practically bankrupt. In a lecture given by an eminent physician, who was then leading a four-month-long national doctors' strike, the first reason quoted by her for the impossible financial situation was the fact that the *haredim* simply don't pay taxes. The situation in education is not much different. When required to follow the norm — for instance, to be budgeted according to the number of pupils in a class rather than by the number of classes that are, in their case, for some reason, tiny as compared with those in the general education — one of their most influential legislators actually called for the elimination of Israel's Minister of Education! Not a plane flies, not a boat sails and not a military unit is fed without their adverse interference. No wonder Israel needs billions in foreign aid in order to exist.

The main reason for the aforementioned poverty is Halachically endorsed. A man's main duty is to study the Torah, not to earn his living; and, while doing so, produce as many children as possible. For each child, after the fourth one, the family allowance increases relative to the number of children.

Just writing this down makes me feel dizzy, as if entrapped in a diabolical vicious circle. What can be the basic tenets in their "Torah" that encourage such behavior? And, then, what is it in us, seculars, that accepts their highhandedness?

As regards the religious political power, which has a lot to do with it, I will touch on it later. At this junction, however, it is necessary that we acquaint ourselves a little further with the Halachic teaching and its methods. In no way would it be possible for us to do it systematically (through its own lens, as it were); it would take a lifetime. All the same, let us take a peep. Who knows? Perhaps we would be lucky to discover in Halacha some remote leverage, something that might aid us include some of its tenets in an overall new Jewish consciousness.

Let us be a fly on the wall and wend our way through its mammoth volume of the Mitzvot, entombed in hundreds of books that pack the shelves of every rabbi. How, for instance, do they apply to the actual life of the rabbi's own flock?

Halacha is an exclusively Jewish legislation. Whatever God ordered, or just said to any of us humans, turned into a binding Jewish Mitzvah or its equally binding derivation. Someone counted in the Bible "613 Mitzvot." A little relief may be gained from the fact that about only a third survived in practice, following the destruction of Herod's temple, in 70 C.E. From that time, animal sacrifice could not continue, and some four hundred Mitzvot were scrapped for all practical purposes. And this, a mere one generation after St. Paul decreed that animal sacrifice had become abhorrent to God (which seems to be a much better reason than sheer physical destruction at the hands of some *goyim*). However, more than two hundred of the commandments remained — enough to brood over them forever after.

Let us look at Mitzvah number one — to be *"fruitful and multiply."* Contrary to the sacrificial Mitzvot, in which Paul, the founder of the Church, and Halacha accidentally concurred, here Christianity and Halachic Judaism diverge totally. In his instruction to the Corinthians, Paul decreed that sexual relations should only *grudgingly* be permitted — and then, merely for the sake of decreasing fornication! What was the result of these two divergent rulings? They somehow achieved the opposite of their original intentions. From around the time of the cessation of Jewish political independence in 70 C.E., it was Christianity which "multiplied," while Judaism, with its strict adherence to what was left of the Mitzvot, remained the battleground of a mere few. Incestuously multiplying (presumably for the purpose of keeping the purity of the Jewish race) is small consolation.

Sixteen centuries after Paul, the Gaon (i.e., "genius") of Vilna, in accordance with God commanding Joshua to *"meditate on the Torah day and night...and not turn from it to the right or left,"* noted down each second of the day which he did not dedicate to Torah study, to discover that over the course of a year he had accumulated nearly three such minutes. Attending his daughter's wedding was, of course, out of the question for the same reason. One of the sublime heights of his rulings was his discovery that not only Elijah, the Prophet, could return from heaven to earth, but that Jacob, our Father, could also return, as he had kept a ladder for that purpose (as hinted in Genesis). And this, one hundred years after Spinoza! The Halacha considers reading Shakespeare or, worse, admiring a tree in the field, to be a brazen neglect of the Torah — not to mention such non-Jewish poetry as composed by the *convert* Heinrich Heine...

Sometimes, to avoid utter despair, I turn for guidance to some of the great non-observant Jews who have found a well of wisdom in "our bygone Wise Men" and embraced some of the spirit of their interpretation — most interestingly, for me, in the study of the *legends* and other "peripheral" Jewish discourse. This was their way of remaining Jewish *regardless* of Halacha. The twentieth century philosopher, Martin Buber, not only admired the *hassidic* legends for their zest for life, but, in his Biblical research, he maintained that the Bible's *poetry* conveyed historical truth far better than the so-called historical accounts in the Bible. (This preference he applied also to authentic documents dug from the earth. The latter, he claimed, had often been written to satisfy power-drunk rulers and were therefore far less objective than the great Biblical odes, that retained the historical moment itself.) Unlike Buber, Chayim Nachman Bialik, the foremost revivalist of Hebrew culture, grew up within the world of Halacha. Bialik, regarded the legendary treasures within the Talmud as by no means inferior to the Mishna-type, would-be rational argumentation. He attributed to *Agadah* (legend) an equivalent if not superior role to that of Halacha in our national cultural fiber.

The following is an example of the beauty of a certain Talmudic legend:

In the days of the Hasmoneans, Honi ha-Me'agel (the rainmaker) chanced upon an old farmer planting a sapling. "When will this tree bear fruit?" he asked. Said the farmer: "After I'm dead and buried." Honi wondered at the answer, since it meant that the farmer would never enjoy the fruits of his labor, and thereupon fell into deep sleep, from which he awakened seventy years later in the shade of a tree laden with ripe fruit.

One can see how this legend supports the present-day ecological spirit. Still, I find it difficult to appreciate the huge corpus of Jewish legends, since in the main they harp on a single theme — of first the Jew being hounded by the *goyim*, and then becoming superior to them. This Jewish "style" has evolved through thousands of years of persecution. For one not programmed to constantly mistrust the other, this theme is rather boring besides being outright chauvinistic.

Another way of assessing the nature of Halacha may be through an examination of its language. Earlier, in Chapter 7, I commented derogatorily on the poverty of the language used by the authors of the Oral Law. On second thought, I should like to modify this statement. The texts in question were written in the *spoken* tongue, i.e., either in Aramaic, a language that has by now long gone out of common usage, or in Aramaic-*like* Hebrew. The adjective "oral" comes from the practice of learning through dialogue, and indeed, evokes the actual way in which Talmud students lived and studied. There is nothing better than dialogue to lead a student to the meaning of a written text. In this respect, Rabbi Akiva's students were not inferior to those of Socrates. Yet a wide gap existed between the former and the latter. Socrates searched above all for truth, no matter what the consequences; Rabbi Akiva and his students labored only to uphold the commandments of the Torah (which they believed to contain the whole truth), their interpretations and the virtually blind fulfillment of them.

In one of his famous odes, "The Perseverer," Bialik describes the life and the duties of a traditional Jewish student. It is, first and foremost, a complete and exact memorizing of the entirety of the written down "Oral Law." Memorization and adherence — not original thinking — were demanded of every child in Israel. Six... twelve...twenty-four voluminous tractates of the Oral Law, the more committed to memory, the better!

Let us reiterate: all this learning is of the already decided-upon interpretation of the original Bible. The majority of the Orthodox hardly ever permits direct Bible study. If and when such study is pursued in some religious schools, it is only to grudgingly concur with the Ministry of Education's requirements. "Holy Studies" concentrate on the interpretations. The male student must immerse himself in those studies, and mundane matters, such as work, house cleaning, cooking, child-care, etc., are left to the wife. The nature and aim of these studies are remote, obtuse and generally contrary to life itself — apart from the only one of value, viz. to keep God's commandments. (Sadly, as already mentioned in Chapter 8, it seems that the systematic "scientific" *dissecting* of that Torah, the way it is carried out in our secular schools and universities, is a befitting continuation of the Halachic tradition, and, regarding the Bible at any rate, serves no better purpose.)

Let us continue our non-systematic prowl through the Halachic jungle, whose true laws, I fear, are beyond ordinary human ken.

Several years ago, a rabbi in Jerusalem woke up with a yearning to perform a Mitzvah. Searching for one in Deuteronomy, he found that *"if it happens that a bird's nest is before you, and the mother bird is brooding on fledglings or eggs, do not remove the mother with her offspring."* The original intention is clear: one may eat the eggs or take away the fledglings, but one must spare the mother. But where was the rabbi to find such a mother? Immediately, he dispatched hundreds of his students to comb the area. Disregarding danger to life and limb, they climbed trees and clambered onto rooftops in search of fowl. Without delay, they brought to the rabbi all the eggs they could round up. Thus, amidst great fanfare, the good deed was accomplished. Unfortunately, the mother birds had nowhere to return, since the students had destroyed their nests. Bird-watchers later reported that a whole species of wild fowl had suffered great harm that day.

Blind adherence to any law is a sin against God, man and life itself. Many of the Biblical commandments are archaic and destructive. The world has changed, but hardly the Torah! Jewish adherence to these laws, simply because they are found in the Torah and its interpretations, has proven unjustified, even in ancient times. During the Roman siege of Betar by Emperor Hadrian's troops, Bar Kochba (the leader of the rebelling Jews), smuggled angry letters to the people of the Ein Gedi Oasis by the Dead Sea shore, because they had failed to provide him with *etrogim* (ritual lemons used during the Feast of Tabernacles), which was a Halachic requirement. This and similar letters, handwritten on crumbling parchment, nowadays adorn the shaded walls of the Shrine of the Book Museum in Jerusalem. They prove beyond doubt that fulfilling the said commandment diverted Bar Kochba's mind at a time when the inhabitants of the besieged city were facing death. Such adherence to what one regards holy perhaps could be forgiven had it not been for the fact that Bar Kochba's revolt against the Romans was, in the first place, a monstrous error of judgment. It never had a chance of success. It was based entirely on Halachic fanaticism and resulted in the massacre and uprooting of millions of Jews (sic!). But it is still celebrated by Jewish children, singing and playing with handmade bows and arrows, to celebrate the "heroic" futile crime against the nation. Bar Kochba's contemporary, the aforementioned vaunted Halachic interpreter, Rabbi Akiva, gave the rebellion his wholehearted support. This is one of the innumerable examples of the separatist aberration encapsulated in Halachic Judaism that has caused no end of harm in the past forty generations.

Yet a few million throughout the ages have kept to it! And, to some extent, giants like Einstein, Freud and Bialik, as well as myself and some of my readers, have found Judaism not merely of interest, but as a meaningful ingredient in their lives. So the question remains: Where lies the attraction? Can it be that Judaism contains some life-exuding values that are not necessarily bound by Halacha?

It can be said that, at a certain historical moment, a choice had to be made, whether the new Jewish entity recently forged in

Babylon would become a nation like all others or keep its singular features. Choosing to be "normal" would have probably resulted in the Jewish nation, like all other minorities, dissolving into the then ethnic and religious surroundings, after having been cut off from their homeland. What actually happened was that the Jews chose to remain separate, rejecting the possibility of becoming a normal nation and thus chose to be a *nation of priests*.

The problems facing us in becoming *normal* will be discussed extensively as this inquiry continues. My point of departure on that score, however, is that the priestly concept is bound to clash with normal existence. Therefore, if Judaism is to survive in any form, we will have to stop being priests. This is not likely to occur as a matter of course. We haven't touched on *decoding* the secret of Jewish perpetuity. Against incredible odds, it manifested a vitality that has brought us through thick and thin, up to the present era.

The Halacha, I feel, won't help us here, it being trapped in its own priestly conception. Let us venture elsewhere. Marxist theorists have been looking for an *economic* function the Jews must have fulfilled during the Middle Ages, being the only organized mercantile body in the otherwise landed society. Curiously enough, this theory fits in with a much older one, that of St. Augustine's. That great philosopher, of the third century C.E., was concerned with the Jewish *religious* function, not the economic one. He believed that the Jews had had a limited function to fill, but when that function had become obsolete, after the advent of Christ, they were destined to disappear from the historic arena. Both Marx and Augustine were wrong: the whole world has become one marketplace, and the Jews are still here; Christianity became the most dominant of the world's religions, and the Jews have refused to disappear. The flaw in their arguments is that the Jewish priestly principle, unlike the Christian missionary practice, was directed *inward*. Overlooking this national preoccupation caused the mistake in both analyses. The function they attributed to us was wrongly seen as something that could relate to the external physical world at large. What an oversight!

Endless other theories have been put forward to explain the anomaly of Jewish survival. I have already suggested that we do not bend our mind to a cause/effect type of analysis, but, rather, *go along* with the phenomenon, keeping our eyes open, with the hope that its hidden essence will surface.

One thing can be said with certainty: Judaism would not have endured had it not fulfilled some deep need. Judaism imbues every one of its participants with a sense of being *unique* — partaking in the divine, if you will. But this has always been the dream of many; all religions promise a kind of uniqueness to their followers. But Judaism seems supreme in this all-too-human failing. This observation, however, is a somewhat mechanical appraisal. Surely, we should look for something organic in Judaism as a whole (as suggested in Chapter 1) from which to reach down to its various parts. This whole may turn out to be quite obvious, albeit hidden in the vast forest of phrases and clauses.

The principle Halachic claim that is that it derives entirely from Moses. From its own point of view, this claim is its main source of strength. Let us *go along* with that for a moment. Moses' initial act was to deliver the Hebrews from slavery. But then, throughout the ages, when gazing at the world around him, the Jew, the descendant of those slaves, has realized, time and again, that he was still waiting to be delivered from *"the house of bondage"* — a process that only *started* with the Exodus. Now, if this were the Jew's function in his own eyes — i.e., to keep the process alive — then it may offer some explanation for Jewish perpetuity. But, while many Jewish revolutionaries have applied this awareness to the world at large, Halacha hasn't; it has kept looking *inward,* barring with all its might whatever concerned non-Jews and, thus, while able to perpetuate *itself,* failed utterly in bringing true deliverance to its followers.

This brings us back to the main issue of this study: the need to become universally interconnected, as opposed to remaining and viewing ourselves as a separate entity from the rest of humanity. My contention is that it has now become clear that if we, Jews, do not succeed in crossing the barrier between us and the rest of the world — and that, under our own volition — we will fail to fulfill the task we ourselves initiated: to become full partners in the universal delivery from bondage.

The Halacha is an old hand in constructing barriers against crossing over, or opening up, to anything that is not Halachic. In accordance with my suggestion that Halacha does not constitute Judaism, Jewish perpetuity should, likewise, be distinguished from Halachic perpetuity.

Finally, trying to assess Halachic specific strength of perpetuity, let us return to the key Halachic phrase, *"Torah to Moses from Sinai,"* and its twin-like phrase, *"Halacha to Moses from Sinai,"* with the hope of discovering in them at least a trace of the secret that guards Halacha from all external influence. Both phrases rate as *codes*, indicating how close a Halachic *new* ruling is to what was originally stated in the Bible. But they serve another purpose as well. In the ramshackle dens that so many Jewish students study Torah from the tender age of four, these phrases serve as one of the Halacha's most efficient tools in "beating the Torah," as the Hebrew phrase will have it, into the minds of its students. These phrases are of a mantra-like nature; their actual meaning is not readily clear; moreover, they imply things that they do not actually say.

"Torah to Moses" could of course mean that the Torah was given *to* Moses; and "from Sinai" that it has come down to us in its entirety from that divine source, albeit through Moses. But if the mantric phrase had been clear (i.e., that every rabbinical statement concurs with the Torah received by Moses at Sinai and handed down to us in an unbroken line by our ancestors and learned teachers), it would be difficult to prove this contention. Worse still, it might provoke questions of an undesirable nature. In contradistinction, the vagueness of the ungrammatical expression serves as a whip in the hands of rabbinical authority. It empowers the rabbis to stand above ordinary criticism. The ubiquitous usage of these phrases has created forms of thought that could hardly inspire in-depth research. Rather, such usage invites sterile memorizing and citing of quotations out of context, often to the point of blatantly contradicting the original Torah injunctions themselves.

The written Oral Law creates the impression that in ancient times there was little in the life of a Jew except for the study of the Torah, and that the Jews did no more than examine written texts endlessly in accordance with whatever criteria their rabbis put before them. The reality was often quite different. For one thing, the rabbis themselves differed: Hillel differed with Shamai. Hillel's life span overlapped with that of Jesus of Nazareth and his ideas must have influenced the latter. Hillel introduced new standards and invented the *reservations*, aimed at adapting the ancient laws to the realities of life. An "erring son," for instance, was no longer sentenced to stoning, as the Torah prescribed. New ways were found for redeeming sinners which suited an open-minded nation inhabiting its own land. (An interesting, seldom mentioned point in Hillel's biography is that he came from multinational Parthian Babylon to Jerusalem. Can it be that being a non-local imbued his thinking with universal values lacking in this strife-ridden country?)

While living in their own land, the Jews sometimes managed to interpret the Torah flexibly, to support life. This trend, however, has increasingly deteriorated due to Halachic intractability and, more so, due to all the misery that followed the destruction of the Second Temple.

Despite the sanctimonious tone of most of that which has reached us through the Talmud, as the "wise" sayings of the time, life in Eretz Israel before the destruction was not only rich, but also veritably *pluralistic*. Many factions existed in Judaism then — the

Essenes being only one famous example. There is ample evidence of a prosperous culture, developing some of the most advanced agriculture in the entire Roman Empire. (The Romans uprooted the famed olive trees of Judea to construct the ramparts for the siege of Jerusalem, *as well* as to deprive the country's inhabitants in future generations from their chief source of livelihood.)

Not everything derived solely from the Torah's laws, but it became increasingly hard for a good Jew to function other than in accordance with rabbinical rules. In the end, despite endless discussions and conflicts, the Pharisees got the upper hand and imposed their worldview on all the Jews. Their spiritual descendants still work tirelessly in the same, sterile vein.

It is important to note that nowadays, in our justified thirst for spiritual values (often so lacking in our present-day "advanced" civilization), one frequently falls into the trap of equating spirituality with Halachic injunction. My search has led me to believe that life-oriented and life-exuding spiritual values are to be sought, overwhelmingly, elsewhere.

Chapter 10

On Two of Second Temple Era Innovations
The Messiah and the Afterworld

One way to become oriented in the Halachic maze is to highlight both its entrance and exit gates. We have passed through the former, and realized what a deep gulf separates Halacha from that which came before it. The gulf itself is guarded, so cunningly, that it is hard to spot its location; it is man-made, devised by the earliest *haredim*, who somehow foresaw the need both to create the gulf *and* to hide its existence. Their purpose seems to have been to bar any independent future researcher from freely examining the pre-exilic Holy Writs.

It was in Ezra's time. Our Babylon-based Jewish lawmakers struck on the brilliant idea of *changing* the Hebrew script — thereby rendering all the earlier written works, including those of our Prophets, unintelligible to the common people. Since that time, whatever was not passed on by means of the *new* script (possessing the square letters, sometimes, erroneously, called "Assyrian") has been lost to us. Most people are not even aware of the change — and that the drawing of the tablets, containing the Commandments, which adorn most synagogues, are inscribed in the "Assyrian" letters, which are totally different from the ancient Hebrew script they were originally written in. And, so, while denying the uninformed access to the past, the erstwhile Halachists hoped to ensure their control over it forever. This fully allows us to doubt the validity of their claim that their teaching derives entirely from past sources *and* the extent to which Halacha upholds the original Biblical spirit.

Let us consider the two Second Temple era innovations in Judaism: the Messiah, and the Afterworld. Both have become so central to Judaism that it is hard to believe they bear little to no relation to what came before that era. The two ideas existed, in some form, in other ancient religions; we know that the Afterworld (or, at least, the Underworld) constituted the religious foundations both in Babylon and in Egypt. (Something about the nature of our forefathers' momentous break with it is described in Chapter 2.) On the face of it, the Messianic concept, too, can be said to have its roots in the pre-exilic lore. There is next to no detailed written evidence of the life in Judea for well over a century after Ezra and Nehemiah — but enough is known to allow us to *surmise* what must have happened then.

There is no denying that, at a certain time after the Jews had returned from Babylon, both ideas acquired a new lease on life, to eventually become part and parcel of the Jewish religion. Some claim that neither rate as Halachic *rulings*, but rather as rudiments of the Jewish *faith*. Be that as it may, their influence on Halachic *acceptance* by religious Jews has been dogma-like — referring to both the Messianic *hope*, on the one hand, and the *threat* of losing one's place in the World-to-Come, on the other. These beliefs still play a leading role in all Halachic discourse.

There is an element of *fantasy* in both ideas that, in a sense, makes them stand out of Halacha — which, on the whole, deals with practical, down-to-earth Mitzvot. And, yet, it is that very *unreality*, which makes them so powerful, as to pose a bastion against Jewish renewal.

The original function of the World-to-Come (this newcomer to Judaism), was largely to serve as an interim location, *until* the

Messiah's arrival. But somehow, that location has also acquired a great import of its own. At his grave, relatives of the departed, with words prescribed by the Halachic grave-master, pray for the dead person's intercession up there on their behalf. Also, every good or bad deed on *earth* affects the status of the deceased.

None of this existed in pre-Halachic Judaism! It bears the hallmark of desperation, of holding on to some unattainable, ideal resting-place, by a people whose roots have been irreparably damaged. Even in Israel, until quite recently, there was no way whatsoever for an Israeli Jew to be buried outside the "comforting" official Halachic graveyards (barring some *kibbutzim*); and even today, secular burying goes against the grain, requiring complicated formalities and is still out of reach for most.

How can we say that all this is totally contrary to the Biblical spirit?

Let us trace the more familiar and more easily identifiable Biblical roots of the *Messianic* idea. In the three leading references, outlined below, the Messiah's chief mission is to implement the rule of justice, predominantly referring to our people.

1. In Isaiah's prophecy, the Prophet speaks of a *"shoot from the stock of Jesse."* (Jesse was King David's father — hence the Christian concept of the Messiah descending from David.) This "shoot" is clearly to be a *living human*, who will rule in the future kingdom of justice. While the reign of this ruler is described metaphorically as a world wherein both *"lion and ox will eat straw,"* this does not make the ruler otherworldly. The word "Messiah" literally means "the anointed one," i.e., a *living king*.

2. In the Book of Micah, the Messiah is also a mortal. Along with many others, he will return from exile. This Messiah, too, will hail from Judea, but will not necessarily come from the royal House of David; he will be a ruler over all of Israel.

3. Zechariah, prophesying on the threshold of the Halachic era, specifically foretells that the Messiah will not have *any* royal attributes, but rather will be "*a pauper riding on a donkey.*" He goes on to point out that *horses*, being the Biblical symbols of corrupt government, will have no place in the kingdom of justice, for it will be ruled by a humble donkey-rider.

(The last point is widely explored in the recently published Hebrew book by S. Rachlevsky, entitled, "The Messiah's Donkey." This describes how the humble symbol of the pauper's donkey was transformed by Halacha into a mean and foul beast — meaning us, seculars — on whose back the righteous will ride to glory.)

We see here how the original belief, according to which a *royal mortal* will deliver the people from their suffering, has begun to erode even in the Bible itself. However, some hope lingered. But then, the descendants of David disappointed the people and ultimately disappeared altogether. After the Hasmonean kings who intermarried with the House of David and ruled with a cruelty hitherto unknown by the Jewish people, the faith in a *living* Messiah was given its last shake-up.

Where on earth could now the Jews look for their savior? Not, it seems, in what the Prophets had postulated, i.e., not in *this* world.

The *world after death* was never a Biblical concept: it was the severely criticized domain of the pagan world. Only here and there do vague Biblical references to another world exist, wherein spirits roam, as well as some Satanic ghost and his unidentified myrmidons. Paradise, for one, is described in the Bible as a *geographical* location in the east, sadly barred to man. Gehinom (Hell), likewise, is the name of an actual valley, near Jerusalem, where humans were sacrificed, and originally had nothing to do with the idea of hell. Our Biblical forefathers believed that when a person died, he returned to dust. But to a persecuted people, waiting hundreds of years for redemption, which had been explicitly promised them, the prospect of nothing to hope for must have become less and less endurable.

Non-Jewish as well as New Age Jewish friends, who inquire of me about Michael, Gabriel and the other Heavenly figures, are often surprised to learn there is *nothing* about that Heavenly crew in pre-exilic Biblical writings. Scant few of its members appear in the Bible *later* — and just once, almost in passing — in the apocalyptic Book of Daniel, which is written in Aramaic and refers specifically to events that took place in the last days of Babylonian dominance and the first years of Cyrus, King of Persia (i.e., just prior to the Second Temple era). In historical context, the Book of Daniel indicates the power the local influence had on the Jews who, then, had lived in Babylon for some fifty years. On the other hand, the Bible's support of the view that the Messiah is a *living* person is expressed in the Hebrew words of none other than the Prophet Isaiah (the Second), who hailed the Persian King Cyrus himself as Jehovah's Messiah! But, following that last pronouncement, such hope was not aroused again for long centuries of suffering to come; any living person assuming the title "Messiah" was branded as *false*. So, sad as it must have been, neither a foreign nor Jewish *true* Messiah has arisen to deliver the nation from those far off days and up to the present.

In the Second Temple period, a basic factor in the spiritual life of the nation must have undergone deep change. Since, as said, the first centuries of Jewish existence under Persian and Hellenic rule are the least documented in our history, the following should rate, at least in part, as guesswork. Let us go on *imagining* the national mood in Jerusalem after Ezra's time.

After their exhilarating return to Zion, people found that everyday life in the shadow of the newly constructed ("Second") Temple was not as rewarding as they had been promised it would be. This may explain why most of the exiles had remained in

Babylon, savoring its fleshpots. The governing power in Judea was predominantly in the hands of foreign rulers. But then, some two hundred years after Ezra, the Jews enjoyed close to a century of political autonomy under the Hasmoneans. These monarchs hailed from *Kohanim* (ordained and practicing priests), but quickly became totally Hellenized and corrupt. They were followed by an Edomite dynasty that went on to marry the seed of David, and finally murdered them, down to the last. By that time, surely, hope in terrestrial delivery from suffering reached its nadir.

Faith in a Messiah who would rearrange everything needed a new vestige urgently. Since the House of David had vanished from the earth, it was only reasonable to assume that Messiah Ben-David was waiting somewhere else: above perhaps, in God's neighborhood, ready to come down and finally save us.

But how did he live way up there? Was he all by himself in the company of angels, or were other souls of *tzadikim* waiting there with him? It is my belief that this gathering-place, i.e., the World-to-Come, achieved prominence since it emanated from fervent Messianic hope. Having only a little basis in the pre-Halachic writings and sets of beliefs could not curb the impulse, which grew out of sheer need for something to hang on to.

At the end of the Second Temple era, however, a Jew named Yeshua claimed that he was the waited-for Messiah. His teaching went contrary to the basic Halachic teaching, viz. that all Israel's God demanded of His people was to fulfill the Biblical Mitzvot. For this heresy he paid with his life. He also created the most popular "exit gate," leading away from Halacha.

From that moment on, monotheism has adopted two divergent Messianic concepts. The main difference between the two is that, in the new one, the Messiah has come and gone, whereas in the old one he was yet to make his appearance.

It is my conviction that neither brings salvation any closer. On the contrary, it seems to be pushing redemption away. The power to determine one's own fate diminishes when one chooses to lean on such a crutch. Priests and rabbis, who, while employing it to raise the spirits of their downtrodden flock, also use it to perpetuate their adherents' dependence on them. This conviction of mine has not been shared by the great monotheistic religions in the last two thousand years.

In order to come closer to some understanding of the power of the Messianic ideas, I propose that we further examine the way they originally differed.

In the Gospels, the other world ("Kingdom of Heaven") occupied a central place from the very start. Its connection to the idea of the Messiah, who came and left and will come again, was seminal. While in some way, in Christianity, the humanness of the Messiah became vital again, their Messiah had already completed his works on earth: the actual Day of Judgment was not dependent on what a Christian was told he must do down here.

The relationship between the Jews and *their* Messiah was totally different: the deliverer and his flock never stopped being interdependent on the works of one another.

It is generally accepted that the Gospels were set down a century or so after Jesus' lifetime. In contrast, St. Paul, the founder of the Church, lived in Jesus' time (though the two never met). Paul's epistles therefore constitute the most authentic evidence regarding the rudiments of the new religion, in particular, indicating how it departed from Halacha.

Paul, a Jew himself, first addressed his fellow Jews, denying their leaders' exclusive right to interpret the Torah. Furthermore, he contended that these leaders had lost their ability to understand it. He then traveled westward and northward, away from the Land of Israel, while Judaism maintained its dominance over the Jews in the East, i.e., in Judea and Galilee, and, farther east, in Babylon.

Paul's new teaching broke away from observance of most of the Mitzvot — even with the overall commandment to fight for justice

— but, instead, it expounded God's mercy, love and forgiveness. Animal sacrifice, circumcision and Kashrut were no longer to be practiced. Paul retained the Sabbath, transferring it to Sunday, but did not insist on strict observance. He wholeheartedly believed in the imminence of the Kingdom of Heaven and felt no haste to change the world's *existing* social order prior to the Messiah's Second Coming. On the contrary, he recommended keeping it the way it had been, maintaining that all human beings had a place in the divine order, slaves as well as masters. The way to change was through the heart, not the mind; love — not war — was all that was required of man while awaiting the advent of the Kingdom of Heaven on earth.

Paul preached that sinners should accept the new faith of their own volition, as indeed the Roman Emperors did some three hundred years later, when they embraced Christianity.

Paul's elimination of those Mitzvot which were hardest to keep no doubt played an important part in a large number of people even considering embracing the new religion. Somehow, the inviting idea of the existence of another world gave Christianity a far stronger hold on this world than Judaism did, with its strict Mitzvot. In Judaism, both the concepts of Messianism and the World-to-Come remained a kind of *yearning*, a soft container, as it were, for the hard, separatist Mitzvot.

Regarding Christianity may have helped us in highlighting the Jewish claim that the Torah was given to us and to no one else, that its observance — through the Mitzvot — is the one and only way to bring redemption — again, to us alone. It puts into focus the "value" of the Mitzvot, in particular of those that bar us from inter-connecting with the rest of the world.

We are confronted by an awesome fact, viz. that the message of a poor Jew from Galilee captured the Western world, whereas Judaism remained the domain of a small minority, dispersed to the four corners of the earth. It has just occurred to me that, while the

Christ, after his immense suffering, was left the sole task of forgiving (or damning) all humans on the Day of Judgment, our Messiah has still to labor hard in this world, to gather us from our dispersion and bring us to one place. And since our deeds on earth deeply affect the chances of His success, it follows that a life of a Jew is, by definition, much harder than that of a Christian! I would call this state of affairs utterly unfair — had it not been the result of our own choice.

Let us get back to what actually happened to the concept of the (Jewish) World-to-Come and the Messiah, after the Jews renounced the Christian option.

To start with, the two ideas supported and, indeed, complemented each other. Only after the second exile, i.e., after 70 C.E., did they start to assume different roles. The former did not differ all that much from the Kingdom of Heaven, wherein all the righteous would end up enjoying eternal peace and other holy pastimes. (In the Jewish version, the righteous would also spend some of their time interceding for a good place for their relatives.) Our Messiah, though, still had a great deal of work to complete down here — in the main, to return us all to the Land of Israel, which had become increasingly inhabited by non-Jews. By and by — while doggedly keeping the Mitzvot and creating new ones — our ancestors grew to believe that Eretz Israel would finally be filled with Jews only when the Messiah arrived. It would then become a blissful terrestrial extension of the heavenly World-to-Come.

Unlike the Jewish religion, Christianity was never bound to any particular territory, thriving quite happily everywhere. And the question arises: How is it that, during all those thousands of years, in which many Jews *could* have returned here, only a few did, while the majority waited for the Messiah in what they regarded as exile?

Over the centuries, some Jews did travel here, mostly in old age, to be buried in the Land. The reason for that custom was the childish belief that the Messiah would start his workings here and, therefore, those interned here would be first in line. On the whole, Jews accepted harsh foreign rule, wherever they lived, as God-ordained. The idea that a Jew should live in his own, autonomous country remained totally unreal, until the unpredictable advent of non-Halachic political Zionism, which turned the tables.

Very rarely did the Messianic concept motivate any Jew to liberate himself or his people. Yet once the Jews started to settle in their Land in large numbers — an occurrence the religious believed would and could happen only with the Messiah's appearance — the Jewish mind was called upon to settle this glaring discrepancy between fact and dogma. What the religious arrived at was truly ingenious: they *reversed* the formula. Instead of the Messiah bringing us here, the sheer existence of a substantial Jewish community in Israel proved, as it were, that the Messiah had already arrived! But something still remained unaccomplished: our sovereignty over the *whole* land.

After the 1967 Six Day War, when Israel occupied just about all the area of Biblical Eretz Israel, the passive Messianic idea suddenly waxed active and quickly reached unprecedented strength. Through sheer temporal power, fueled by the newly-formulated Messianic-Halachic combination, the Messiah's belligerent messengers (achieving their status on the backs of the secular donkeys of my father's generation) discovered that they could bring about His kingdom, here and now. All which was left for them to do was to rid the Land of those who did not share their Messianic beliefs, or, at least, diminish their influence as fast as possible and, if need be, by violent means.

Chapter 11

Eretz Israel and the Halacha

Since Roman times, throughout the Middle Ages and in more recent times, too, the apocalyptic arrival of the Messiah has been bound with the idea of settling in Eretz Israel ("Eretz" in Hebrew means both "land" and "country"). As we have seen in the previous chapter, the order of events was: keeping the Mitzvot would pave the way for the Messiah who, in his turn, would gather us from all corners of the earth. We have also discovered that this order has recently undergone modification: the Messiah's arrival and the settling of the Land have become, each, a possible precondition for the other. While both formulations have always aroused the same irrational, fundamental longing, looking at them closely will show how different they are from one another.

The Messiah is portrayed as supernatural; he is not only immortal, but possesses other super-human powers as well. He will arrive once and for all time. The Land, on the other hand, has always been there; it is real and has been accessible to all who wished to live in it, provided temporal conditions (such as a foreign ruler) allowed it. This reality is not based on anyone's belief. Throughout the millennia, many ordinary people have partaken of this privilege, some better known than others. Among Jews, one remembers Yehuda Hannasi, the great Talmud compiler, who thrived in Eretz Israel around 300 C.E. under Roman rule, and Yehuda Halevi, the exalted Hebrew poet, who some eight hundred years later died in Jerusalem on his pilgrimage from Spain. (Both Spain and Palestine were then under the illustrious Islamic rule.) But a certain number of ordinary Jewish individuals, as well as small communities, have always managed to live here, despite restrictions by local rulers. And yet, this never amounted to anything resembling an *en masse* return of the Jews to Eretz Israel. Effecting this was left for the Messiah.

The fact that the Jews remained, on the whole, away from the Land is connected to the Halachic wavering attitude toward the question: its ruling on the subject of settling the Land has never been clear. Awareness of this fuzziness is of the highest importance for anyone who maintains that Jewish identity in Israel needs no Halachic endorsement. Yet the roots of the enduring attraction to this Land (which is certainly not Jewish alone) must be of interest to us.

Halachic literature is full of statutes as to how the Jews should regard "the kingdoms," i.e., the temporal rulers in their separate countries of residence. On the whole, we were to accept their "yoke" regarding all non-religious matters. Those rulers have nearly always been "foreign" (i.e., non-Jewish) and the temporal laws in Eretz Israel did not much vary from those applying in all other lands — as long as the Messiah has not arrived. This poses a tricky problem: it seems that the Messiah could effect his main deed of bringing us here only when *all* Jews fulfilled *all* the Mitzvot — except the one commanding us to settle here!

But does such a Halachic commandment exist at all? No one is quite sure. The quotes from Halachic legislators are often contradictory: the Rambam says one thing and the Ramban, the opposite! No one seems to want to interfere with the Messiah's workings, and what's the hurry, anyway? Let's wait and see.

For a non-observing Israeli all this seems incredible, remembering, among other things, what a special status the injunction to settle the Promised Land has in the Bible. There are few Biblical commandments, save those of a purely religious nature, which are as sweeping and clearly stated as the one commanding the Hebrews to settle Canaan. In most commandments, the believer was told what *not* to do: he was *not* allowed to make a graven image and/or bow down to it; he was to keep the Sabbath by *not* working on that day; he was *not* to murder, etc. Some commandments are more lax, due to their very nature. For instance, a Son of Israel was to visit the Temple in Jerusalem three times annually, but, quite obviously, only some, even when residing in the Holy Land, could carry out this commandment to the full. Honoring one's parents? Of course, but how does one implement it exactly?

In contradistinction, conquering and settling the Land of Israel was to be carried out bodily by every Hebrew, without exception and without reservation. None could be left behind to die in the wilderness. Obviously, this commandment applied primarily to nationals living *outside* the Land. It was they who must go, conquer and settle there.

And yet, through all of the last two and a half millennia, a good Jew could somehow adhere to all the other commandments *without* going to, or living in, Eretz Israel (provided he memorized the non-binding directive to do so, with the belief that "some day" we would all, the living and the dead, get there). As we will see, it was not just insurmountable barriers that necessarily stopped the Jews from settling the Land.

What we should be asking here is: How the same Halacha which purports to be unalterable since Mount Sinai allowed the matter of physically settling in Israel to be set aside for generations; and how, suddenly, within a mere two generations of Jewish political dominion over the Land, the abstract issue has become immediate and paramount to Halachic legislators? This extreme Halachic about-turn is totally alien to the spirit of the people who brought about the possibility of such a dominion, i.e., the last century's Jewish pioneers. The contemporary champions of the Messiah claim that they are the latter-day *true* Zionists, a claim that cannot be all that easily refuted. But, if what they say is true, then the whole of Zionism amounts to nothing more than a Messianic movement. For one who grew up in this country since way before the Zionist movement succeeded in creating a state for the Jews, this is patently not the case. We will enlarge on this issue in the following chapters.

Dedicating a whole chapter to the territorial question may cause uneasiness — in particular, in regard to one's emotional attachment to one's land. There is nothing "wrong," of course, in loving one's country, both its physical features as well as its history and culture. But since the Nazis, who hallowed their *Vaterland* as part of their racial ideology, one has become suspicious toward an overdose of this particular ingredient in one's overall attitude. In the course of history, and in particular in the century that has just ended, love for one's country has often turned into hatred of the *other* and, at times, to total negation of basic democratic tenets. The recent swing in Israel towards brazen nationalism (bringing this country dangerously closer to the brink of civil war than it has ever been) requires that we give the subject special attention. Also, land, in the sense of the soil one treads on, has become of major concern to present-day ecologists. Today, our Messianists vociferously declare they love "our Land," and one should be doubly careful in clarifying what particular kind of love one is talking about.

Let us examine the earliest mentions in the Bible connecting Israel to the Land of Israel.

While the Book of Genesis often poses contradicting views, its editors seem unanimous as regard to our right over the Land of Israel. They put this right forward as the foremost element in the exploits of our forefathers and weave it into their tales at every opportunity, whether relevant or not. As we have already seen, it took hundreds of years for the message to sink in — first, when the Land was taken by Joshua, Israel's quasi-historical military leader, and, then, when Ezra, the historical chief editor of the Torah, returned here from Babylon to reclaim it for the Jews.

In all this, however, a dominant Jewish trait is totally ignored — that of the Hebrews being, from the very outset, a wandering people. The Hebrew root of the word "Hebrew" ("Ivri") denotes "that one who passes from place to place." At one point in our history, as discussed in chapter five, a graft was made: the faith in the desert God of Justice grew into the belief that His place of residence should be Jerusalem, and that belief evolved within Judaism into a yearning for the Holy Land. But, returning to Genesis, it looks as if God's promise to Abraham that the Land was to belong to his descendents did not feel quite "organic," for, if it were, why should Abraham have to be reminded of it endless times?

The Diasporic nature of the nation persisted throughout our history. When the Prophet Jeremiah arrived in Egypt before the destruction of the First Temple in 586 B.C.E., he found an established community of his compatriots already settled there. They were alarmed by the news from Jerusalem and by the stream of fugitives pouring in from devastated Judea, but did not seem exceedingly concerned about the fate of "their" country. Over six hundred years later, toward the end of the Second Temple era — but while the Temple still stood erect and fully functioning — Paul traveled across the Roman Empire, where he preached predominantly to Jewish communities. These two examples refer to two of the most momentous periods in our history. A lot of other evidence shows beyond doubt that, for various reasons and for protracted periods, the majority of the Jews have chosen to live elsewhere, even when "their" Land was in Jewish hands.

The conclusion of the above is inescapable: the most specific of the positive, non-religious Biblical commandments — i.e., to settle Eretz Israel — has been the one least adhered to, as long as the Jews had a choice to stay away. The next question before us is, therefore: has anything changed in recent times? And, if so, what?

External conditions had a great deal to do with Jews

immigrating from time to time to this country, far more than the dubious Halachic injunction, which, as we have seen, had been mostly ignored. The first exiles returned to Zion from Babylon, when Cyrus, the Persian Great King who conquered Babylon, declared they might, in order, among other reasons, to create a reliable bulwark on the western flank of his empire. On their part, the returnees had been taught they would constitute a *kingdom of priests* here — not a normal kingdom, which is ruled by kings. Perhaps this is when the real trouble started: from the first moment a Jew stood on holy ground, an impossible admixture of corporeal needs with holy duties marked his existence.

Let us see what happened when devout Jews ruled over Israel. The longest Jewish (as distinct from Judean or Israeli) political rule over the Land, lasted under a hundred years. It came into being after the Maccabean (or "Hasmonean") victory over the Seleucid Hellenic rulers of Judea in 165 B.C.E., and lasted until the Romans annexed Judea, in approximately 80 B.C.E. In no time at all, the God-fearing Hasmoneans became Hellenized; their kings despised the Pharisees (the animosity was mutual) to such a degree that the Book of the Maccabees, which describes the most successful national/religious wars in Jewish history, was left out of the Bible. Political independence, by itself, was of next to no importance in the eyes of the religious.

Altogether, Jewish life more often than not bloomed under foreign rule, inside and outside of Israel. The Babylonian Talmud was of more importance than the Jerusalem Talmud, despite the affluence and influence of the Mishnah's authors who lived in Israel. (A visit to the court of Yehuda Hanassi in Beth She'arim was such a lofty affair that, according to the legend, was sought after even by the Roman Emperor himself.) King Herod the Great, who reigned under the auspices of Rome and was inevitably abominated by the Pharisees, rebuilt the Second Temple to please the Jews. But the Temple, though rating as one of the most impressive edifices in the whole Empire, signified not so much *national* sovereignty as a *religious* center. Regular, religiously sanctioned contributions from the Diaspora were the chief source of its immense wealth and influence.

After the fall of the Temple, the Sages of Israel went on busying themselves with interpreting the 613 commandments in the Torah. Remembering that the core document of the Torah, the Ten Commandments, makes no mention of Eretz Israel, it is not difficult to imagine how the settling of the Land was smoothly relegated to an undefined future. Even today, adherents of tradition still sing "Next year in Jerusalem" — as if temporal sovereignty over the city is meaningless to them. So, what is at all meaningful in the Biblical commandment to settle the Land?

The process of physical control of the country originally gendered the Halachists' rage: They termed it "pushing the end." But, as already mentioned, having become fact, the same control was turned by some of last-century's leading rabbis into a prerequisite, a *maturated* condition as it were for "the days of the Messiah."

In their view, will the Messiah's rule embrace every human being? Certainly not in the eyes of most Orthodox Jews. In contrast to Christianity, which welcomes anyone who wants to join as long as he or she is baptized, the Jewish Messiah will embrace our people only, i.e., those legendary six hundred thousand males (as a friend turned Orthodox confided in me) who were present at Mount Sinai. According to this "ruling," having been always isolated will finally pay dividend: this time, God willing, only Jews will inhabit the entire world.

Other than the territorial need for the Messiah to function, Halachically it is irrelevant that we have been a people of persecuted wanderers, until someone up there decrees otherwise. But, as is well known, contrary to the religious perspective, at the beginning of the last century, a few Jews suddenly found the strength to forgo — indeed to transform — that attitude, and settle in Palestine where they would become a free people. Those early pioneers had no intention of being bound by Halacha; nor did they wish to rid the land of non-Jews. They dreamed of another kind of Jewishness, upholding the kind of freedom to which every individual and nation is entitled. Such freedom, they felt, could not be based on an eternally binding, ancient covenant, but rather had to rest on a new lore, which the non-religious spiritual leaders of that time searched for, and to some extent created.

It should be added here that, during the time of the Halachic total sway over Judaism, the nation also produced original and open-minded thinkers, but very few of them raised the banner of return to Zion. Sa'adya Ga'on, who over a thousand years ago led the most important religious school in Babylon and heralded a new openness in Judaism, did not put any stress on Jewish residence in Eretz Israel of all places. His philosophical inquisitiveness influenced Jewish thinking for some two hundred years. Toward the end of that period, another great thinker, Maimonides (the Rambam) virtually saved many of Aristotle's writings by translating them into Arabic. He also had a rapport with Thomas Aquinas, the great Christian rationalist. All that time, none regarded settling in Eretz Israel as a great imperative. When the Holy Inquisition began persecuting the Jews in Europe, the Jews were thrown back into their old, separatist paradigm. The vague possibility of settling the Land under the amenable Islamic rule was put off again for many centuries to come.

By and large, since those far-off days, Halachic thinking has stopped connecting with advanced non-Jewish philosophy. On my part, drawing on the Halacha's intrinsic nature (including its abstruse attitude toward the Land), I doubt that a fruitful fusion between Halacha and truly democratic values can ever be achieved. Yet, for present-day *progressive* Halacha followers (and there are some such wonderful figures in the midst of the raging Messianic zeal) it certainly poses a challenge: to prove to their satisfaction, the life-exuding power hidden in the Halacha.

Here the question of individual responsibility comes into focus. It has been fostered in the West for generations and, to some extent, has a religious aspect. Since the Reformation in the beginning of the sixteenth century, Christianity has increasingly held that a person is responsible for his own deeds. The Messiah has long come and gone and a believer chooses to walk in His ways. A sinner, of his own volition, must confess to his sins. The Jewish religion paints quite a different picture. It also *preaches* personal responsibility (sometimes called "free choice"), but it actually works quite differently: Messiah has yet to make his appearance, and the believer has no choice but to be held responsible for his coming, by observing the Mitzvot.

But then, the ordinary Jew is not entitled to know exactly what to do, until his rabbi tells him. The rabbi's authority covers all areas of life — from artificial insemination to political decisions on a national scale. Since the key to the Jew's place in the Afterworld is also in the hands of his rabbi, if one does not listen to what the rabbi says, one will both obstruct the Messiah's Coming *and* go to hell. The constant fear of the Orthodox Jew has always been a symptom of this malaise, never to be lifted. The Hebrew expression regarding this is quite clear: a believer is a *"yere shamayim"* (one who fears God); and a *haredi* is one who does so *tremblingly*.

How different is the mood of a present-day *haredi* from the one that Ezekiel created in the community of his time! The first Jews ever were specifically taught to develop individual responsibility for their deeds. (What Ezra did to them 150 years later is yet another swing of the historical pendulum.) Sadly, most American Orthodox Jews, who nowadays leave their home to go to Israel, follow Ezra's teaching, not Ezekiel's. Most of them will take the step only on the instruction of their rabbi. (My father, for one, chose differently: he went to Palestine against his rabbi's dictate.) All this may explain why so many Orthodox Jews who come to Israel from abroad are conditioned to carry out one single task: to become obedient, fierce soldiers in the Messiah's host.

The second largest Jewish community in the world lives in the U.S. Most of its members believe they are respected American citizens. The State of Israel serves them as a crutch for their self-respect and gives them some comfort through an ephemeral sense of ethnic identity. Free of the pressures that plagued Jewish existence throughout history, some of them have created truly innovative ways of expressing their Judaism. Such is "Jewish Renewal," which espouses spiritual cooperation with other religions and supports social and ecological causes. "Renewal" constantly criticizes both Orthodox bigotry, at home and abroad, and Jewish official attitudes towards the Arabs in distant Israel. The other, older movement is primarily of an intellectual bent: "Reconstructionism." Its members search for modern elements in Halachic Judaism and view Judaism as a separate, progressive civilization, with a unique function in the West. Leading representatives of both movements visit Israel occasionally: the former to sing and pray and expound their New-Age beliefs and the latter to present their philosophy more sternly. I envy them. For them, the world is a good place in which to live. I agree with that, too. But, then, I do not believe that they are sufficiently exposed to life's hardships — enough to effect true change in Judaism. Both movements seem too comfortable in their country of origin to lead such a process. A new, vital concept of Judaism, which can check the Messianic surge, must have its roots within a community whose struggle for spiritual and physical renewal is a matter of survival. The only place where Jews deeply feel this way is Israel.

But doesn't Zionism fall within the new paradigm's attributes? Many of the arguments I have set forth to the effect that Halacha is predominantly inimical to "normal" life have already been widely expressed in secular Zionist writings. As opposed to the ideas of the abovementioned American groups, Zionism demands a real change in a Jew's life, viz. his personal involvement in the creation of a normal nation, living on its own soil. Why, therefore, can't we find in present-day Zionism the new Jewish paradigm we seek? The following two chapters will be devoted to that question.

Chapter 12

The Modern Return to Zion

The twentieth century's Return to Zion (Zion being one of Jerusalem's many epithets) was in no way a product of Halacha. It had certain Jewish elements propelling it, but was no less induced by other, universal ideas. As mentioned before, while a longing for the Land of our Ancestors had always smoldered in the hearts of all Jews, it had never been strong enough to effect massive emigration to Zion. The change came from new and unpredictable directions.

In the eighteenth century, the Emancipation movement in Western Europe opened doors for the Jews into the societies in which they lived. It encouraged many to abandon old forms of Judaism and go even further in search of a life without religion. A considerable number converted to Christianity, but in most cases the conversion was for economic and social advantage, not religious belief. Heinrich Heine, the brilliant Jewish gadfly in German society, believed that his conversion would secure him a state position. He was sadly mistaken and died in exile, in France, where a new anti-Semitism had begun to raise its ugly head. At the very end of his life, Heine felt himself to be a Jew. His poetry increasingly expressed love for his roots and for his people's culture. His poem about Yehuda Halevi is one of Heine's most memorable works.

The story of the Mendelsohn family represents another variation on the theme of conversion. Mendelsohn-the-grandfather created a new German translation of the Bible, believing that the time was ripe for the Jews to become an inseparable part of world culture. He didn't convert to Christianity, but his sons did. His grandson, the brilliant musician, at the end of his life, composed an oratorio on the theme of Elijah the prophet, whom he regarded as one of the moral giants of antiquity. For him, there was no longer any gulf separating Jewish and non-Jewish humanistic values.

We have already mentioned Karl Marx, whose youthful Jew-hatred stemmed from his belief that the Jewish people were the outspoken exponents of capitalism, which he abhorred. All the same, he did retain the zeal for social justice characteristic of many of his race.

Emancipation did not take long to reach Eastern Europe, and many Jews, predominantly in Poland and Russia, came under its spell. But in those countries the Emancipation seldom led to assimilation, for Judaism had deeper popular roots there than in the West and, at the same time, the societies in Eastern Europe did hardly ever encourage assimilation. The early eighteenth century's Eastern European Hassidic movement had already demonstrated the Jewish acumen for breaking away from the Halachic straitjacket — though it did not relinquish Halacha altogether and most certainly not its Jewishness. Without elaborating on Hassidism's breakthrough, it should be mentioned that it, too, fell prey to the aforementioned historical pendulum: the originally emancipatory nature of the movement metamorphosed within two hundred years into radical fundamentalism.

The nineteenth century is often regarded in Europe as the century of national, or nationalistic, awakening. General democratic tenets became inextricably intertwined with national aspirations. Toward the end of the century, however, another factor came into play: globalization. The process, which moved a divided world into one integral entity, had certainly begun before World War I. In 1905, Lenin ascribed that shift to the power of what he entitled the (new) imperialism, sweeping the world in the West's pursuit of markets for its capital investments. Whatever its cause, global awareness also played a part in the Jewish national awakening. Close on the heels of the mid-nineteenth century rise of nationalism, a combination of increasing anti-Semitism on the one hand and the potential for action on the global scene on the other, prepared the way for political Zionism. (More of this, in the next chapter.)

Generally speaking, in Eastern Europe the Emancipation among the Jews switched direction. It moved from the Western impulse of departing from Halacha to a kind of return — to a new Jewish awakening, based on ancient values. Books and newspapers in Hebrew started to be written, published and read. They often drew on ancient sources of Jewish history — such as *"Shivat Tsion"* (Return to Zion) and *"Ashmat Shomron"* (Guilt of Samaria), the epic novels by Abraham Mapu, as well as David Frishman's deeply humanistic Bible stories, which were but a few drops in a veritable literary outpouring. The shift from this Hebrew literature to what later became Zionist literature was only a matter of time. Altogether, it was all part of the new, revolutionary global awareness: a Jewish renaissance! In very much the same way that the Renaissance in Europe had sidestepped the Dark Ages and drew its vitality from pre-Christian European cultures of ancient Greece and Rome, the Jewish renaissance drew mainly on pre-Halachic Judaism, sidestepping the Halacha. Plunging into the ancient Biblical spirit and metaphor, it created Zionism. And contrary to Halacha, it made the return to Zion its chief goal and aspiration.

The aim of the Zionist movement was to gather the Jews from all parts of the world into their old home, Eretz Israel. The flourishing Hebrew culture — especially that of Eastern Europe — found a new avenue of expression in the new political movement, which, on its part, had an all but ready-made cultural base to build on. The new sweep gave rise to an astonishing kind of leadership, when each Zionist became an all-rounder, versed in everything — from agricultural and other manual crafts to the secrets of statesmanship and high finance, and perhaps most importantly, the ability to draw on varying sources, Jewish and non-Jewish, young and old, East and West alike. The leading figures of the new Jewish awakening hailed from all over. For instance, the founder of political Zionism was the Viennese (i.e., Western) journalist-cum-novelist, Theodor Herzl. The giant of the Zionist literature, Chayim Nachman Bialik, as well as the leader of the Zionist spiritual ideology, Achad Ha'am, were both from Russia (i.e., Eastern Europe).

Clearly, Zionism constituted a paradigm shift in both Jewish thought and practice, though it did not immediately become dominant in the life of every Jew. For the most part, only the liberal ones — those who were able to free themselves from the fetters of the old paradigm — began to leave their homes and "ascend" to Palestine. At first, they came in scores, then in hundreds and in thousands. Many were unable to endure the hardships of the new life in the Land that had been all but neglected and grown to seed under Turkish rule. Out of more than ninety thousand who came to Palestine in the Second Aliyah (i.e., the second wave of emigration, from 1905 onward), no more than about five thousand remained. By that time, millions of Russian Jews had immigrated to America. But then, following World War I, in the wake of the pogroms and increasing economic restrictions, and the new reduction of U.S. entry visas (and later, of course, the rise of Hitler in Germany), immigration to Eretz Israel became a mass movement. There were many more who stayed in, rather than left, Palestine.

The paradigm shift reached its zenith. It had already started with the First Aliyah at the end of the nineteenth century, with the new concept of the "productive, creative Jew." After World War I it gained strength with the images of the tiller of the soil, the road-builder, the crop-gatherer, the worker in the new Jewish industries that were developing in Eretz Israel. The shift found expression in the credo of egalitarianism, which in turn led to the creation of rural collective farms (*kibbutzim* and *moshavim*), and the cooperative movements in the new Jewish urban neighborhoods and townships.

The new Hebrew culture, having become part and parcel of the Zionist paradigm, sought general human values as well as new Jewish ones. But to crown all, attachment to the "Hebrew soil" became a virtual religion for the new Jew. "...Pale night covers the fields of Emek Jezreel, / Dew from below, and, above, / A moon — from Beth Alpha to Nahalal..." wrote Natan Alterman. A new idiom developed, expressing a true love relationship with the Motherland.

Both in theory and practice, the Zionist paradigm embodied many of the attributes of the present-day new paradigm. But then, in the space of only two generations of political independence, its new paradigmatic features lost their original spirit, turned anachronistic and have today become so radically altered that they are able to provide ammunition for belligerent, fundamentalist Messianic ideologies.

Was this yet again the pendulum of history? Indeed so! But what did the Zionist paradigm lack? What were its inherent weaknesses that resulted in such a total reversal? Did the negative components come from our history? And is it possible to build a new spiritual edifice — a new Jewish paradigm — from the dregs?

Perhaps this is the right moment to dwell on the origins of paradigms. According to Thomas Kuhn, a paradigm is seldom a conscious creation; rather, it is the result of an evolutionary process of which many factors are, at best, only partly conscious. To me, however, having grown up in the lap of Zionist thought and practice, it looks as if many processes within the Jewish nation have been predominantly conscious. Starting with the description of how the Ten Commandments were handed down to us (and even with an earlier one, that of Abraham's departure from his father's house), and all the way up to the Jewish pioneers leaving their homes to "ascend" to Eretz Israel, there has been a stress on a clear *idea* — whether initiated by God or man — behind those acts. In that sense, our history proves that, at times, a paradigm can be *created*.

This rather idealistic view finds support in Fritjof Capra's book, "The Turning Point." Capra laid out an inter-disciplinary approach to the new scientific paradigm, arguing that, though the turning point has already taken place, in another sense it will not exist unless and until it becomes fully conscious through persisting effort. Such a process, regarding the new scientific paradigm, is in evidence worldwide, but hardly in Israel. On the face of it, this delay cannot be attributed to the old Jewish paradigm, since there are Jewish movements, mentioned in the previous chapter, which embrace the new thinking.

Can this resistance have something to do with the fact that the Zionists, in their enthusiasm to create a "normal nation," still were not able to rid themselves of some ancient mental structures? Or, perhaps our present-day inability to open up to new ideas has to do with the unaccustomed reality of being, as Jews, in political territorial dominion over others? Be that as it may, we Jews often give out the impression that we have nothing to learn from others, since we have been through it all for much longer than anyone else and, anyway, the world has been, and always will be, against us... The Israeli, popular version of this fatuous creed is that we can fight all our enemies and win! It is both diabolical and fatalistic; it brings to mind the Second Temple zealots, who gendered barren revolt, bloodshed, devastation and bitter exile.

This fatalistic tendency certainly does not apply to all Jews, or all Israelis. For the first time since the establishment of the Jewish state, a considerable part of Israel's population supports the efforts for lasting peace with our one-time enemies. Some of our leaders dream of a new Middle East, free of war and fundamentalist terror. But this is not enough. During the Great Revolt against Rome, the majority of Jews did not support the uprising, either, but failed to arrest the surge of zealotry, which was bred on Halachic separatism.

While a multitude blinded by Messianic fervor is not very likely to be dissuaded by historical parallels, we, the sane ones, with our reluctance to employ the conscious effort referred to above, may become the latter-day zealots' accomplices.

The question here is: What is the cause of our Jewish-Israeli persistent blind spot in regard to partaking of the new thinking? Can anything be done to cure this blindness?

My contention is that all is not well with our ideological (Zionist) vision of peace. Obviously, the decision in favor of the Oslo Accords, attained in Israel's parliament with a one-vote majority, is a shaky one. Most Jewish members of the Knesset were, and are, against it! They are no fools. Most of them are not religious either. And yet they are utterly blind to the fact that, unless a totally new perspective is employed, we here face inevitable destruction.

Therefore, before we delve into the overall nature of the new paradigm, drawing on which we may hopefully envision a new Jewish paradigm, let us take a hard look at classical Zionism, with the clear question: Has it harbored from the start at least some of the germs which, through slow but continuous fermentation, have inevitably brought about the present situation?

Chapter 13

The Zionist Paradigm

To begin with, I had planned writing two separate chapters on Zionism — one dedicated to its initial strength, and the other to its basic flaws. But, then, I found that those conflicting features were so intertwined that there was no way I could pursue such a plan successfully. Instead, I decided on a composite chapter, realizing that, in it, the critical would outweigh the supportive; for had that not been the case, there would be little point in seeking a totally new approach in contemporary Judaism to supplant Zionism.

The present chapter will be central in that, on the whole, it will take leave of studying the past (which we have done so far), neither will it attempt to formulate a future perspective: its focus will be present-day Israel, covering last century's Zionist achievement, progressively moving from the pre-state years to what has emerged since 1948, when the Jewish State was established. It will be divided into sub-sections, to mark different areas of thought and action.

To judge by what most commentators agree upon today (June 2000), Israel constitutes a society undergoing disintegration. Such a sweeping statement may sound exaggerated and arouse the suspicion that whoever is making it cannot be relied upon. Disintegration? It can't be! Someone is bound to turn up and pull us away from the brink. Yet the ground *is* quaking, and there is no one — I repeat: no one — who is not aware of it.

Some among us may welcome this situation. The Messianists often talk of "the footsteps of the Messiah" that are said to bring about an Apocalyptic state, just prior to the Golden Age. The extreme Leftists are known to have waited for a "revolutionary situation," to enable them to bring about *their* kind of Elysium. Needless to say, a proponent of the new paradigm sides with neither.

The most talked about political issue that is shaking the nation today is the viability of peace with our Palestinian neighbors who clamor for a state of their own. Most political spokesmen in Israel declare that *of course* they support peace, but not at all costs. For instance, those on the Right claim that peace can be achieved with the Palestinians without "giving" them a state, for this will endanger our State for all time. More of this view (or is it a philosophy?) further on.

The peace negotiations (which anyway seem to be heading for total collapse) are by no means the only divisive factor in our shaky situation. Deep gulfs split apart all areas of public life here — from politics to economics, from education to social welfare, from views regarding the military and the judiciary and all aspects of cultural life. What a far cry it is from the early years of the State, when Israel seemed a sane, democratic and responsible society, catering equitably with all its members.

In order to understand Zionism's indigenous weaknesses, it is necessary to demonstrate that such a blissful state never existed. The roots of the present situation reach down to inherent flaws in the Zionist philosophy and practice, notwithstanding Zionism's substantial humanism and outstanding achievements. My criticism, therefore, is not toward those who oppose the Oslo Peace Accords, the ultra-Orthodox or the "settlers," who occupy what the world has come to regard as Palestinian territory. My disagreement with them is unchanged; on the whole, they're quite consistent, and the more extreme in their views, the more honest, let alone outspoken, they are about expounding them and struggling for them. No, my words are meant for my own camp, which outwardly struggles for peace and democracy. After all, from its rank arose the leaders who were in power within the Jewish entity in Palestine from long before the Jewish State, the very same who dominated Israel for close to thirty uninterrupted years and, since they first lost their overall power (in 1977), they still wielded some power, intermittently, until before and immediately after the Oslo Accords, which were signed barely seven years ago. Hence, the present situation must be to a great extent the result of their ideology and its more or less consistent implementation.

I have recently discovered that what seems to me to be common knowledge — i.e., that in the first years of the State the overwhelming majority of Israel's population was both non-religious and upholding Western democratic values — is not shared by some intellectuals, particularly those who arrived here in the last two decades. For those who believe that most of Israel's original population was religious, the following reminder should be useful: In 1949, out of 120 seats in the Knesset, 46 were Labor (exactly twice their present number), 19 belonged to the Zionist Marxist Left (again, twice their present strength), the Liberal Center numbered 12, while what can be taken to be the "religious" numbered no more than 20.

If we shy away from questioning the basics of the then dominant Zionist ideology of the time, we are in danger of tumbling into the same pitfalls which that ideology has created. Worse still, present-day reality is not reversible; trying to revive classical Zionism cannot correct its inherent mistakes.

As said, it is chiefly to the liberally minded, from Center to Left, that this chapter is dedicated. But not only to them. Numerous groups and individuals who desperately seek an alternative exist in Israel but are deeply baffled by not being able to make head or tail of how, why and when Zionism went wrong. Among them one can meet the as yet little-discovered grass-roots who practice new ways of life along with many others besides — authentic protest groups, as well as progressive members of what is called the *Sephardis* or, more recently, *Easterners* (i.e., Jews of Middle Eastern descent). The latter are often attached to traditional customs and frames of thought, but simultaneously vehemently oppose the fundamentalist surge among their lot.

The difficulty in discovering where it all went wrong stems greatly from having been fed on the pioneers' lofty ideals of merely three generations ago, on which the established cultural and educational apparatus seldom fails to lavish unmitigated praise. One grows up in Israel picturing those idealists, totally in love with their land, steeped in their belief that self-reliance, attained through cooperation between all members of society, men and women alike, will solve all past problems and rectify, once and for all, Jewish anomaly. Wasn't their message bright and clear? "We must grow our own food!" "No hired labor!" "No class distinction!" These indeed were their ideals, and for some short decades, they seemed to be turned by their proponents into everyday reality.

Neither are we allowed ever to forget the negative impulse behind the Zionist drive: the enormous suffering which our immediate predecessors and their communities endured in their countries of origin for the sole reason of being Jewish. But this alone can neither explain Zionism's strength nor its basic flaws. We must look into the movement itself, its specific ideas and practices, in order to discover what made it first succeed and then go sour.

Our Mode of Inquiry as regards Zionism

Before delving into some salient aspects of early Zionist thought and practice, I should make it clear that I do not do this in order to find fault; neither do I intend to prove anything, "good" or "bad." Nowadays, a trend of pulling the Zionists apart with great relish has arisen, proving, as it were, how totally rotten Zionism was from the outset. (In the West, it used to be a Communist prerogative; today this pastime has become more general.) The best known among Zionism's Jewish detractors is a group of academicians who call themselves New Historians.

What I wish to do is something quite different — similar to what we did when looking at the Bible: i.e., *go along* with the Zionist phenomenon, in the light of some future-oriented integral worldview. I propose that view to be the Deep Ecology vision, for I believe that a mental framework of that nature should endow the past as well as the present with added value. To use a metaphor: spoiled fruit can be regarded as garbage or, conversely, as life-enriching humus. It is largely a matter of choice — and choice, indeed, is a basic attribute of the new paradigm thinking. This rather revolutionary manner in viewing both science and human affairs will be discussed in some detail in the next chapter.

Sources

Let us note, however briefly, the main *positive* influences on Zionism's early ideas. We have already touched on the trends, which transformed Europe in the eighteenth and nineteenth centuries. First, it was Liberalism and, at the end of that period, globalization. Midway through that period, two revolutionary movements evolved: Nationalism and Socialism. The former became the dominant force in Europe since the French Revolution; the latter was born out of the struggle of the new *proletariat*, predominantly industrial workers in the West, which slowly gained momentum and reached Eastern Europe as well. Caught in these movements, in which they sometimes played a leading part, some Jews began asking themselves: How can we, scattered and deprived of basic rights, adopt these ideas for *ourselves*, and become, for the first time since antiquity, a productive people, living in our own land (i.e., a "normal nation")? And should we not, at the same time, create a *just* society, from the bottom up, given the fact that social justice was imparted by our people to the very societies in which we live, but wherein we have remained strangers?

Ideology

It seemed that Zionism could not but adopt and develop these two ideals, i.e., Nationalism and Socialism, simultaneously. And yet these progressive principles never looked to the "returning" Jews as quite applicable to the indigenous residents of the Land. How very Jewish to keep up ancient traditions! Remember the "return to Canaan" over three thousand years ago? And that of Ezra, some six hundred years later? True, the Zionists never dreamed of anything like ethnic purge; their ideas drew on European Liberalism and Socialism. And, yet, little thought, if any, was given to the "primitive" inhabitants of Turkish Palestine, those unfortunate members of an antiquated feudal system. And, even when universalistic sentiments were voiced toward the Arabs, they remained peripheral. For my Socialist parents there was no barrier whatsoever against enthusiastically repeating Herzl's dictum, by which the Zionists were "a people without a land coming to a land without a people." But there *was* another people here! This "minor" oversight turned out to be by far Zionism's worst original sin, whose bitter fruit we are eating to this day.

Herzl, the brilliant founder of Political Zionism, was far from being a Socialist. In his view, settling in Eretz Israel could never come about without a massive investment of Jewish capital, as well as deals struck with the imperial (or "imperialist") powers: the Turkish Sultan, the Austro-Hungarian Kaiser, the British Crown, and France. Once the Jews were allowed to migrate here, the obvious next step was to acquire land for them to settle on, with the generous aid of the aforementioned capital. Did the first settlers, who had no capital of their own, try to address the conflict between Capital and Labor? Or did they, in fact, join forces with the rich in the great Zionist synthesis? The answer to both questions is yes, however paradoxical this may sound.

Encountering the desolation of the land that the pioneers had dreamed about gave rise, first and foremost, to the will and the passion to reclaim it — to "redeem" it was the commonly used expression. Redeem it from whom? The answer was inevitable: from the hands of those non-Jews who had literally corrupted it. The zeal which motivated the new Jewish farmers and their determination to "bring forth bread" from the land clouded their universal vision. Fifty years later, when a third of our nation was butchered by the Nazis, the old national belief that "all the *goyim* are against us" understandably grew stronger, relegating the universal message altogether to some far off, unprescribed future. (This last statement, like others besides, must be taken to indicate the *general* trend: there were always groups and individuals, here and elsewhere, which varied with the majority.)

But let us not forget the spirit of those first pioneers, who were toiling to create the earth-bound base for their nation's revival, soaring on the wings of the rejuvenated Hebrew language. Indeed, there is no other example in world history of a dead language — scarcely in daily use for thousands of years — being so revived and employed to weld together a national entity. The process of "making the desert rejoice" (a quote from the Hebrew Bible) already had its cultural counterpart in the hearts of the new arrivals in Eretz Israel. Yet, even within that land-bound, formative creation — i.e., the agricultural achievement — there lay a dormant flaw to which we will return toward the end of this chapter.

Let us stop for a moment to address possible objections to my singling out Jewish separatism over other separatist ideologies, which propelled pioneering movements worldwide. "Why don't you deal, for once," I am often reprimanded, "with the White-Christian separatism of the first settlers in North America, toward the continent's native inhabitants? Can you even compare what they did to the Indians with what we have done to the Arabs?" Strangely, despite the near-obtuseness of such an objection to separatism, it is the one most repeatedly raised against arguments for the possibility — let alone the need — of lasting peace in the region. What is intimated here is that no Arab will ever give up his dream of destroying us. The fact that I know this to be an utter falsehood has little effect; neither does indicating how we, too, often destroyed others when the chance presented itself. Sadly, we as a nation are some of the last in the "enlightened" world embracing veritable racial tenets — unless they are directed against *us*, of course. At the beginning of the Third Millennium, separatism does not hold together any more; it is sure to backfire. Not only is it no longer supportable, it is outright dangerous for our very existence. But is there, in reality, anything else we can put in its stead, to keep our national spirit alive?

Let us proceed to survey several salient aspects of Zionist thought and practice — leaving the most revolutionary one, the agricultural renewal, for last — keeping our eyes open toward what else may explain our progressive State of Israel virtually plummeting down to the level of Messianic isolationism.

Defense

Mainstream Zionism never advocated taking the land by force. On the contrary, its philosophy was peaceful. How then did Jews first acquire the land, which had been owned by Arab feudal lords, often living far from this malaria-blighted region? Simply by buying it. This was rarely done directly with the miserable lot who had tilled it for generations; they were told to leave and live elsewhere, presumably to crowd in with their relatives living in areas not yet purchased by the Jews. Soon, however, the dispossessed organized to attack the new settlers, often under the leadership of the very traditional clan chiefs who had sold the land to the Jews in the first place.

There was now no choice for the new settlers but to learn the use of weapons in self-defense — and the defense of their land, which had now come to be regarded as "Jewish land" as distinct from "Arab land." This is the chief reason for the fact that, ever since those far off pre-State times, we consider bearing arms as self-defensive. To this day, the Israeli army, by far the most powerful military force in the area, is called "Israel Defense Army." The flaw here is obvious. Since no mighty military force is likely to remain defensive forever, entertaining such an epithet (however "justified" historically) is blatantly wrong, particularly while occupying another's territory, as has been the case with us since 1967. One might argue of course, that international law permits a defender to remain in the aggressor's territory as long as peace is not established. But why have we not attained comprehensive peace with our neighbors in over fifty years of independence?

This subject is an extremely complicated one, involving not only the warring parties themselves, but, also, the world's great powers and their interests in the area. It won't help our inquiry to enter a detailed political and military discussion. Yet this major issue cannot be altogether overlooked. No doubt, the Arabs are no easy partners for peace, and certainly bear great responsibility for the continuing warring relations with Israel. But there were many occasions when peace offers on the part of various Arab countries and organizations that Israel's leaders rejected bluntly. In all these cases, Israel's rejection was based on the argument that the Arabs can never be trusted; that they would always revert to their old ways. Had it not been for our old paradigm's claim that throughout our long history we had always been the victims, this argument would hold more water. It inevitably brings to mind Isaiah's wailings over Jerusalem two thousand seven hundred years ago, even when she had long reached military superiority over her neighbors, indicating that we, come what may, will always remain the innocent prey.

The new paradigm proposes thoroughly to review the old lore of military conquests — e.g., the one concerning Columbus, the European pioneer whose actions are today widely criticized by proponents of the new thinking. Other historical figures, such as Henry V of England (who ruled close to a hundred years before Columbus' time), come to mind. His "right" to Normandy, France, enabled him to invade it and spill the blood of thousands in realizing his claim. This English monarch's exploits cannot serve any more as a model for contemporary rulers. The Plantagenets no longer inspire the youth of England either. But they would do so here! King David, who preceded Henry V by some two thousand five hundred years, does — and that, in song and dance, as if the man who created the first Israeli empire never died. (The expected Messiah, one should remember, is called the Son of David.)

In suchlike manner, our teachers find no barrier in Israel's ethos to counter the claim that we are all defenders, *whatever* we do. In doing so, they perpetuate a would-be historically-founded buffer against peace. Admittedly, equating the Plantagenets with the highly motivated Jewish defenders of a hundred years ago may sound far-fetched. But Bar-Kochba's rebellion (mentioned in Chapter 9), nearly two thousand years ago, being adorned with Halachic mantle, gets closer to fitting the equation. According to what he symbolizes, we will eternally fight the *goyim* in the spirit of the Torah, be it at the cost of clear and obvious physical self-destruction.

No reversal of this trend can ever be achieved, until we look at the early Zionist defenders, and ask: Were "Hebrew arms" always as pure as we are taught to regard them? Today, few believe that this, in fact, was the case, remembering that those who fought us were often considered by us no better than pests. Though the use of arms was not one of Zionism's declared aims, most sadly, present-day ubiquitous reliance on it — fitting into our old image of being the eternal victims — may have altered Zionism's original, declared aims beyond recognition.

Legality; Legal Structure

Another glaring flaw in the Zionist ideology stems from Israel's initial legal structure. It is also ascribed to the State's unceasing state of hostilities — though, in this case, not so much having to do with those which surround us as with those "neighbors" living in our midst.

From its very outset, Israel — under the auspices of the 1947 U.N. resolution — was to be a *Jewish* State, as distinct from an *Arab* State, which was to be established in another part of the defunct British Mandate Palestine. By its very definition, then, Israel can be said never to have meant actually to become the state of its non-Jewish citizens as well. Few intended this to be the case, of course. The 1948 Declaration of Independence (which, somehow, has never become constitutionally binding) expounds the opposite. And, yet, despite Israel's Arabs' formal — predominantly voting — rights, in reality they have been deprived of many civil rights, e.g., being allowed to emigrate freely into and out of the country. It is crucial for our discussion to stress that we do not ask whether that policy was necessary (or even, as some would claim, unavoidable); what concerns us is the resulting legal situation and its intrinsic nature, whatever its causes.

One of the first basic laws of Israel was the Law of Return, which permitted all Jews to become its citizens automatically — this being the prime purpose of creating the State in the first place, enabling the hundreds of thousands of Holocaust survivors in European D.P. camps to come home freely. Little mattered the fate of an Arab student traveling overseas to study. Would that student have the right to return to Israel, after completing his or her academic education? In many cases and for many decades the answer was no. There was scarcely a legal way to contravene an authority's ruling barring that student from returning home. And what of family land that Arabs had owned for generations — if it were not specifically registered by the Turks or British all those years ago — or, alternatively, land that was confiscated for Israeli military maneuvers? In the light of the Right of Eminent Domain, practiced throughout the West, the chance of a local Arab in appealing for the reclamation of these lands, in the face of growing "redemption" now in the hands of the State, were practically nil. For Israel, "the only democracy in the Middle East," this legal situation is untenable, causing deep injustices and inevitable grudges, with no end in sight.

In regard to the status of religion in Israel's taut democratic fiber, one must recall that Ben-Gurion, our unchallenged prime Socialist statesman, made several fundamental decisions in the early days of the State. One such decision concerned Israel's political orientation. With uncanny foresight, Ben-Gurion realized that the Soviets — despite their early political and military support for Israel, believing the new state to be "anti-imperialistic" — could not be trusted for long. Thus, he unequivocally oriented Israel towards the democratic, though "capitalistic," West. But, on another front, Ben-Gurion did not prove so far-sighted, namely, conferring power upon religious circles far beyond political necessity or prudence. According to his view, separation of the State from all religious institutions was considered for Jews an unaffordable luxury. What no other democracy could countenance, our special history allowed. From that early moment on, Israel has had *two*, parallel legal systems — in other words, no *one* binding legal system, no *one* law, applying to all.

From the very outset, Israeli religious parties were awarded sole control over personal status affairs, such as marriages and burials. Worse still, in practice, they were given the authority to determine the question of "who is a Jew?" which, in turn, determined who could benefit from the Law of Return. Even today, when Reform Judaism is struggling for its right to convert non-Jews to Judaism, it is still accepted that the power to determine who is a Jew — with all that ensues — rests in the hands of the religious.

Another "small" privilege, granted to the ultra-Orthodox, was exemption from military service. This "insignificant" minority immediately used this anti-democratic tool to increase its number — done through a complicated and blatantly anti-social set of financial handouts. The ultra-Orthodox have gradually become one of the most influential factors in every area of Israeli life, including critical decisions regarding war and peace, while they themselves do not serve in the armed forces. With their basic anti-democratic ideology, they pose a real and immediate threat to Israel's democracy.

The fact that Israel lacks a written constitution is also a result of the seemingly inalterable grip the religious have on our legal system, through holding the parliamentary balance of power. Legally, this is Israel's original sin, which nothing other than a real and profound change in our perception of ourselves will ever expiate.

Culture

Despite its vitality, the new Hebrew culture has not escaped a similar fate to that of legality: its existence is ambivalent (*unprincipled* might be a more fitting adjective). It is an extremely complex subject — culture being Spirit incarnate: whether matter assuming spiritual qualities or the spiritual endowing matter with its own properties. In short, culture engulfs almost anything humanly created. For our discussion, however, let me put forward the proposition that the covert ambivalence of Zionist/Hebrew/ Israeli culture lies in the inability of most Israelis — or is it their innate unwillingness? — to distinguish Judaism from Halacha, as a matter of *cultural principle.*

In the beginning, Zionist (Hebrew) culture did not draw chiefly on Jewish sources, to the extent that Tolstoy, with his earthbound social teachings, was far more of an inspiration for the first kibbutzniks than Moses. Zionism was a movement of national, social and personal revival, not a religious one. Its culture was modeled after shining European Liberal, sometimes National, examples. At times, Middle Eastern influence came into play and, as said, the ancient Biblical spirit, particularly concerning agricultural festivals, had its hour of revival. Poets, novelists, dramatists, painters, composers and choreographers had a veritable field day: the new Hebrew secular culture flourished.

Halachic Judaism was pushed aside. When the State of Israel was founded, most of its Jewish citizens regarded themselves as non- and even anti-Halachic, though a dividing line was never clearly drawn — i.e., to what extent does Judaism exist outside of Halacha. Being Jewish still meant that, to some extent, we owed our existence to Halacha, remembering that so much of Jewish life had evolved during thousands of years of Halachic dominion.

But then, close on the heels of Israel's independence, something happened to the world, with what was then called the scientific revolution. It gathered momentum reaching the present stage, in which both culture and education seem to be that which can be zapped onto, or derived from, the small screen. Parallel to this, with the influx of the materialistic "values" let loose in the democracies of the West, our new, initially spiritual but non-Halachic Hebrew culture began crumbling in the face of the surviving Halacha, which seems to have been lying in waiting. Quite suddenly, Halachic norms turned out to offer the spirituality, which was not present in what, for brevity's sake, I'll call "T.V. culture." This phenomenon is not altogether unlike the spiritual quest in the West for Far Eastern semi-religious disciplines. But in America, Buddhism, for one, is often taken to be an enriching addition to one's way of life, while Halacha wishes to replace and utterly change the life of a non-observant Jew — to *lehachzir betsuvah* (to make him or her repent and return to ancient, separatist practices). Halachic rule, the way one experiences it in Israel, is a *totality*; it does not allow any other options to exist side by side with it. The result is that, while in the well-established Western democracies the danger of fundamentalist take-over is unthinkable, here it poses a real threat. For one must remember that Halacha has deep roots; and it is a lot more Jewish than Buddhism is American! (More will be discussed on this subject in Chapter 15).

But how, one might ask, with the rest of the world virtually riveted to the small screen, could Zionism be held responsible for not defending staunchly its incipient, emancipated Hebrew culture? Ascribing blame is not the subject of this chapter, of course. Rather, we are trying to discover what flaws in classical Zionism made it fail so dismally to supply answers to most of present-day pressing requirements. Recently, it began to seem as if the Zionist official culture of Israel — under its Ministry and well knit set of semi-legal trusts and funds — has in fact thrived in limbo (albeit with a strong Western bent) and proved to be poorly equipped against a virtual Halachic takeover.

A relevant aspect of Israel's cultural scene, hardly mentioned so far, may shed light on the cultural about-turn indicated above: the rise of Middle Eastern culture. To many it seems to have quite unexpectedly acquired a major position in Israel's cultural life, having sprung from a virtually unmapped region. To the question, "Why has this happened?" a great many contradicting answers are being offered. But, adhering to our mode, let us simply observe this phenomenon and internalize it, with the hope that, at the end of our discussion, we will be wiser about it.

This about-turn is clearly part of the awakening of the hitherto under-represented Jewish *Easterners*. This underdog population arrived in Israel after 1948 from North Africa and other Middle Eastern countries, and had long been regarded by the *Ashkenazis* (i.e., *Westerners*) — who were until quite recently the uncontested tone-givers of culture — primitive and even Arab-like. Our Moroccan community which amounts to a million, i.e., some twenty percent of the State's Jewish population, to this very day bears a deep grudge concerning the degrading the way their parents were received by the *Ashkenazis*, in particular, being sprayed with D.D.T. on arriving in Eretz Israel.

Not surprisingly, most of our cultural chiefs were taken completely unawares by the sudden surge of *Eastern* culture, which is disseminated chiefly through audio-cassettes and pirate radio stations that tirelessly broadcast simple, undulating love songs and, side by side, speeches, encouraging listeners to return to the fold, with a clear anti-*Ashkenazi* edge. These cassettes and radio broadcasts reach an audience of hundreds of thousands and indeed are the symptoms of a deep, cultural, revolution.

For those not versed on present-day Israeli politics, it should be mentioned that following this cultural upheaval the most ominous, *Eastern* brand of ultra-Orthodox organized power emerged, threatening all of Israel's democratic standards. The rise of this power is commonly attributed to the wider *congregational* problem, as it is sometimes called, referring to a variety of socio-economic factors. Consequently, the "cures" for this malaise are sought within the realm of higher budgets for social welfare — budgets that are far more spoken of than actually distributed.

In the context of this discussion however, what this new power represents is still characteristic of the old Jewish paradigm. It, too, manifests the historical, as well as present-day flaws, inherent in our national make up. It thrives on conflict and on factional one-upmanship, with little true regard for the other, always in the name of justice embedded in one's sole ability to interpret some Torah or another (the Hebrew meaning of "Torah" being, simply, "doctrine" or "teaching").

Classical Zionist culture is obviously on a downhill trajectory. Like the other aspects discussed here, Israel's cultural survival can be envisioned only in the context of a total change of paradigm.

I trust that the short survey we have just made of some aspects of Zionist thought and practice sufficiently indicates that the State of Israel — Zionism's sole and cherished offspring — does not yet constitute a democracy. At best, it is a kind of "Jewish democracy," wherein each faction increasingly holds its fort against all other factions. The ominous *Eastern* ultra-Orthodox political manner, for one, is all too reminiscent of our traditional factional, destructive splits — even from Biblical times and, in my own living memory, to dozens of kibbutzim splitting asunder over a Leninist or even a Stalinist dogma!

But what, pray, have I done regarding my intention constantly to bear in mind a future-oriented, ecological worldview, referring to all events and processes, past and present? I confess this is not an easy task concerning my own people. My choice of subject for carrying out that intention is what many regard as the greatest miracle brought about by Zionism — that of making the wasteland flourish. What has helped me in this choice is the initial ecological awareness, which, to some extent, underpinned that achievement.

The Agricultural Miracle

In the Diaspora, Jews had to excel; otherwise, they could not survive. Often and repeatedly, sovereigns accepted Jews and even invited them to help in advancing commerce, crafts, medicine and education in their countries. After all, throughout the Middle Ages, in every country of Europe, only the Jews were totally literate — young and old, rich and poor alike. But, for a long time, Jews had not been *productive* — i.e., farmers or, in more recent times, industrial workers. But then, as soon as they set foot in Palestine, they had to engage in those crafts. With incredible speed, they acquired the new knowledge needed for normal national existence. And they did more than just acquire knowledge: as usual, they excelled and adopted the most recent discoveries in the fields they had entered.

Let us consider one of these fields: dairy farming.

The way the Jews, arriving in Eretz Israel, transformed, concurred with a not altogether dissimilar process in the West. In post-World War I Europe, it became clear that many dairy farmers, who had just returned from the trenches, could not make ends meet using their antiquated methods. Soon, a scientific approach was developed to increase (among other things) dairy produce. This method introduced new grazing crops, which the cows relished, that increased their milk production. It quickly substituted the traditional fodder, temporarily alleviating the troubles of the dairy farmer. The adverse ecological effect that resulted took much time to register. Great efforts are now being made to redress the damage done and heal the badly affected eco-system.

News of the advanced methods reached the pioneers and, as soon as the Mediterranean waters had been cleared of mines, a number of Palestinian Jewish students set sail to enter European universities in order to acquire the new knowledge. Initially, they chose to study in Holland, which ranked first in dairy farming. Several years later, Dutch bulls were shipped to Palestine in order to improve the milk production of the native ("Arab") cow, which gave on average a meager 650 liters per year (equivalent to the yield of a common goat). Not more than two generations went by before the new *Hebrew Cow* (named and bred by the pioneers in Emek Jezreel) had surpassed all her European rivals, yielding twenty percent more than its North American counterpart, sending the Dutch cow to the bottom rung of the ladder.

What has all that to do with inherent flaws in the Zionist paradigm? Is it conceivable that the newly-acquired productivity of the pioneers could cause anybody any harm? Surprisingly, the answer is yes. The question before us is, what, at bottom, motivated the improvers and at what expense were the improvements made.

The Zionist imperative was clear: those initial few thousand pioneers knew they were literally preparing the ground for millions of survivors to come. And they did. No other consideration mattered. In the early days of the State, flying over this narrow coastal strip called Israel, one could not but be stunned by the difference between Arab and Jewish lands. A fascinating checkered matrix lay below — small flourishing arable areas, rich with vegetation, spotted with new, dazzling buildings — flanked on all sides by large patches of gray, where our neighbors dwelled. And yet, that very sweep, unchecked by overall ecological awareness, and fueled, as it turned out, by endemic separatism, has boomeranged. It sometimes seems that Zionist values turned on themselves: what had started as a drive to save *others* turned into narrow *self*-interest.

Seemingly petty reservations in the way of technical/scientific progress were swept aside: the composition of the milk produced by the new methods suffered; its percentage of antibiotics was of little importance; what happened to a cow which never went to pasture (such progress has not reached far-off Europe), whose udders had been, contrary to nature, inflated to drum-size, did not matter; what occurred in the eco-system, when soil was subjected to scientifically chosen crops, was hardly heeded.

In the beginning, the kibbutzim engaged in what was then called mixed farming, so that their land would provide them with most of, if not all, their needs. Since the founding of the State, however, this policy has completely given way to production of only that which would yield the highest profit — a policy involving economic adventures, which sometimes brought about financial crises from which the kibbutzim could not extricate themselves. The famed Jewish mind, which had brought forth some of the world's most advanced agriculture, became interested only in the increase in marginal profits. Due to the employment of ultra-scientific methods (chemical fertilization, insecticide spraying, artificial ripening and dyeing, and, most recently, genetic engineering), Israel's agricultural produce — once the pride of European food shops — is presently often rejected in Europe for non-compliance with international health regulations. A bitterly remembered example of over-development is cotton growing, which suddenly became attractive to Israeli farmers who pursued it at break-neck speed, at the expense of the irreversible closure of many traditional branches of agriculture. When cotton prices collapsed on the world's markets, some kibbutzim went bankrupt overnight and the national water system was left in tatters.

What happened to the hallowed principle of self-reliance and the next-to-holy principle of manual labor, which the new Jew had adopted? Within one generation, manual labor passed into the hands of Israeli Arabs and, after 1967, to those living in the "territories." It was this new brand of Gibeonites, hewers of wood and drawers of water, who built modern Israel. From the original idea that we, the new masters of the land, will tend and build it, we have retained only the element of the master, who is just concerned with his so-called living standards and is oblivious to the damage his unchecked economic activity may cause forever.

The Zionist paradigm, which began with an unreserved love for the land, has turned that very land into — at best — a saleable commodity, to the degree that even national "redeemed" land is for sale. The reason for this momentous about-turn can be clearly traced back to the predominance of the Zionist division between Jewish vs. Arab land, with little to no regard of the land *per se*. Once we reached political independence, since most land has become Jewish anyway, it is no longer sacred. From then on, it was each for himself. (The Jewish Messianic attachment to the "Land of our Fathers" in the thickly populated Palestinian areas makes this less apparent; but there, too, the selfish economic element obtains, despite Messianic protests to the contrary.)

Once again, the reader may comment that such things happen all over the world, so why single out the Jews for such special criticism? That comment has only some truth to it. It perhaps needs to be repeated: early Zionism's profound love for the land sprang from the need to create a territorial base for the scattered nation. There was no time to indulge in the deep-seated antipathy toward over-use of land that existed, to some degree, in old, landed societies. We cannot ignore the fact that the moment we became politically independent, a process of crass self-interest increasingly swept moral values and other far-seeing considerations aside. Of course, the reigning economic philosophy in the West, above all upholding economic growth and wasteful mass-production and mass-consumption values, play a part in all this. Our intention in espousing a new Jewish paradigm is to put all earth-oriented forgotten considerations — with other, new ones — high on our national agenda.

Before ending this survey, let me touch, in the briefest possible manner, on the way that one who grew up in this country was exposed to Zionist thinking in two areas which range, perhaps, highest in a nation's spiritual life: the intrinsic attitude to the *other* and *education*.

The Other

I grew up in a kibbutz lying in a conclave between two Arab villages. To this day I cannot believe the lack of any real interest in the material and spiritual culture of our neighbors, despite the slogan adorning my kibbutz movement's daily paper, "For Intra-National Fraternity!" I could see a tiller plowing with a single-bladed wooden contraption, harnessed to a woman and a donkey across the fence, and all I could think of was, How primitive! Despite some effort on the part of my progressive teachers, hardly any of the great Islamic culture and history ever penetrated my consciousness. The fact that our greatest philosopher, the Rambam (Maimonides), and so much of Western civilization have their roots in magnificent Islamic scientific and philosophical achievements still evades me at subconscious levels. My *mental framework* indicates that we were always at the top of some spiritual edifice, while they were at the bottom — which is sheer reprehensible nonsense.

It is clear to me that, had it not been for this deeply-rooted false conception which I am tempted to term *chronic xenophobia* (which however dormant it may periodically lie is still all-pervading) as well as the deep flaws mentioned earlier in our legal conception, the peace process would have started long before it actually did, and would have met with a great deal more success.

Education

Due to the momentous sweep of the renewed Hebrew language, all schooling was nearly exclusively aimed at propagating covert Jewish values, then still naively entitled Hebrew values. The internalized belief that we Jews (and, more so, those born in Israel), are different if not better than all others, is the direct result of three to four generations of Jewish/Hebrew education, albeit new in form and overtly progressive.

In recent years, the teaching of democracy has been introduced into the curriculum. It is, no doubt, a welcome addition. And yet, democracy is another field that, like Biblical studies, is regarded as a plague by our youngsters. And rightly so: for the teachers seldom internalize that subject. In a society that, deep down, regards itself as elitist, egalitarian values can hardly have the ring of truth.

It seems that we still have a long way to go to join a world that is awakening to the need of a new concept of itself. Clearly, we are not the only ones in need of the new idea — by which one human's relationship to one another, a human's relation to his and her own group; one group's attitude toward another group, and the way we all regard the earth we live on — all must undergo a deep change. This need is universal. The fact that we Jews (or Israelis) have special difficulties does not make us special; for every group has its specific problems but, in basic matters, what applies to others, applies to us, too. Each must examine their sectorial difficulties on the way to change and, in doing so, contribute to the general effort.

Only a realization that we, Jews, are an inseparable part of life on the planet could pave the way toward departing from our old separatist paradigm — the old Jewish paradigm — of which the Zionist experiment has failed to cure us.

Chapter 14

The New Scientific/Ecological Paradigm

We are now departing from the familiar ground of our people's history to venture forth into areas somewhat alien to the homegrown Israeli. Going abroad, I often discovered how hard it was to face slighting attitudes towards the State of Israel. They often came from intellectuals, particularly on the New Left, who went as far as expressing regret over the actual creation of a Jewish State — and that in the late sixties, twenty years after it had been established! I could not believe my ears. Who, in Heaven's sake, set them up as judges to "approve of" or "oppose" the existence of a living body? The right-wingers were no better of course. Their Prussian-type slap on the back, congratulating me on Israel's military achievements, was outright nauseating. On the whole, I felt that I had little to learn from them, not about our situation, at any rate. There I was, the son of early pioneers, plunged almost straight from the battlefield into the lap of secure European culture, discovering to my dismay an all but complete lack of understanding by those who, at the same time, passed Olympian judgment on issues they could not possibly appreciate. It was hopeless. My reaction was to retire into whatever occupied me at the time, totally rejecting the vanity of the West.

However, my curiosity was aroused. On the one hand, it was clear that Western consumer society was far from perfect. Deep flaws were apparent, which caused great suffering, especially for the dark-skinned foreigners who had started pouring into its cities. The new problems persuaded even some of the more comfortable members of that society to ask new questions. And then, returning home, I realized that Israel's traditional Left had become totally incapable of handling the important issues in our lives, not having the slightest idea — let alone overall view — how to change the constant of a people living by the sword. It took a good number of years for a new understanding to emerge.

At that time I was studying the phenomenon of the Ethical Prophecy in Israel, wishing to penetrate the hearts of those who had created the concept of universal justice. During that period, the futile war in Lebanon broke out and then, totally unexpectedly, the "Socialist" Soviet Union disintegrated, practically overnight. This collapse dealt a deathblow to the ideology of the Left, and along with many of my friends who had periodically demonstrated for peace, I found myself bereft of what remained of my old ideological compass. A few more years went by when, one morning, I woke up to discover that peace was on our doorstep. I could scarcely believe it: how had salvation managed to appear so unexpectedly? Only one question, tucked neatly away under the conference table, seemed to mar the idyllic picture: the future of Jerusalem...

Deep down, I suspected that peace, with all of its glamour, was still a good distance away. After the assassination of Yitzhak Rabin (the man who had led the peace process with the Palestinians), I realized it was time to resume what I thought I had left behind — our *necessity* to become a part of new ideas that were developing elsewhere in the world, however irrelevant they felt at times.

But why, one may ask, should the murder of someone leading a move toward reconciliation — a move I had wholeheartedly supported — have sent me searching for new ways of thinking? Should I not have just continued supporting his old views, while increasing my opposition to the views that had prompted the murder? Was not Rabin's courageous stand proof enough of the validity and vitality of his views?

The truth of the matter is that it was not the murder itself that spurred me on — for it simply vindicated my already firm conviction of the lethal nature of Messianic zeal — but what followed immediately after. Rabin's supporters and colleagues (still in power) turned out to be pitifully incapable of explaining — let alone effectively countering — what had happened and what had caused it. Rather, they seemed to be bending over backward, trying to appease those who had called *Rabin* a murderer before the assassination — all in the name of "national unity" — thus increasing the mental disarray among their followers. Nothing like the aftermath of the murder could more clearly testify to the ideological vacuum of the Peace Camp. Soon enough, Labor leaders were accused by the Opposition of not being *real* Jews (a claim that was supported by an overwhelming number of rabbis) and consequently suffered a humiliating defeat at the polls.

It was then that it became doubly clear to me that something basic was wrong in the way we regarded our politics; that the classical division to right and left stopped supplying the necessary tools for understanding everyday realities. I had already noted, while in Europe and the U.S., that, on the whole, the proponents of new paradigm thinking tended to shun the old divisions of right v. left, secular v. religious, etc., and altogether seemed to evolve new ways to address human and planetary problems. Breaking away from most accepted theories and practices, which still led the world, they showed acumen for ameliorating existing conflicts and injecting new vitality into systems and individuals. They espoused interconnectedness as *containing* conflict and hierarchy, rather than annulling them. With regard to inter-human relationships, they decried both totalitarianism and competition in favor of cooperation as the mainspring of life, health and creativity.

I started to wonder what it was in the new thinking that had kept me from embracing it wholeheartedly. Basically, I found it was the gnawing feeling that, as a Jew (or Israeli), I could not accept the reluctance of its leading proponents, such as the Austrian-American physicist Frijof Capra and his colleagues in California, to regard *our* place in the world: they felt as though Judaism had ended its role long before — thousands of years ago, in fact. Yet my grasp of our problems had begun to slowly transform under the influence of their seemingly remote principles. I had also personally met with some leading new-paradigm intellectuals who, for the first time, were ready at least to listen to my questions, although their answers were painfully slow in coming. Neither were there in Israel any who felt a strong need to change their ways of addressing our spiritual crisis; for this, of course, would demand of them a total reassessment of their old philosophies and well-entrenched positions. But then most people are loath or just unable to do that, even when tragedy stares them in the face. I had to make up my mind: should I take up the challenge alone — until the time when, hopefully, others would join? The result is this book.

The new scientific paradigm represents an overall approach, serving as a clear guide in an ever-increasing number of fields of thought and action. Since the underlying objective of this study is to discover to what extent the new thinking can apply to Judaism and, also, why, at least in Israel, the new concept is a virtually unknown entity, it is necessary to clarify its rudiments, so that they serve as road signs toward our objective.

The idea of a paradigm, in the sense we use it here, was first introduced in 1962 by Thomas Kuhn, in his book "The Structure of Scientific Revolutions" (University of Chicago Press), denoting a conceptual framework shared by a community of scientists and providing them with model problems and solutions. The term "new paradigm" has never attained a clear-cut definition. Instead, it nowadays refers to that which contains "all thoughts, views and values which together form the picture that represents the frame and the direction in which society apprehends and organizes itself" — as Fritjof Capra put it in 1988 — and that is in reaction to Kuhn's purely scientific way of employing his paradigm. As said, in Israel the new approach is all but unknown. It is felt to be too soft a contestant for our age-old Talmudic mentality, which on the whole seeks and accepts authority. (Incidentally, Capra's "The Tao of Physics," published in 1976 — one of the most popular icebreakers of the new thinking — took some twenty-five years to receive its Hebrew publication.)

It is no accident, of course, that the definition of the new paradigm is so broad, enabling the user to maneuver quite freely within its parameters. By its very nature, the new scientific paradigm does not employ set definitions. One of its major attributes, with which we are already familiar, is aiming at the *approximation* of truth, rather than its finite formulation.

Whereas in the past, scientists attempted to attain an absolute truth (or, at least, believed it to exist), one of the most important scientific developments in the twentieth century — the Quantum Theory (studying the sub-atomic nature of matter) — has peaked in Werner Heisenberg's Uncertainty Principle. The Quantum physicist accepts from the start that he/she will never reach an exact description of what is; instead, he regards all matter as a *set of probabilities*. This by no means indicates that these scientists follow fuzzy, groundless assumptions. Far from it: they conduct precise experiments, down to the last particle of matter.

Shifting attention to a *process* rather than to a permanent situation is another main attribute of the new sciences. One no longer regards reality as a solid structure, the kind that might be constructed out of building blocks. Rather, one views reality as a *network* of intertwined processes interacting with each other. It is clear that the instant a cube structure is freed from the earth's gravitational pull, it will cease to be a firm entity, but its parts will continue to relate to each other, though their relationships will be different. In the shift from structure to process of a new scientific paradigm, "every structure is seen as the manifestation of an underlying process. The entire web of relationships is intrinsically dynamic," as Capra puts it.

The new paradigm researcher regards every detail primarily as *part of a whole*. This enables him or her to understand the detail not only *differently* from considering it in separation, but to a fuller understanding of each part. In the field of medicine, there is an increasing understanding that treating a specific illness will seldom heal the patient's overall ill health (of which the specific illness can be said to be a symptom). Sometimes there is a need to treat a particular ailment: there is nothing wrong with an emergency measure, just as there is nothing wrong with a building that stands firmly within the earth's sphere of gravity. But in order to truly understand and truly heal, it is necessary to grasp the broad context in which the person or the structure exists. For that we need to look at the parts in their relationships both to each other and to their surroundings — to a larger whole within which they operate.

The principle of uncertainty regarding all matter and processes — the understanding of which opened the way to discovering parallels between present-day scientific discoveries and ancient mystical revelations — in no way encourages relinquishing responsibility. On the contrary: the new scientific paradigm upholds the conscious and active part of the human observer in the reality that she or he is observing. In the early days of the Quantum Theory, scientists were surprised to find that "still" matter appeared differently to the same viewer according to the "questions" put to it! This led to the far-reaching conclusion that human consciousness affects objective reality. Thus, the new paradigm submits that a conscious human being is an integral part of the universal whole. This statement does not imply manipulative knowledge; rather, it is a deep understanding connecting every human being, in a comprehensive, reciprocal and creative way, to his and her environment.

Consequently, this new understanding does not concern only scientific research and its findings; it most emphatically derives from, and affects, what is happening in our everyday life — the very life which has become so deeply affected by science and technology. Today, news from far-off countries reaches us more swiftly than it does people in those same lands, if by chance they are not watching T.V. at the time. An all-embracing conception ensures that television news is not accepted as the truth, whereas it is actually a one-sided aspect of the truth, amounting in most cases, to a tendentious distortion of the truth. As someone who was personally involved in television, I have learned what "good T.V." stands for, viz. whatever happens to look good on the screen! What is not visually exciting does not make news and, to many people, does not exist. But the most significant of life's processes and events cannot be televised.

Here springs up the contention that ultra-Orthodox Jews forbid — actually abhor — watching the tube. (Recently, this prohibition has spread to the computer as well.) Is that not proof of the soundness of their view concerning the world? It certainly isn't; for any examination will easily show that their objection derives from a diametrically opposed reason to the one that we have voiced here, i.e., that television does not enable one to see events in their true light. The ultra-Orthodox view is that there is no *need* to explore any outside phenomena, since they are all clear anyway, as set down in the Torah. For them, ours is an unchangeable world and there is one superior force — known only to them — which controls and explains everything in it. It has always done so and always will. Therefore, there is no need for television to change all that suddenly.

The new scientific paradigm is sometimes referred to as the *ecological* paradigm, for ecological awareness is an essential aspect of the new world conception. It too is reaching our country with some delay. Up until a few years ago, the general attitude here was that ecology did not really concern us, as we were continually called to address more pressing issues. Hopefully, when it becomes apparent that a factor, which has never seemed to be connected to our distress, is in fact a *cause* of it, the Israeli would be prepared to go a very long way to find out all about it. Indeed, here and there, one can detect signs that this kind of ecological awareness is reaching even this strife-torn region.

Ecological awareness is the prime example how the new ideas can move a person to take responsibility for his life and her surroundings — be they near or far — rather than relying on some father-figure to care for him or her. This kind of a patronizing mental figure had previously taken the shape of God, His Torah (through the medium of the rabbi), the Welfare State, or even, nowadays, the United Nations. But one who believes that the earth and the world are one intimate entity, inclines himself to searching for ways in which he or she can contribute to the general betterment as a matter of personal involvement, wherein cooperation substitutes competition. Today, the world can appear to be a home for one large family. Recently, with just a day's notice, the heads of eighty states attended the funeral of our murdered prime minister. They came not because Rabin had been awarded the Nobel Peace Prize, but because he had given his life for a cause clearly affecting every single person in the entire world. The gathering was an example of the network attribute of the new thinking.

Seemingly small forces are involved in carrying out certain tasks: they are no less important than the "big" ones. This is a meaningful ecological teaching. The way in which one nowadays addresses a child or an animal, one's attitude towards a single shoot, express to an ever-increasing degree the modern humans' relationship to the world as one whole. Today's child — the citizen of the future — absorbs more than what meets the eye; he and she are capable of sensing fundamental truths beyond old-fashioned inflated verbiage.

Satish Kumar, an enlightened and learned Indian monk, founded one of the most advanced colleges in the world, in which the researchers work on problems of deep ecology. The college is housed in Devon, England, and is named after Fritz Schumacher, who wrote the book, "Small is Beautiful" (1975). Schumacher revealed the futility inherent in pursuing unlimited economic growth with no regard for either humans or the earth's limited natural resources, such as oil, gas and coal. He maintained that the world economy has to relate always in-depth to the underlying ecological and social processes in operation, and to rely increasingly on human resources and creativity ("labor-intensive" rather than "capital-intensive") and, of course, on recycling. Kumar — who had been one of Gandhi's close followers and had succeeded in persuading rich landowners in his country to give up millions of acres of their land to the landless — once described what he would do if he were to become the head of state. Matters would be arranged so that each child would go *on foot* to a school, in which there would be no more than a hundred pupils. There, he and his friends would learn to prepare food — organic food, filled with wholesome ingredients — and after a time, would learn how to grow those ingredients. He would be taught how to work with his hands and to fashion all things necessary for his life. As for the teachers, they would teach what they know! That was all.

Schumacher's ideas demand action in concert with others — always considering human beings before "pure" economic interests. Is such an ideal practicable for most individuals in our present-day world? As a single individual, can everyone be responsible for the way electricity is generated? Can I possibly manufacture the car I drive or necessarily fly the plane that takes me, for instance, to my studies at Schumacher College? There are no immediate practical answers to many of these questions. The teachers of the new paradigm do not aspire to fix a definite course for, or to alter, human behavior in one stroke. They do not stop driving cars either, though a good number of them travel to work on bicycles. Their approach is holistic. They believe in personal example, teaching each person and organization to take responsibility for immediate problems within their reach with the general good in mind. They naturally stress the supreme importance of what can be termed participatory education.

Today, there are varying methods of recycling. Likewise, there are many ways to grow organic food, generate electricity from wind, reuse sewage, and so on. Manifold practices and experiments in these realms are being carried out all over the world in an effort to prevent a planetary ecological disaster, for which the policies of international conglomerates (whose sole motive is showing profit to their shareholders) must be held responsible. Ironically, another cause of impoverishing the land is the perpetuation of antiquated modes of production, when human and natural resources are exploited indiscriminately to bring livelihood to the poor, as is the case in the nearby Gaza Strip — the tiny Palestinian area at the southern tip of Israel's Mediterranean coast. There, ecological ills, caused by overuse, are considered by many to be beyond repair.

Addressing this problem, Schumacher developed the concept of an *intermediate* technology, being the ecological solution for the world's two billion villagers, by utilizing their traditional production methods *in combination* with advanced technology, in a way that would keep them on their land, rather than be uprooted to fill out the mega-inner cities with no hope in sight for improving their lot.

What, at base, are ecological principles? In the words of Arne Naess, the Norwegian founder of the Deep Ecology movement and philosophy: "Every living thing has intrinsic value." "Living thing" applies, of course, to plants as well as animals. With the Gaia

Hypothesis proposed by the British astro-physicist James Lovelock in 1979, Naess' definition extends to inanimate matter too. "Shallow" ecology is concerned with the preservation of the eco-system; deep ecology, on the other hand, reaches farther: it represents the deep tenets of life and the role of the conscious human being in promulgating it. Ecology, to some extent, can be said to constitute a practical aspect of the wider, deep ecological philosophy. All humans are called to share all ecological concerns, since they deal with life itself.

As a child, I was taught that our bodies needed three basic nutritional stuffs — carbohydrate, fat and protein — as well as some minerals and five or six vitamins (and, of course, sunlight, oxygen and water). Today, we know that our bodies function within a complex system that includes innumerable and for the most part minute ("trace") elements, which in the first half of last century we neither dreamed of nor realized were vital for life. Several years ago, a doctor told me that there were twenty-seven enzymes present in our saliva alone, as opposed to the single enzyme I had learned about when I was young (at the time it wasn't yet called "enzyme") — the one which converts starch into sugar. Like the living body, the soil is also a complex system, whose elements — organic and inorganic — are interdependent. The most complex processes occur everywhere in nature at every second. The mechanical approach, which views soil as a mechanical mixer, is totally counterproductive in the long run. It is possible, of course, to increase crops by employing pepping-up techniques — such as adding whatever chemical the specific growth needs to the soil, and getting a better result which will bring the farmer larger profits. Ecology concerns itself with more complex and far-reaching issues: the behavior of insects, in and above the soil; natural growth; small and large animals; the mutual influence of the biosphere and the atmosphere, which taken together guard the soil so that it can continue producing what is essential for life. Intensive study of the ecological system is only in its inception; however, it is already clear how great a role the tiny organisms and larger insects — so often regarded as "pests" and sheer nuisance — play in the natural cycle and in creating the components necessary for our existence within the soil.

New research, carried out in England by one of Schumacher College associates, has demonstrated that the quantity of minerals vital to our life, found in vegetables, is some fifty percent less than it was fifty years ago. The reason for this decrease is the attitude of most profit-oriented food producers. Our bodies, as well as the very earth we walk on, are put in sterile isolation. Western man has next to no knowledge of what he eats, despite rather empty gestures on the part of health authorities, in the form of statutes, which demand that all is specified in writing on the actual product.

The soil has ceased to be the intimate "mother of life" and has become one among many commodities in the economic system.

From time to time, we are assured that in place of the natural minerals we are given artificial minerals, such as, for example, those added to cornflakes. But this information is misleading. It is seldom possible to replace that which nature can no longer supply us with. Consumption of sugar is a good example.

In order to have the strength for most activities, we need sugar, which in combination with oxygen gives us energy. With our modern lifestyle that typically seeks instant results and gratification, the consumption of "refined" sugar has grown by hundreds of percent in the last generation. Sugar — especially white sugar — drains the calcium reservoir in our bodies. Undoubtedly food, which contains sugar, strengthens us for a while. But in the long run it does not supply the body with what it needs to prevent illness and rebuild dead tissue.

In some respects, general health in the West has worsened in the last fifty years, in direct connection to pollution, artificial foodstuffs and mental stress — all resulting from our modern life style. Enough to realize the increase of cancer and heart diseases in recent decades. The most conservative — or "conventional" — health reports advertise a twenty percent rise in cancer in the last fifty years. In cases of skin cancer, the rise is a lot higher. Ecological concerns are not only vital for the environment; they have a direct influence on life itself.

The decimating of rain forests — by far the world's largest reservoir of natural medications — is a well-known virtual crime against human and other species. A possible cure for AIDS was denied us, since the Malaysian gum tree — which was found to contain a natural chemical that stopped the development of the HIV virus — was eliminated by a "development" program that took place before researchers returned for it when their experiments had proved its wondrous potential. The list is long — growing and not diminishing, despite international environmental conferences — and is, indeed, threatening our lives. Science, out to improve our health, comes forward with cancer cures at the very same time that it practically ignores the deep-seated reasons for the increase of cancer, which are rooted in blatant unecological practices.

But, surely, all this depicts universal crisis and concern. So, how can this necessarily be considered as something to encourage a new *Jewish* paradigm?

Well, it seems to me that there is something specifically Jewish that stands — in Israel, at any rate — in the way of the new conceptuality; not just the type of crass nationalism that opposes progress, but, rather something deeper — *paradigmatic*, in the sense proposed above, i.e., "…the frame and direction in which a society apprehends and organizes itself."

The two main worldviews, which all but govern life in this country, are the overall Zionist and the religious respective points of departure. The two are moving towards each other to a point where it is sometimes difficult to distinguish between them. Notwithstanding, we need to assess that which still separates them and in particular what separates both from the new conception.

Chapter 15

Secular Zionism v. Religion
Rituals and Community Life

From the new paradigm point of view, both the Zionist and the reigning religious outlooks are venerable members of the Old Paradigm Club, despite their seeming to hold contrary positions regarding central human concerns. The main difference between them is a matter of age: the Zionist paradigm is much younger and, for a while, exhibited appropriate vitality — but not for long. Today, with the appearance of the even younger (the ecological) paradigm on the horizon, the more experienced, religious conception, in its fierce battle for rehabilitation, is sweeping aside the Zionists. It despises them and calls them *shallow*, though, at times, makes them useful partners against allotting equal rights to non-Jews and other such "heresies." All in all, it is not difficult to realize the ascent of religious ideology in modern Israel. It is useless to pretend it is not there, nor does it seem possible any longer.

I do not consider "the religious" to be homogenous, of course. There are deep differences among people and groups holding religious beliefs. My argument, inasmuch as it concerns religion, pertains to the *leading* attitudes in the religious camp, which are direct and outspoken in their opposition to any new, free thinking. Also, my use of the terms "we" and "they" is for the sake of brevity alone. My overall intent is to advocate *another* approach, one totally different from both the religious and the liberal-Zionist.

Not trying to define, or do justice to, either reigning concept, one thing must be stressed: in comparison, fissures have appeared in the liberal worldview, whereas the extreme Torah adherents find little reason to forego their old beliefs. Furthermore, the believers in the unchangeable Torah succeed in wreaking havoc within the Labor camp to a degree, which demands rapid and thorough reappraisal of its former, liberal tenets. One of the most difficult sentiments to combat is the offhand, widespread expression (voiced by liberals), "They (the ultra-Orthodox) are the *real* Jews," which allots my father and his generation the menial task of having been (unbeknownst to them) the Messiah's donkeys. It puts people like me in a position of trying to desperately salvage what is left from the rich lore of those who founded Israel. It is at such moments when, instead of screaming in anguish, adopting new-paradigm attributes is needed, with the belief that this fresh view can supply us with a positive stepping-stone from which to wage an otherwise rearguard, lost battle.

A chance encounter I had some years ago may best illustrate the corroding force of the religious view eating into our secular life. It was a chat I had with a soldier to whom I gave a lift. The time was before the general elections, and we talked politics. I asked him if he favored *Eretz Israel Hashelaymah* (i.e., that we, Jews, should rule the whole of British Mandated Palestine). "Yes, of course," he replied. "Why?" I inquired. "Because God promised the Land to Avraham," he responded without hesitation. He wasn't wearing a skullcap, so I asked him if he was religious. "Of course not," he said. "Then how can you believe in God's promise if you don't believe in Him?" I insisted. "Because it's written! He promised it to Avraham!" As far as I could see while attending to my driving, the soldier said that without batting an eyelid.

There was no time for a lecture; but even if there had been, there would be no way I could reach him. In fundamental matters (like the right to the Land), the arguments of the non-religious often seem lame, in the face of the Divine Promise. Even if I had presented a case for dividing the land, based on history, morality and straightforward expedience, and argued most flawlessly, I would never have been able to convince him, so long as his rational and emotional *framework* (the meaning of the Greek word "paradigm") remained unchanged.

The core of the present, or the "old," paradigm is *I* (or *we*) against all others. Presently, at the religious end of the spectrum, the Torah appears to be in full support of this divisive view — as opposed to tattered remains of arguments at the non-religious end. For, in fact, as Schumacher has shown (at least in the field of economics), the only remaining value guiding Western thinking is greed.

In what hidden recesses then does the vitality of the followers of the Torah lie?

Their first claim is that our Torah is *holy*. All of their thinking and actions are based on this "fact." On the liberal side, only a few will own up to the fact that we have not of late evolved any overall conception resembling that of the sacred Torah — an entity that is not only holy, but one comprising an airtight moral and legal code. Normally, liberal thinkers will claim that they, too, have a complete and elevated worldview. But the realities of life have recently demonstrated that the classical liberal view of *laissez faire* no longer provides an integral worldview. At the extreme end of liberal thought, the *postmodernist* claims that values simply do not exist! But this is no more than an intellectual manipulation. For there is at least one value guiding the majority of contemporary Western thinking: selfishness. That is the reason why most run-of-the-mill proclamations of Western leaders not only fail to inspire trust, but also are manifestly unable to provide any sustainable answer to personal, national and planetary problems. Consequently, not only in the Middle East, but also throughout the West, all brands of fundamentalist (Christian, Islamic as well as Jewish) movements rush in, as it were, to fill out a veritable ontological vacuum.

In days gone by, the Israeli freethinker (again, I include in this term, for argument's sake, anyone with from Center-to-Left convictions) relished discussions with the religious. But today the chances of holding — let alone prevailing in — such a discussion are at their lowest ebb. Not only classical Western philosophy has lost its gusto, but there seems to be in existence less and less common ground for a formal discussion. What is there to discuss, anyway? For every quote the liberal could offer, his opponent would marshal five, usually way out of context, unless it is *his* context, i.e., his belief. One way or another, the real issue does not lie in the realm of formal logic, but on another, somewhat evasive level. Here is my suggestion as to how this epistemological issue — i.e., that there must be, somewhere, common ground for all human understanding — should be broached.

Let us start with the following question: Why examine religious ideology at all, if one realizes the pointlessness of such a discussion? My answer is that we should not do so in order to *challenge* the religious views, but rather, to give us an opportunity to *learn* from them, to understand the wellsprings of their strength. While there is something obviously amiss in the Liberal views — those very same that motivated secular Israelis in the first years of the Jewish State — there is an *interconnectedness* that seems to exist in religion, which gives it its vitality. So, it is not the "right" or "wrong" we are after, but, rather, an assessment of those deep values, which are overwhelmingly lacking in contemporary, a-religious modes of thinking.

This brings us to the second "incontestable" argument in the religious arsenal: *continuity*. Those, to whom Moses' Torah is holy, claim to be *connected* to it by an unbroken chain. While this contention is far from being factually true (as widely discussed in the opening chapters), it is not totally groundless, for the editors of the Bible and adherents of the Oral Law took great care to make them *appear* continuous. It is therefore quite useful — indeed, necessary — to detect the discrepancies, contradictions and paradoxes in the Biblical accounts, in the way we have done. But to realize that their moral content is often self-contradictory and that most of their legal tenets and inferences are separatist and essentially inimical to contemporary life, does not seem to convince the deeply religious, which still comprise well over half of the world population. The question is, why?

Rational argumentation will seldom bring relief to a heart longing to belong, whereas the sense of continuity will fill a deep need that little else can replace in the vacuous "spirituality" of modern living.

Having learnt the immense power deriving from the relation to a continuous whole — in our case, the Bible — we have also learned that there is nothing that should bar a non-believer from drawing on its richness regardless of its "incorrectness" — save from the stultified, "scientific-progressive" methods of teaching the Bible, such as prescribed by Israel's Ministry of Education! In the same way that a modern farmer is misguided to regard the soil as a conglomeration of isolated elements, so do most modern Israeli secular researchers view the Bible. The result in both instances is similar. In our schools the Bible teacher ends up handing down an accumulation of lifeless material, and this plays into the hands of the extreme religionists: the living Bible is becoming their possession, despite feeble secular protests to the contrary.

Let me mention the Book of Job in this connection. As to its *ecological* depth, I will touch on it in the following chapter. What I wish to emphasize here is the common inability to appreciate its boundless beauty — regardless of justified reservations toward its capricious God, Who was so easily provoked by Satan into torturing His human, faithful servant. My dispute is neither with Him nor with those who believe in Him. Rather, it is with my own camp, which will, at best, analyze Job to death, with the result that my own, intelligent children have no idea what this Book contains, as they do not have much use for the rest of our cultural heritage.

Despite the pain that I feel when realizing that my own daughter finished high school without knowing that there are two Isaiahs in the Bible — she hardly knew of the existence of either — I should add that I do not blame her teachers for it. The aridity of present-day secularism is not their invention. Indeed, the pendulous movement that swung our immediate predecessors *away* from religion, nowadays, in its *reverse* movement, causes many, like myself, to view religion with growing interest. The task before us, I say, is to see to it that this reversal does not throw us back into our old, destructive separatism; rather, it should encourage us to truly *connect* with this movement and find in it future-oriented and life-exuding qualities.

This brings us to the third claim of the contemporary representatives of God: their right to the *truth*, due to their fulfilling all the so-called Biblical Mitzvot. As we have seen, a simple examination of the Biblical statutes will testify that most of the existing Mitzvot do not derive from Moses at all. Wearing the skullcap — the most obtrusive symbol of Jewish adherence — stems from an anti-Semitic regulation, enacted in the Middle Ages, that ordered Jews in Germany to put on a special hat. The Jews, in turn, converted the edict into a Mitzvah, in order to sweeten the bitter pill. What has that to do with Moses' original, revolutionary teaching? Another example is that of the wearisome Passover Haggadah, which followers of tradition read from cover to cover every year. The document reached its mandatory text many hundreds of years after the destruction of the Second Temple. Until that time, Jews told the story of the Exodus as their fancy took them, without a prescribed, sanctified text. This seems to have been their custom (as described in the Haggadah itself) so why should we, here and now, not follow their example? In a similar manner, most Jewish dietary laws were unheard-of during the period of the First Temple. As described in Chapter 9, the prohibition against mixing meat with milk is, at best, *hinted* at in "Moses' Torah," in prohibiting the cooking a kid in his own mother's milk. Indeed, examples of arbitrarily and strictly ascribing Jewish traditions to the Five Books of Moses go on endlessly.

But is there anything we can learn from the power emanating from obeying the Mitzvot, despite their doubtful origins? Surely, a freethinking person will never adhere to them blindly. For instance, the pious expression, *"Succah k'shayrah"* (i.e., building the ritual shack by following all the compulsory rabbinical specifications) looks plainly ridiculous to anyone who knows that the water-bound plants and fruit adorning the Tabernacles came from *pagan* Babylon — not from the *desert*, as explained away in the Book of Leviticus. Nevertheless, there is a touch of holiness in them, a kind of adhesive strength, is there not?

The predominantly cut-and-dried secular approach stops many from absorbing some of the richness of these symbols. In Israel, this reluctance is enhanced by the knowledge that those who demand their total acceptance for themselves, tirelessly try to impose their mores on all others. But, nowadays, in the reigning cultural atmosphere we, seculars, seem to be the losers. Recently, a tendency for a lateral (i.e., not a yes/no) approach to those rich, ancient symbols has evolved in secular Judaism, but it lacks an overall new perspective. People will often speak for "Tradition!" which is all too often turned into the belief that "the real Jews are them," i.e., the ultra-Orthodox.

The effort of developing a new, lateral tradition is bound to be a lengthy one; yet, to my mind, all efforts in this direction are invaluable, and that is for a number of reasons.

Contemporary psychologists and sociologists have rediscovered the value of community life, explaining many of the ills of modern society by its absence. To many of us, however, it often feels that stringent community regulations would limit personal freedom. Thus, the lack of community life is the price we pay for our personal liberties.

There is a decisive socio-economic factor for the breaking up of traditional communities. It came into being with the industrial revolution in Europe, which affected Jewish communities of the poorer countries of Eastern Europe and the Middle East far less than it did the richer Jewish communities in the West. For the "less developed," their immediate community was and still is an essential ingredient of their daily life. The weakness of the West-oriented, non-religious camp today stems partly from the lack of community life — but a community cannot be artificially created, whereas strict adherence to the Mitzvot fosters community life naturally.

The pioneers of the Zionist paradigm were community-minded to the core. But since early Zionist days, something has changed radically. The message of the early trendsetters lost its original spirit; at most, what has remained is the "socialist" preoccupation with the material needs of the worker. Despite any pretension to the contrary, today's standard of living is achieved well within the framework of the existing paradigm, putting the "I" or the "we" way before the general good. And, then, when something for the spirit is required, one easily returns to a bit of *Yiddishkeit* (i.e., traditional Judaism). There is almost no barrier that stands in the way of the old religious mores penetrating into the arid secular soul. Some mention of the value of any human being as such persists, but the realities in which the young kibbutznik concerns himself primarily with his private bank account can hardly evoke concern either for man's soul or for the soil beneath his feet.

Every attempt to create community life is vital, even when it appears lackluster. Most of us seem to be concerned with raising our own material standards of living endlessly, rather than discussing such boring subjects as local taxes and the neighborhood streetlights with our next-door neighbors! All the same, the proponents of the new paradigm will always encourage community life, involving a great variety of subject — from recycling and childcare to improving the social services, all the way to creating local cultural activities, and, last but not least, waging community-based struggles against corrupt authorities in order to maintain and improve the quality of the life of the community. This, in my view, is sorely needed for spiritual growth.

Like developing a new approach to tradition, community life cannot come into being overnight, of course. But, when an understanding of the decisive matters in our life enhances, it would naturally foster a new kind of community life.

We indeed need Mitzvot, but not necessarily those imposed by the adherents of the Torah and its derivatives. They should sprout from our spiritual needs and understanding. On our holidays, for instance, how can we continue to sing texts defying all progressive human criteria? We do not really mean to say such words as, *"Prepare us a slaughterhouse for our canine enemies/ so that we may dedicate the Temple in psalteries and singing."* But we sing these words nevertheless, every year, when lighting our *Hanukiyyah* candles. Why? For the sake of the children? Not so! In fact, the reverse is so: we must *change* these texts for the sake of our children.

Let us look again into the matter of texts. Holy Scriptures exist in almost all religions. As in our case, a great deal of what is written existed orally long before the creation of the written texts. And even after they were set down in writing, they did not become canonized immediately. They became so in a later era, with growing literacy; and, only after a formative period of argument and prevarication, have remained more or less unaltered. Over the ages, when people of integrity discovered contradictions in them, a clever technique was devised to counter those discoveries in order to bridge over the gaps. In time, the Holy Scriptures became so powerful that religions and empires broke up over their interpretation. Nowadays, however, if we do not wish to be ruled by ululating ayatollahs, our choice seems quite clear: nothing is *necessarily* sacred regarding a written text. Any believer may choose a religion for himself, including its canonized scripts, and also choose a rabbi and follow all of the Mitzvot according to his rabbi's interpretations, believing that these Mitzvot are holy. But for the non-believer, a prescribed Mitzvah is not holy in the least, and there is no reason why he or she should heed the local rabbi, even when threatened with ostracism. Furthermore, if a believer chooses another rabbi (a Reform rabbi, for example), chooses different Mitzvot and elects to drive his car to the synagogue on Yom Kippur, he may be embracing the new paradigm, as long as he does not force his beliefs on others.

The unalterable written Mitzvot are the bulwark of the old Jewish paradigm. The new paradigm, on its part, strives for new, flexible molds, often through dialogue — an oral torah so to speak — which are continually renewed, without resorting to sanctified restrictions. These molds need to be perpetually created, and this can come to pass primarily by communal effort.

One often wonders whether Jewish culture might not lose some of its life-exuding qualities without the prescribed, heart-warming ceremony around the Passover table, or the blood-curdling ceremonies in the synagogue on the Day of Atonement. I will be the first to admit that such time-forged rituals cannot be too easily supplemented. But the fact is that they have *always changed*, to some degree. Those changes infiltrated the canon, spread wide and far, and enriched both Jewish and non-Jewish cultures. Musicologists tell us what a deep influence the Hebrew prayer of *Shmone-esrey* (lit. meaning 18, but referring to the thrice daily 19-blessings contained in the Standing prayer) had on the underlying structure of the Christian Mass. A reverse example is the immense influence of Arabic poetry on Jewish literature and liturgy during the Jewish Golden Age in Spain.

Obviously, such enrichment is more than just possible — it is highly profitable; it fills up a vacuum. A people, who produced spiritual giants such as Bialik, who quit the fold to lash out at old Jewish customs (not to mention Einstein and Freud, who never were traditional in the least) should not balk in the face of a temporary cultural vacuum, but rather gird up in search for new forms, to express ever-renewing content. Observing Jewish holidays did not altogether cease with the immigration to Eretz Israel early last century, when most of the pioneers who came abandoned most of the other Mitzvot. The kibbutzim printed rich Haggadot, filled with both universal and Jewish content, old and new. Today, in the United States, there are many New Age Haggadot — each a far cry from the original one. It is, notwithstanding, important to remember an opposite trend, when even the most progressive creations — such as "Germany, Germany above all the rest," first sung on the barricades in 1848 by those who fought the outdated German feudal-system — lost their progressive nature, when sung by thugs and murderers. Of one matter one should be quite certain: if, within a people's tradition, there are clear retrogressive, inhumane elements, it behooves one to consciously relinquish them. Most of our holidays are touched to some degree by the values of the old separatist paradigm. It is, therefore, necessary at times to give up some cherished historical relics, whenever they bear within them the germs of, say, ethnic cleansing.

How does one go about effecting these changes in practice? With dedication and patience. A few years ago, I composed a new text for the beloved Passover song *"Had Gadya"* — the old text seeming to me to epitomize the old paradigm, being based on the eternal mutual enmity among all species. In the traditional version, a certain old man buys a kid in the market, a cats spots the kid and devours it, a dog devours the cat, a stick clubs the dog, then fire consumes the stick, water quenches the fire, a bull comes and drinks the water, a butcher slaughters the bull, the Angel of Death kills the butcher and, finally, God butchers the Angel of Death, Alleluia! In my version, I proposed that rather than being put out by water, the fire invites the water to brew tea together, and the water, in turn, invites the ox to drink its fill, since there is plenty for all. My song never became a hit; I expect it was a little disturbing for some of the kids who simply *adored* the old version — particularly for the reason that, at the end, instead of God killing his angel, in my version, Rabin's voice calls from afar for the implementation of peace. Well, it seems that, like achieving peace, it all takes patience and dedication. And I am glad to inform the reader that my bland version *is* already sung in *some* seders!

My gentle approach of denouncing eternal war — in this case, among the species — can be said to be "new paradigm." On the whole, I think it is true to say that new paradigm thinking — like many New Age ideas — is not overtly revolutionary. It aims at depths, where changes occur slowly — slow *evolutionary* changes.

In Israel, singing and the composing of new songs, spanning our variegated past and charged, at the same time, with contemporary meaning, ranks high in our cultural output. It may indicate a measure of spiritual yearning. Yet, in all this local creativity, new paradigm themes are noticeable by their scarcity. In this context, let me refer to a problem, which was put before me repeatedly by various Jewish Renewalists during a recent visit to the United States. Their query concerned the gulf, which they felt existed between them and the usual type of the progressive Israeli. "How is it possible," they wished to understand, "that whereas for us, *tefilah* (prayer) is the one assured way to social, communal and ecological action, it is anathema for all Israeli Peace Now activists whom we meet?" I believe that in the answer to their question may lie a clue to our spiritual impasse. It is more than likely that, apart from new *consciousness*, we need new *tefilot* as well — *secular* tefilot, if need be! Lifting our spirits in a positive way is a necessary addition to protests, which, while drawing on real needs, seldom help us cross the threshold of our as yet limiting cerebral conceptualizations. It is more than possible that *singing* while crossing that imaginary Rubicon into a New Age, is a prerequisite for *internal* change, which will, in time, bring about *external*, political mobilization.

Chapter 16

In Search of a New Jewish Paradigm

In the course of this discussion, I have often referred to the *old* Jewish paradigm also as the *existing* Jewish paradigm. While the term "old" may imply the existence of another, totally new concept, from whose vantage point one should be able to view the boundaries of the old, receding entity, the adjective "existing" may indicate the opposite, i.e., that what we are regarding as old still exists and may well remain dominant and unaltered in the foreseeable future.

What do we actually mean by "old"? Do we consider a paradigm to have a certain age at which it becomes old? Does a paradigm die? What is the interrelation between various existing paradigms? The very names of some disciplines indicate a close link between certain *sciences* — such as astro-physics, physical chemistry etc. — but can an old *paradigm* interrelate with a younger one, or does the new annul the old altogether?

"Old" is obviously a relative term: for what is considered old now was certainly new when initially conceived. When a new theory shakes up the existing principles by the root, a new overall conception is born — a new paradigm — but the old one may linger on for a considerable time, and the new entity is likely to preserve *some* of the terms, the qualities and the attributes of the old concept.

Let us consider two paradigm shifts, which occurred in recent centuries to basic approaches in two leading sciences — chemistry and physics — and ask, how instant was the birth of the new overall concept and how long it took the old one to finally die out.

In the eighteenth century, a chemical theory reigned, by which combustion resulted from the emission of some substance, dubbed *phlogiston,* since it had been observed that the burned residuals of any matter were lighter than the weight of the original, unburned matter. The burned matter was said to have *lost* its phlogiston in the process of burning. The new chemical paradigm, proposed by Lavoisier in 1790 — that of burning being a process of *oxidation* — transplanted the preceding one almost immediately, and today has reached a ripe old age of over two hundred years, while hardly changing since its inception.

In physics, the new paradigms occurred along a different timetable: there were two paradigm shifts within just over two hundred years. The first was Newton's ("classical") physics, which came into being about a hundred years before that of Lavoisier's chemistry, but itself met with a deep paradigmatic change when reaching just over two hundred years of age with the introduction of Einstein's and the *quantum* theories early last century. So, while Lavoisier's paradigm of chemical combustion shows little signs of dying, Newton's physics is now considered "old paradigm," though, contrary to what happened in chemistry, Newton's "old" principles are still being taught at school, while a few people living today have ever heard of the forlorn phlogiston.

There are many important aspects in these diverging fortunes — the main one concerning us is the fact that, at the time, there was a certain *convergence* of sciences under the influence of Newton's physics. Chemists, for one, were deeply influenced by Newton's thinking; otherwise they would not have been able to regard their field in the way that enabled Lavoisier to come up with his new discovery. (Lavoisier's discovery was by itself the end of a thinking process, in which others had partaken.) But over the last two centuries an opposite process came into being. Chemists, among other scientists, now having their own, sound, scientific theory, started to *diverge,* not only from physics but also developed their own varying sub-disciplines — became what is now called "reductionist" in nature — to the extent that nowadays one chemist often understands precious little of the another chemist's work.

What is the deep nature of these diverging trends? Originally, physics — sometimes called "the mother of all sciences" — dealt with things one could see or touch — such as stars, billiard balls, light. Until quite recently, these "tangibles" were thought to be made of basic "building blocks" moved by energy, all of which were believed to be either visible, tangible or, most importantly, unchangeable. Chemistry, on the other hand, dealt with what happened *between* substances and how they changed. There was a general agreement that chemical processes took place, on the whole, where the naked eye could not spot them at all. But, suddenly, since the beginning of last century, this distinction held no longer, for it was discovered that what was taken to be the smallest indivisible and utterly unchangeable units of matter — its basic building blocks, the atoms — were the most divisible, changeable and unpredictable. From that moment on, due to the epoch-changing discoveries of Einstein, Neils Bohr, Heisenberg and their no less brilliant associates, no conceivable phenomenon could be regarded as unchangeable any more.

And, since everything is today known to be subject to change — and, indeed, is always undergoing some change — no firm definition can be applied to *any* phenomenon at any given moment. Hence, the new scientific paradigm's chief aim is to reach an approximation. As we have seen, even the terms "old" and "new" are relative: they keep interconnecting and mutually affecting each other. Reality itself has stopped being "objective" and is now often referred to by means of *metaphors*.

Before we return to the main subject of our discussion — our envisioned new national paradigm — we need to re-establish our usage of scientific criteria as applicable to inter-human relationships — for these relationships, surely, have to do with emotions and, more so, with questions of faith. Following what we have already discussed in Chapter 14, what should aid us in bridging over the gap between our old concepts of spirituality v. reality is the realization that it is *science* that seems to have drawn closer to faith rather than the reverse. Recently, intuition and even emotions have come to be regarded as leading forces in all our achievements, including scientific research and discoveries. In a dialogue between the physicist Fritjof Capra and the Christian theologian, David Steindl-Rast ("Belonging to the Universe," 1991), Capra, referring to the new scientific paradigm, described the *subjectivity* of all our observations, by enumerating the new sciences' chief attributes, of which I will here refer to two:

The shift from objective science to "epistemic science," and,
The shift from building to network as *metaphor* **of knowledge.**

Enlarging on these two points, Capra explained that (a) the study of the process of knowledge (epistemology) had now become part and parcel of what used to be regarded as the *object* of scientific research (even when this object seemed utterly independent of the researcher), and (b) that that very knowledge can be described only *metaphorically*, in this case, comparing it to some network.

It is in this spirit — of which, to start with, I myself had only an intuitive hunch — that I suggest we continue to envisage the emergence of our new national paradigm. It is an inter-disciplinary approach — one which, unfortunately, still fares badly in most institutions of learning in today's world — that is advocated here. This approach takes into account all other discoveries made in other fields, be they scientific, spiritual, specific or possessing a more general nature. Contrary to the reductionist approach, the new paradigm upholds viewing all human achievements to date as converging again, being reborn, as it were, to assume a unified worldview. The term New Age carries with it this new sense of unity.

In the chapter following this, we will grapple with the crux of our as yet uncracked three thousand-year-old national code. In preparation, having just acquainted ourselves with the new paradigm's ways and means, let us go over some "pointers" in our history, which have emerged throughout our discussion, in order to discover how they may converge to present us with an overall picture of Judaism. They were:

(1) Loyalty to the nation;
(2) Unity at all costs;
(3) Underlying contradiction;
(4) Obeying all of God's commandments (Mitzvot);
(5) The notion of a Chosen People;
(6) The rule of justice;
(7) Being the victim;
(8) Wandering by nature.

The above list is the result of the "strolling" manner in which we have surveyed our history. Many reservations may be put forward regarding it and may alter that list. For instance, it could be observed that some major characteristics were not enumerated there at all, such as the belief in one god. My reason for this omission is that that belief has become central to other major religions as well and, hence, is no more specifically Jewish, as such. A devoutly religious Jew would seldom concern himself with such a consideration; for him, God is *ours* and nobody else's. Conversely, some of the categories, which *did* get into the list, also characterize *other* peoples — such as unity, loyalty and justice — so why did I include those? After all, one may claim that every nation tends to view itself as just and united, and that our periodical outbreaks of fanaticism — which derived, at least in part, from adhering to our Mitzvot — have certainly been equaled, if not exceeded, by other religions and nations at one time or another, keeping to *their* commandments. On the other hand, the same Mitzvot have made

members of our nation, among *themselves,* equal before the law —
an elevated principle, which today obtains more or less universally
— and justice, as such, *is* included in the list.

In sum, my choice seems quite arbitrary; but then the element
of choice is, indeed, basic to our inquiry.

The entire list — with the possible exception of the third and
the eighth items — indicates *separateness,* dividing us from the
larger humanity and, hence, constricting. Now, what happened to
the universal attribute, which is absent in the above list? As
remembered, while originating in Israel midway in the eighth
century B.C.E., it all but petered out with the first return to Zion
some two hundred years later. But should we not re-introduce it
into Judaism or, indeed, discover that it still lingers on and simply
needs resuscitation?

Obviously, if we weigh the above-listed Jewish qualities against
a universal perspective, separatism will easily prevail in branding us
a separate human species. My intention, however, has been from
the start to view them by means of a change-oriented mode, in
order to divest them from some of their binding, separatist
qualities.

We may be close, but I don't think we're ready yet. We still need
to clarify the means with which to do it.

It may be said, for instance, that I have erred in making a list in
the first place, for it rather looks like resorting to exact definitions,
which, as I have claimed, would get us nowhere, certainly not in
perceiving a new paradigm for our nation. But, then, these qualities
have characterized us through the ages and still embody, to some
degree, our existing paradigm. They may have undergone some
transformation — our nation did have periods of openness toward
other people — but, in the last analysis, most of them have
persisted, often defying all logical explanation.

What may have occurred here is that, in trying to assess our old
paradigm, I was unable to extricate myself from employing old

paradigm criteria, while what I was required to do was to employ a totally new approach. It is not always easy — or even possible — to give up past criteria. But, in reaching toward a new paradigm, one is called upon to do exactly this: to *gently* consider various elements, past as well as present, *gently* separate noble metals from dross, wheat from chaff, and, then, *gently* construct a new mental edifice, in which we would feel at home, safe enough to extend a hand to the rest of the world.

Let us then cast a new look at the "list." The most *change-oriented* quality in it is undoubtedly the third element of *underlying contradiction*. Not long ago, conflicts were regarded as threatening the weaker with racial extinction. But in the new understanding, contradiction is the very last to give cause for worry. After all, in the quantum view, a thing can look — and in fact be — one thing *and* another at the same time. With this in mind, contradiction becomes widely expected. It has now discarded its Medieval cloak of threatening the existence of a divine whole and, at the same time, lost its more recent Darwinian status of being the leading force in life. It is, simply, part of life. All this holds, despite the fact that, in today's advanced life-sciences, life-processes are discovered to be harmonious, even symbiotic, rather than conflicting. In other words, both contradiction and symbiosis are seen to be vital forces in all living processes. (Symbiosis was considered until quite recently to be good for microorganisms, but not for us humans, among whom it had foreboded physical and mental aberrations.)

The new paradigm refrains from analyzing living phenomena in a mechanical, black-and-white manner. By employing circular, more intuitive modes of thinking and observation, the new worldview often finds that what looks inimical to a system is what that system needs most sorely.

This kind of mental ambiance, of *containing* conflicts and contra-dictions, may open new doors, new ways of introducing universal attributes into Judaism. The new mental readiness toward containment of contradictions should serve as a green house for an altogether new spiritual framework within which to proceed in our quest.

Here I would like to relate to the aforementioned dialogue, which more than any other has encouraged me to believe in the possibility of a new perspective for Judaism. Its subject was the development of new theological (Christian) paradigm in its relation to the new scientific theories. "Belonging to the Universe" condensed a five-year encounter between David Steindl-Rast, the Benedictine monk, and the secular sub-atomic physicist, Fritjof Capra. At that time, I was already familiar with Capra's work and also had the good fortune of learning from Brother David an Israeli dance and a Hebrew song. The lyrics of the song came from the Biblical Lamentations, and went like this: "Restore us to Thee, O Lord, that we may be restored!" Neither being a scientist nor expecting God to restore me, still, meeting with these two thinkers on the occasion of their mutual publication has become a deeply treasured memory, encouraging me to look to the future with hope.

What was so special in their dialogue was not just the ultra-modern approach of both the scientist and the theologian, but, more so, the *manner* in which they interrelated. In the book's opening section, in presenting their worldviews, the two seemed to have quite a lot in common, but the differences between them were quite clearly outlined as well. Then, all along, they kept *complementing* each other, by exploring in-depth the points they agreed on while heeding the issues on which they disagreed — all in a kind of pre-knowledge that they were treading a similar path. As the dialogue progressed, there were more and more points on which they saw eye to eye, and, although the points of dissent did not disappear altogether, their exchange looked more and more like two separate streams ending up in one, powerful flow.

The way these two representatives of varying ideologies

cooperated made them spokespersons for the selfsame new paradigm! To illustrate the interchange, let me cite two theological points that came up in discussion.

The first one was that of *Limbo*. Limbo used to be considered the place to which the souls of infants, who died before baptism, were consigned. In the old Christian view, because the infants had not received the sacrament, their souls could not ascend to heaven, and yet, since they had not had the occasion to sin, their souls could not be dispatched to hell either. This inhuman concept caused bereaved parents great suffering, and led to it being completely discarded in the new theology.

On the other hand, the new theological paradigm has not altogether done away with the concept of Original Sin. At the same time, this fundamental dogma has undergone a thorough transformation. Brother David likened Adam and Eve's disobedience to God to the Buddhist concept of *dukkha* — the image of all things being a wheel that grinds on its axle. According to the monk, every religion, including Christianity, began with the assumption that man was imperfect and was searching for his way home. In answer to Fritjof's observation, that it was unfair to impose such human imperfection on an infant, David said: "But children are born into this condition because our society is out of whack.... That [concept] corresponds much more closely to the original Biblical notion of what we've come to call original sin." He went on to explain that this view, according to which society was responsible for the human imperfection known as "original sin," was gaining ground in Christian thinking, and was much stronger than ever before.

On re-reading the above passages it dawned on me that the matter they spoke of dealt with two of the most basic tenets of the Christian Church. Yet the first had been totally discarded for being inhuman, and the second — perhaps the most central in Christian theology — was now attributing man's weakness to the imperfections of the social order humans are born into. To arrive at his conclusions, the monk had been helped by a Buddhist (pagan) concept, supported by the Hebrew original! All this rethinking and reworking was managed with the enviable ease of a dancer. The monk's views, of course, have not yet become the declared official views of the Vatican. Brother David is part of that ever-growing movement in the Church, which spearheads the struggle for social justice while remaining an integral part of the official Church.

In considering a new Jewish paradigm, I have often asked myself what the possibilities were for such liberal attitudes in any sector of Orthodox Judaism. Compared with the link between Brother David's ideas and his dedication to social improvement (together with so many priests and monks who commit themselves to working within impoverished communities worldwide), I could not, to start with, see it occurring here.

As long as Judaism lacked power bases that exist today (in Israel and, in another sense, in the U.S.), parallel with breaking away from Orthodoxy, many Jews joined the social and revolutionary movements in the countries in which they lived. This situation no longer pertains. Nowadays, the life and status of Jews as such are not endangered any more than other minorities'. In fact, the greatest danger to Jews exists here, in Israel, at the center of Jewish political life, where we have considerable economic and military power. Israel's self image of being strong and secure is bolstered by American Jewry as well as the non-Jewish American taxpayer — but is threatened with nuclear powers-to-be to our east. The question arising here is, whether, in this situation, we still have a natural need to join the underdog and progressive social movements as we did fifty and a hundred years ago. Moreover, is it at all possible for us, having reached our elevated status, to rid ourselves of our traditional sense of superiority?

Looking for an answer, I have discovered several denominations in religious Judaism, based abroad (mentioned in Chapter 11), partaking in social struggles within their own countries. Altogether, these movements (as represented, for instance, in Tikkun magazine, edited by Michael Lerner in San Francisco) developed clear thinking on new paradigm lines — in many cases, well beyond the ordinary Israeli's perception. Yet, notwithstanding the importance of these other than Orthodox denominations in Jewish religious life (including the most encouraging fact that some secular Israelis have started to join those movements and support their cause), a vital *a-religious*, *overall* new Jewish paradigm is not yet being articulated And, since the likelihood of the greater part of Israelis ever becoming religious is nil, it is necessary we continue to search for a new Jewish paradigm here, encouraged by these incipient breakthroughs elsewhere.

As said, some Jews abroad still wage social struggles. They do so while cooperating with other groups and other religions — Chinese, Muslim, Buddhist, Protestant and Roman Catholic. They partake in a paradigmatic change, not only in alleviating a spiritual impasse but also in looking for practical economic alternatives in the new eco-social spirit.

Such cooperation is scarcely known in Israel — either with other religions or in cooperating with sectors of other Jewish religious groups. As regards the guardians of the ramparts of Jewish Halacha, they are normally bad partners for dialogue in anything and with anyone non-Halachic. Supplying examples of Christian efforts will only evoke their rage. But how many among us, the secular majority in Israel, are open to the new thinking? What is happening, for instance, to the followers of A.D. Gordon, Ben-Gurion, Tabenkin, and Meir Ya'ari — the stalwarts of Socialist Zionism, whose teachings are still referred to in our schoolbooks? Jewish separatism has its stamp on many of those disciples, too. Sectarianism, envy, and the unwillingness to develop *new* universal views seem to be our daily fare almost wherever we turn. The Peace Camp is no exception to the rule. I use the phrase *almost wherever* as a kind of safety net, for without putting it thus, I would have to stop right here and spend the rest of my time lamenting the vain search for new concepts in Judaism.

The reason I do not stop is my belief that a change of conception is existentially vital; but, having said that, the question remains: Which elements in our society are naturally open to the new breakthrough? Where are they to be found? To which socio-economic group do they belong?

They do exist in our midst, wherever an individual or a group searches for a different way, for an alternative. Many have willingly given up the so-called Western way of living and renounced the materialistic values of the consumer society. In their lifestyles, they are proponents of the new paradigm. While they do not necessarily term their ideas Jewish, they see themselves as Jews; therefore, their conception represents Jewishness of a new kind. Their relationship to fellow humans, animals, plants and life itself is one of partnership. Often, they are materially poor, but rich in spirit. They search for deeper meaning in their lives, though their way of life may not always be termed "alternative." In "small" matters, they express the conception that *small is beautiful*. It should always be remembered that the new paradigm is not a detailed program for any one individual or organization; rather, it is a way of life and a way of thinking.

Above all, a new element has recently come into being here, which will not sacrifice itself on the altar of archaic, corroded values. This group is intelligent and positively oriented; it possesses the proverbial Jewish capacity for friendship. They are the tens of thousands of young people who stood silently at Rabin's graveside for weeks on end. They are confused, for they don't quite understand what is happening. In addition to my father, who smiles wanly at all this from on high, I dedicate this book to these youngsters.

Chapter 17

The Maze
A People... A Religion...

Grappling with our persistent dichotomy (people/religion) has turned out to be even more trouble than I had expected. It felt rather like entering a purgatory, wherein doubt darkened the way before understanding, but insisted on being a prerequisite of knowledge. The process was quite painful, but I still invite the reader to join it, for I believe it is not in vain.

In the previous chapter, two interrelated questions arose: (1) Who would be the natural partners to the new paradigm, and (2) would religious people, too, be able to partake in it. In order to answer these questions, we need to settle two preliminary ones, which have underlain the whole discussion. They are:

(1) Is it possible to find a common denominator for all members of any nation — let alone ours, dispersed all over the globe, which has been known for its fatal splits?

(Most remembered is the tragic civil war, called the "Great Revolt" against the Romans, which brought down Herod's Temple and made Jewish political independence a distant dream for close to two thousand years.)

(2) Is it at all conceivable to consider a Jewish paradigm when we have discovered no satisfying definition of its subject, i.e., Judaism?

The aim of this chapter is to try and unravel the tangle that keeps these twin-problems forever intertwined.

The notion, even among non-religious people, that the real Jews are those who are religious is widespread (in Israel, this normally applies to the Orthodox). Yet many secular Israelis try to shrug off the question altogether. "I'm a human being!" they protest, sometimes adding: "an Israeli" or "a citizen of Israel." And, while every citizen in a democracy is certainly free to maintain such a view and determine whatever he or she takes Judaism to be, surely, this attitude can hardly promote future-oriented Jewish values, let alone a whole paradigm.

No one can be said to be excluded from a paradigm, for it obtains to any member of a given community on a par with all other members of that group. Our first question, though, is whether it is at all possible to create — or detect — a paradigm that pertains to an entire *people*.

My initial impulse to look for a new Jewish paradigm stemmed from the parallels drawn between science and Christian theology. But these did not touch on anything resembling a national paradigm. Neither did the extensive survey of our history provide us with a comprehensive answer. At times I have wondered whether I had not ventured deep enough, where it hurts — allowing myself the luxury of viewing Judaism as an uninvolved observer.

I have entitled this chapter The Maze; let me enter it then, vowing this time not to leave any stone unturned. I am not at all certain where all this bravura will get me: after all, for so much of its history, Judaism was Halachic and nothing besides. What are then anyone's prospects of hitting upon a totally different common denominator? The huge effort to create predominantly non-religious criteria for Judaism by the secular founders of the State of Israel seems, alas, to have floundered. We refer to them as giants — so how can we, mere life-sized humans, challenge the emotionally

charged and associatively laden statement, equating Orthodoxy —
or, at least, religion — with Judaism?

So far, I have tried to refrain from binding definitions, wishing
to apprehend the whole of Judaism, to sense its essence. But now it
feels that "sensing" is not enough! What, then? Also, I have been
defending Judaism from its detractors. Now the time has surely
come to hark to some of the more scathing remarks concerning us.
After all, as Aristotle has taught, horrific experiences may bring
relief!

The following epithets are taken out of utterances made by
people who have neither disowned their Jewishness nor their
Israeliness.

The veteran columnist, Uri Avneri, who has for decades been
advocating peaceful Arab-Jewish coexistence, once wrote that a
little racist hides within each of us. Not so long ago, such a
statement would have aroused indignation in the hearts of most
liberals; today it is difficult to refute. The more I consider this
statement, the more gnawing the suspicion regarding its validity
becomes. We know only too well that most (though not all) Jews,
feel that they are not only different, but, in fact, better than others.
For them, the whole of history has demonstrated that the Holy
Torah has put us above all others, and that no other explanation for
the perpetuation of Judaism will hold.

But racism is a disease, and I sometimes feel — as has been
often flung in my face — that there is something well nigh
pathological in compulsive wrangling with Judaism. But ignoring a
disease won't cure it! We must discover non-racial traits in Judaism,
though they are not likely to be found scattered on the ground
among the thickets of Halachic Judaism for all to see.

In moments of despair, it indeed appears that the Jew is, like
Jeremiah, "a man of strife and contention to the whole land." If he does
not get up in the morning, shouting "Gevalt!" — blaming someone
or something for his troubles, always justified in his own eyes in the

face of a hostile and sinful world, unable to trust anything unless it's his and his alone, and never trusting a stranger — he will not feel to be a Jew that day. After ingesting this daily portion of anger, he is all ready for business, in which he will excel in the face of untold restrictions. (The link between the Jewish talent for business and the Torah is an enigma that I leave to mystics to solve.) And in better moments, I feel a heart-warming identity with my people. Who else in the world is so concerned with his (Jewish) brethren, anywhere in the world? While this is the result of being persecuted for generations, this very persecution has inflated our sense of superiority as well. Even outstanding Jews, like Heine, Freud and Einstein, were not altogether free from this double-edged ethnic trait, so implicit in our mental make-up.

Many "good Jews" who wished to free themselves from these and other traditional shackles, ultimately cut off all their roots. Others, who had abandoned their Jewishness, sometimes repented and returned to the warm embrace of the Halacha, wearing skullcaps. But, as we have seen, not all those who left Halacha behind fit into these categories. Many of us here do not follow tradition in the least, but insist on being Jewish. For many Israelis, speaking Hebrew and remaining loyal to the State of Israel sums up their Judaism. Of late, however, the sound of these positions have grown hollow, as the secular citizen is constantly beset by the question of what makes him or her Jewish. The non-religious Jew is suddenly jolted out of his intuitive acceptance of Judaism, because, he/she is told, he/she can't be Jewish unless he/she observes the so-called 613 Mitzvot, about which he/she often knows next to nothing!

There may arrive a time when national traits won't matter any longer; it hasn't arrived yet. Our traits, at any rate, give us a lot of trouble — whether in the manner indicated above (when the validity of secular Judaism is attacked by the religious) or when vitriolic attitudes are directed at *all* Jews (this phenomenon is referred to all too easily as anti-Semitism). Either way, the need to question thoroughly our national traits — both as a whole and as regarding their varying parts — must not be abandoned.

But is a balanced overall view of Judaism — devoid of inferiority or superiority — possible at all? It often looks as if we are touching upon an intimate emotion, similar to love, which the author of the Song of Songs declares is *"as strong as death."* In the same verse, however, he implies that love leads to jealousy, and the latter emotion is described as *"hard as hell!"* Well, there's the rub! Whereas death occurs in a flash, the netherworld (or "hell") is a continuing affair, lingering after death forever and ever. What follows is that jealousy, this inseparable partner to love, is unrelenting, like hell itself, and out of our control — as is love. Indeed, Judaism seems, first and foremost, jealous — like its God, Who is both jealous and vengeful, notwithstanding some more benign attributes ascribed to Him, such as "patient" and "merciful." It is this jealousy of His that hurts — and sometimes kills — mostly those who believe in Him, His flock.

This is the main reason why I did not follow my initial plan, to tread cautiously in the footsteps of the monk and the scientist, mark down meeting-points between science, Christianity and Judaism or, conversely, spot the differences and then draw my conclusions. I had considered this plan to be quite a sensible, but, after numerous attempts, and an even greater number of torn drafts, I realized that in such a way I could weave, at best, a synthetic vestige for Judaism, an external garment. Even if it were to look good on paper, such an analytical attempt would not touch Judaism's core. For I now have come to identify the chief contradiction that runs through Judaism: **our longing for a just world, which will always crash against our own walls of separateness.** This contradiction is so powerful that the chances of envisaging Judaism as possessing modest, harmonious and conciliatory attributes (those that characterize the new worldview), seem to be remote if not altogether out of reach.

But what has happened, one may ask, to our good-old selves, i.e., to the Jewish renowned moral and spiritual qualities? Amos Keynan, one of the country's most caustic commentators, contends that the modern Israeli resembles the ancient Philistine more than he does the traditional Jew. His contention is that here, in all but two generations, the Jew who investigates, who hesitates, who is bound by moral restraints, has become arrogant and obsessed with a lust for dominance. While this description does not necessarily fit *all* Israelis, looking around for exceptions, I have found that those few who have retained some concern for fellow humans mostly developed a decidedly non-Jewish trait: indifference.

How does one escape such a web? Is it conceivably possible to find solid common ground in such a tangle of conflicting attributes? Is there any wisdom in attempting to graft the principles of the new paradigm onto such a hoary and stubborn wraith? Nonetheless, as the saying goes, once you've begun a Mitzvah, you have to complete it! I do so with trepidation, but, at the same time, am encouraged by the Satish Kumar's gentle voice, saying, "Don't fret, Mokadi. With everything you do, you bring forth the new paradigm. Every word is a seed; continue to sow; don't wait for something to happen in the future: you are already a part of it!"

If it is not totally wrong to apply the new paradigm attributes to our people, it certainly needs to be done gently, by careful elimination. It is possible, for instance, that not all new paradigm attributes can be applied to Judaism — at least not immediately. But, since the new paradigm's basic principles presumably apply to *all* universal phenomena, they must also apply to our people — but not all at once, please! There are no identical living entities in nature: sweeping, "foolproof" mechanical application to them all is bound to fail. Let us then check out the differences between the

disciplines discussed in "Belonging to the Universe" and Judaism
and see where this gets us.

Capra and Steindl-Rast drew on their two respective disciplines:
science and Christianity. While for long centuries, these had been
subjected to logical and philosophical analysis, in Judaism, the
situation is different. In spite of the greatness of many of its
teachers (above all, Maimonides, the Rambam) Judaism scarcely
contains a theological system. Our universities teach *Jewish thought*
rather than *Jewish theology*. It is, therefore, not certain that Jewish
theology can ever be formulated, unless, of course, its proponents
accept the nation/religion dichotomy — and this, to my knowledge,
has never been done thoroughly. From a purely religious point of
view, it *cannot* be done, of course, since, for the religious, our nation
is its religion. But here, from, as it were, the very bowels of this
hopeless argument, leaps its *quantum* opposite: it could be that
because the term Judaism *also* encapsulates religion — remembering
that some major religions, *un*like nationalities, *have* constituted
philosophical disciplines — there arises the prospect of conceiving
a (new) Jewish national paradigm, *as long as it retains at least some of
its religious aspects.*

Before we follow this astonishing new opening, I feel we should
try and answer the first preliminary question — whether there are
any national paradigms in existence. An English friend of mine
claims that, for the British, there does exist one: *fair play.* It is not
set down anywhere, but is widely accepted; the judicial system in
his country is intended to uphold it; it is, as he claims, accepted
everywhere and by everyone. To fail to follow it is looked down
upon.

So, there seem to be some national paradigms after all, but, as in
the case of the English, they are not necessarily *formulated.*
Moreover, the underlying nature of fair play, for one, is that it
doesn't *have* to be formulated. It is simply there. The Jewish
paradigm, on the other hand, *is* formulated — but only by the

religious — enlarging on their belief that the Jews are the chosen people. What is still absent is, of course, a distinct a-religious counterpart. As long as only the religious can be said to have a paradigm, the rest of the Jews, trapped in our specific nation/religion dichotomy, can have none — unless we learn to somehow *contain* that dichotomy.

It is not surprising that I was unable to follow the clear and steady path taken by Capra and Steindl-Rast. Their inquiry revolved around *future*-oriented attributes, and these were not necessarily applicable to any whole nation, in particular our nation, trapped in its religious *past*. Anyway, who says that we — as a modern nation — need to formulate a mental framework for ourselves, singling us out of all peoples, as it were? Isn't there something elitist — very "choice-Jewish" if you will — in such a quest?

Every person and every group base their actions on some set of beliefs, even when not fully conscious of it. It may be said that a certain philosophy is the framework within which one pursues the solutions for one's problems, and when that philosophy does not supply the solutions, one ultimately abandons it. Yet most people do not run their lives according to a *declared* philosophy. Nowadays, many unassuming individuals, as well as politicians, scientists, farmers, businessmen, community workers and teachers, make decisions of an ecological nature, regardless of philosophy. Consequently, the fact that presently it is difficult for certain Israeli agricultural products to find markets in Europe derives from an ecological malpractice — not from a philosophical error. We are not discussing philosophy, but, rather, a paradigm, which is an inter-connecting framework. Furthermore: a paradigm is not necessarily a definable philosophy; it may come into being unawares, but its effect on one's life is all pervading.

As we have seen, regarding religion and nationhood in separation has not brought to light any unifying new concept in Judaism. But now, to my surprise, I have discovered that, though being a total non-believer, I have come to accept religion as an inextricable element in my national identity! It indicates that, if I wish to formulate a new Jewish paradigm, it has to somehow include both these Jewish strata. I must then discover in religious Judaism some elements of what I consider to be my *non*-religious nationality. But how can that be? Perhaps what we are considering now is something altogether different, which may *look* like religion, but is, in fact, an as yet unnamed element that harbors some new-paradigm attributes?

What an unexpected turn! I am decidedly a part of the Jewish nation that came at a certain moment in its history, in opposition to its religious leaders, to settle in its old-new Land with a clear intention to break free from the past and live as a free and normal people. This happened despite the fact that for a hundred generations the Jew's religion had been his nationality. And, then, after only two generations of national independence, the *abnormal* nature of the Jewish nation — the old *religious* one — has all but taken over its life and culture. And in this state of confusion, I am now led to seek direction from that very religious ideology which is in diametrical opposition not only to my beginnings, but also to what I thought the very rudiments of this inquiry to be!

Let me try another alley. Politically, it appears that we have two clear options before us: either the religious sector becomes even stronger, in which case our nation will lose its hard-earned Western-type normality, or else the people break away from the grip of religion and ultimately separate the religious from the national aspect, creating a constitutionally-based democratic state. The two opposing trends keep increasing in strength; each side declaring that "it's all mine," pulling in opposite directions. Until not long ago, a delicate balance seemed to have been kept but, now, few feel that it can be maintained for much longer, especially with the apathy characterizing most Labor supporters. What is it, then, that is holding back so many of my enlightened friends from taking to arms? What is missing in our *secular* cultural arena? Some *spiritual* element, perhaps, a religious-*like* enthusiasm, a *longing* for that element? Is *spirituality* then the name of that unnamed something, for which I was looking earlier?

Let us continue to wander, however confusedly, in search of clues. Earlier, in Chapter 13, when discussing the failed Zionist philosophy, I suggested to view it against an ecological whole. Perhaps we should try it again — this time, in order to find out whether we can apply this *whole* (i.e., ecology) to the new amalgam, i.e., our newly-discovered religious/national concept.

By and large, the Jewish religion, as practiced, is not inclined towards ecological principles. A visit to Me'a She'arim (an ultra-Orthodox quarter in Jerusalem) is a depressing experience for anyone looking for ecological consciousness. As far as they are concerned, they have never left the *shtetl* (the small, decrepit Eastern European township). For most of its existence, Halachic Judaism was disconnected from the earthly processes of sowing and reaping, busying itself with teaching and studying, which, at best, dealt with those activities in *theory*. As they did in Europe, contemporary Hassidim persist in waiting for a Messiah who will summarily put everything amiss in order. In their zeal, they attempt to coerce all other Jews to join in the holy task of accelerating His arrival, by keeping *their* brand of Mitzvot.

Still, there are certain ecological signals that can be detected even within Halachic Judaism, e.g., *shemittah* (the fallow year); the legend of Honi ha-Me'agel (outlined in the Chapter on Halacha); and nature-festivals such as Tu b'Shvat and Succot. Nonetheless, they all remain in the realm of strict religious observance, inapplicable to anyone but them.

What we are doing now is, in fact, reverting once again to seeking guidance in new paradigm methods. We could try to utilize its first attribute, i.e., to shift our emphasis from a part to the larger whole, *starting* with the whole. In this case, we will regard the ecological concept, representing the whole, in its relation to the Jewish religion in its declared separateness, representing the part. In doing that, we should continue to review the Jewish religion *in the light* of this whole.

Let us review briefly the familiar ecological teaching and its overall *necessity*. All recent examinations show is that during the last half-century, as a result of a technological explosion, man has exploited the sources of the earth's energy in an unprecedented way, while deluding himself that those reserves are limitless. Concurrently, technological advance has created the notion of the possibility of boundless economic growth. Both views have proved to be myopic. The supply of raw materials from the earth is limited. Once the supplies of gas, oil and coal are exhausted, they will not replenish themselves, but will bw gone forever. Today's various substitutes for current energy sources — such as nuclear energy, as offered by the power hubs of the world — puts life on our planet in jeopardy to an unimaginable degree. At this juncture, when man is the prime threat to the earth and all life on it, humankind is offered a new understanding demanding that we humans should change. Technological man must find a new path; he must refrain *voluntarily*; he must renounce immediate material gratification, as has long been suggested by all the *old wisdoms*.

We know that the State of Israel is considered one of the biggest offenders against ecology within the community of Western democracies. Now, is there in the Jewish *religion* anything resembling the accepted ecological requirements to change this state of affairs? Let us look at some "small," practical aspects. The way of life of most religious families (especially the way of the wife, who is in charge) is frugality and discipline. In an ultra-Orthodox family, if the mother is lucky enough to drive a spacious car, she will seldom use it for vacationing, but rather for driving her twelve children to school. This is one indication that we have something to learn from religious way of life. Another quality, which I invariably find among religious people, is their thirst for their particular brand of learning from ancient sources — as opposed to the shallow "knowledge" many seculars glean solely from the internet.

Now, moving to the "larger" aspects of religion, we find that in many areas of the Jewish religion are interwoven ecological elements, despite the focus on man and his sectarian God. They are hinted at in the story of the Creation (when God instructed man to till the garden *and* keep it) and later upheld in many of the Psalms. The Book of Job displays the most remarkable deep-ecological grasp when God, amidst thunder and storm, speaks to Job of the cosmos as a divine creation, with its *own* reasons and laws, independent of man. Though this is a God-centered approach, the modern ecologist is happy to gain support for his concept in these ancient and profound pronouncements, in which cosmic and global processes are the *equivalent* of God.

The Rambam, too, maintained that there are things in the world which man is unable to comprehend. This view corresponds to at least one new-paradigm principle, that of *approximating* truth. The basic difference between the two views, however, is that Moses Maimonides reckoned we must not question God, since it is separate from us and beyond our ken, while the new paradigm constantly aspires to advance towards fuller understanding of the universe, regarding our conception of reality as a *part* of this reality. I doubt very much that the Rambam would subscribe to that!

Crowning all ecological and deep-ecological pronouncements of our ancients are those made by the Prophet Amos, the first and perhaps the greatest of all universalists. Amos struck an astounding balance between the *anthropocentric* view and the God-centered one. The God of Amos is "*He who forms the mountains and creates the wind* [also meaning the 'spirit'] *and declares to man the nature of his thought* [also meaning his 'speech'], *He is the Lord.*" This balance between all creation and the human ability to grasp it, is of the most profound philosophical and spiritual import. Amos returns to this concept in his cosmic ode when he portrays God as the One *"who builds His ladder in the heavens, and founds His vaults upon the earth,"* and when equilibrium will ultimately carry the day as *"the Lord makes destruction flash forth against the strong, and devastation upon the fortress,"* God will *contain* the one who has become excessively strong, ensuring that human-cosmic balance is restored.

As observed, universal concerns in the Jewish religion have fared badly since before the advent of the Common Era. Consequently, from that point onward, our ability to draw predominantly on Jewish thinking to support both ecology and deep ecology has also diminished — though we have discovered that universalist as well as ecological traits have not altogether disappeared from traditional Judaism.

Notwithstanding the above, it is vitally important we remember the need to always consider our *partly*-religious past, as well as present religious practices, as necessary ingredients in the new national paradigm we are seeking to promote.

In some way, our wanderings in the "religious-national maze" has helped us in clarifying some past and present concepts. What we need now is to find out how it could affect the future. Are we then called upon to become "partly religious?" Of course not. But we have discovered that the reigning secular views fall short of providing answers to most of our personal *and* national needs. In my new understanding, it is the *spiritual* element that is sorely wanted in most a-religious worldviews. The question is whether spirituality can — or, indeed, should — be sought on the wide, national canvas, or, as many will agree, it should be nurtured within small, dedicated groups of spiritual practitioners, or even within oneself, with little need for outside support.

A paradigm, we have said, is something shared by a group. Regarding other national paradigms, I think that the evidence shows that, when national paradigms exist, they often become the basis for one's happiness. The French consider themselves to uphold the principles of the French Revolution; the Americans have their constitution, etc. The Russians, on the other hand, having lost their overall belief in the Leninist paradigm, wade in deep waters. And we, here, are faced with national disintegration, which is due, to a great extent, to not being able to extricate ourselves from our old national paradigm. This is yet another consideration for not giving up the search for a future-oriented, a-religious new Jewish paradigm.

For the remaining part of this chapter, I will enlarge on the merits of the overall ecological paradigm, as applicable to our recent findings.

The deep ecological concept clearly places the reciprocal and balancing forces in nature at its center, in contrast to the primarily linear, mechanistic viewpoint, which pursues *quantitative* economic growth without considering the damage done by such growth. The ecological view is at odds with *self*-seeking. Deep ecology embodies some elements found in the *Old Wisdoms*, which place the general good before one's own. Deep ecology may, therefore, sound moralistic and *impractical* to the modern ear. But, having just discovered that it is the spiritual element that is so wanted in most of our a-religious concepts, we can now envision deep-ecological view, being spiritual by its very nature, as the leading principle in our sought-after national paradigm.

But doesn't ecology normally deal with the *material* aspects of life? Calling ecology "spiritual" might look like contradiction in terms — or *has* looked, until not very long ago. In recent years, many spiritual disciplines have increasingly turned to regard the material aspect as a growing element in their teaching. Suffice here to mention the Dalai Lama who, since his expulsion from Tibet forty-two years ago, has become a chief proponent in all ecological discussions — and many other "material" subjects besides, such as national territorial sovereignty for his compatriots in exile. Deep ecology is indeed a spiritual discipline, in that it regards as fundamental the good of others and the good of the earth as equal to one's own good. (Science has done the same, though in an opposite direction: it has turned *spiritual!*)

The principle of equilibrium embodies the principles of *reciprocity* and of *tolerance*. Amos was the first to preach *fraternity* between Israelites and foreigners — with Israel being at the time the most powerful nation in the region, a veritable empire. It is imperative we remember his words today, when the most salient element in our life is the *lack* of tolerance.

No doubt that, by its very nature, the new worldview is tolerant. The question here is: Can we, Jews, single out this quality of *overall* tolerance, internalize it and transform it into a paradigmatic element in viewing ourselves vis-à-vis others and in relating to the world at large? Many in the secular camp usually answer this question by rushing to declare that *they* (i.e., the religious) are *in*tolerant and nothing will change that. But that statement does not reflect the whole truth. Removing the beam from between our eyes, as advocated in Matthew and Luke, should be practiced here! The non-religious Israelis have not managed to avoid racism either. Many among us practice violence. We do this in our pursuit of a standard of living that wreaks havoc on the earth and on the fabric of society and by competing to eliminate all competitors and within the sphere of all the "small" matters between man and fellow woman — e.g., our driving and abusive language in and out of doors. All this is patently a non-spiritual practice: it demeans the individual and harms our environment, too.

It should be mentioned here that the struggle for tolerance is in progress on many fronts in this country, however scattered. Individuals and organizations involve themselves in granting and guarding equal rights and equal opportunities — to Palestinians, to Jews from Middle Eastern countries, to women, to foreigners and to sundry minorities. The contribution of such activities to our quality of life cannot be overrated. And there are also those who are active on behalf of ecology, including a newly established Ministry of the Environment (with, unfortunately, too small a budget). These activities are far from sufficient, but they are of great significance. Practical and educational efforts gradually produce results. The series of meetings dealing with ecological issues that have been held between Israelis and Palestinians since the Oslo Accords are the first step in regional ecological awareness, a first swallow — perhaps even more future-oriented than the image of the dove bearing the olive branch.

It is wrong to assume that the new paradigm is anemic — a "vegetable" creation, in common parlance. A new paradigm proponent will not refrain from combating those who oppose it. On the contrary, he or she will espouse the method of protest, on personal, community and national levels. She/he will champion personal fulfillment, stressing the importance of participatory education. She/he are normally fully aware of the dangers that derive from frozen, stultifying views, on the one hand, and the sweeping harm done by the theory and practice of market economy, on the other hand.

But most important is the realization that the application of the new concept of life rests in our nurturing it in our daily existence. The imparting of justice, generosity and an alternative lifestyle begins at home, and within our immediate environment. The steadily increasing number of meetings between secular and religious groups reflects a will to remove the discussion away from the gap dividing religious and seculars, away from the domain of public figures — each with their own vested interest — to more personal meeting points. Sadly, it appears that the non-religious participants arrive at such meetings with insufficient preparation; frequently, the religious delegates present their position courageously, while the secularists mumble and grope for a way to adjust themselves to the demands of the others.

Our chief weakness, however, lies in the lack of a compass — i.e., an overall, positive approach to life, both in theory and in practice. We, seculars, in our justified desire to counter a fanatic religious takeover, could have a much greater influence on *them* if we were, first of all, to choose a way of life and an alternative concept of life for *ourselves*. Only then would we be capable of truly attracting the religious differently from the way it is occurring now in religious/secular encounters, which often resemble flies converging on a carcass rather than human encounter.

We have discovered that it is not *necessarily* religion that clouds our horizon. In this context, I wish to examine one of the most familiar examples of the Jewish observance, in order to highlight a possible reservation toward the above statement. It relates to one of the most holy principles of the Jewish religion: the keeping of the Sabbath. The observant Jew respects this divine gift with profound tenderness. In the Diaspora, during weekdays, the Jew endured humiliation befitting a slave, but, on the Seventh Day, he retreated to his home and synagogue, beholding himself as a king. Often, on Saturday mornings, when I see traditional Jews with their wives and their children dressed festively on their way to the synagogue, I feel some envy. But then I remember that this same very gentle and pious Jew can *metamorphose* into a raging, violent zealot in defending that selfsame essence of holiness! This fervor, which perhaps had the power to keep Judaism alive unto our era, bears the odious marks of endemic separatism that flouts the deepest principles of the new worldview. When I said that the new paradigm did not refrain from opposing its negation (e.g., by protest), I was also referring to rejecting this quality of zealous violence, which exists in traditional Judaism.

For our immediate purpose, I propose to regard this manic

quality of swinging from one extreme to its opposite as one of *polarity*. I trust that, keeping it in mind and viewing it in the spirit of containment, will advance our grasp of the Jewish essence — both old and new — which is the main subject of the following and final chapter.

Chapter 18

The Paradigm

We have now come to the question — Judaism, what is it? No, that can't be right. Rather, we are seeking the nature of the paradigm *underlying* Judaism. No, that's not it either. Well, it is the *new* Jewish paradigm we're after. That's it, of course! It is something that we say refers, at best, to an approximation, but at the same time derives from a whole, which cannot be defined, only *sensed* — Hold it, please! Sensed by whom, pray? And how?

I give up — or, at least, I must admit confusion — as if being marooned on a rocky vessel, riding a vehicle whose wheels have not been properly tested, or, to be honest, having got myself into a world of mixed metaphors called the new paradigm... Help!

We'd better stop to take a break for reflection, hadn't we?

Well?

Well, on reflection, I would like to put forward that, prior to trying to reach an overall view of Judaism, we spend a little more time on the new paradigm's proposed departures — in particular, on clarifying what we mean by the shifting of emphasis from a part to a whole. We have discussed it already, but I am not yet convinced that we have — well, internalized it.

A paradigm, we may safely reckon, is not the sum of its characteristics, but, rather, a framework "containing all the thoughts, views and values... [by which a society] apprehends and organizes itself" — a far cry from the mechanical sum of its components. Also, the new scientific paradigm requires that we acknowledge the existence of a whole, i.e., the "sum," prior to examining its various parts. Yet I believe that most of us have been taught to do the opposite, namely, that in order to understand anything we need to analyze it — first dissect it and, then, hopefully, understand the whole assembly from having scrutinized its constituents in separation. Formerly, a square used to be presented as a geometrical form, being the *outcome* of four straight equal lines that met at right angles; and a rose was a plant, which was so high, had a thorny stalk and so many petals with a certain shape etc. (At times we were taught to start by stating to what *family* of plants the rose belonged — in this case, the genus *Rosa* — but then, in the old way, we were also required to define the *genus* by its parts.)

Now we are asked to say that we *know* a rose, regardless of its specifics; and regarding the good old square, today we are taught by means of the Theory of Relativity and fractal geometry that there is *no* such thing as a straight line anyway. So, what is a square? It's a square, isn't it? It's agreed that it fits its Euclidean definition, based on certain axioms — but what is an axiom? Ah. It is something we have *agreed* on, not the actual *truth*. Of course it isn't the truth, for, at best, it is an approximation. We all agree on what we mean when we say that the table is square; but its squareness doesn't make it a table; nor do its other parts. What is required, talking of a table, is to start off with *it* and then describe its parts. Plato would agree with this approach; but Aristotle wouldn't. And, indeed, it needed the introduction of Aristotelian analytical modes into Medieval thinking to precede Newton's mechanics. All this does not mean that the *whole* (the table, the rose or the square) does not possess several identifiable attributes, but these, we now have come to believe, are of a general nature, not representing an immutable truth.

That's it, then! In discussing the contemporary paradigm, all we need to do is to internalize and then apply this approach.

But, surely, some of this sounds familiar. It always has been accepted that, when discussing anything, we need to agree *a priori* on some common denominators, such as the meaning of the words we use. A culture, as C.P. Snow showed in *The Two Cultures* over forty years ago, is primarily a matter of a common language shared by the members of that culture. Now then: when explaining the basics of the new paradigm, Capra refers to *attributes* rather than *characteristics*. Why? Don't these two terms represent the same thing? No; for when we say "a characteristic," we refer to something embedded in the object, whereas when we say "an attribute" the reference is to something *we* attribute to it. And, since this distinction is not necessarily generally accepted, we need to agree *a priori* about what those key words mean to *us*.

When it is suggested that the new paradigm requires that we comprehend (or at least sense) the whole first, we assume a common denominator shared by us *and* by the person whom we are addressing. But, while regarding the square, there should be little difficulty in assuming pre-knowledge of what we are talking about, the same does not necessarily apply to national paradigms.

We are now faced with the following dilemma: we have been given to understand that we should start with a certain whole, but, in order to become familiar with that whole, we need, ourselves, to endow it with certain attributes. How are we to come by those attributes? The answer can be found in Karl Popper's approach to the nature of new scientific theories. This renowned philosopher of natural and social sciences (1902-1994) espoused that a new theory is born in a flash, emanating from all previous knowledge and touched by a new intuition. This newly-born theory now becomes subject to challenges and, as long as it is not refuted, it is retained.

According to this, having fair knowledge of Judaism, and, sharing the intuition that, in order to survive, Judaism needs a new mental framework — a new theory, as it were — all we need to do is to somehow agree what attributes are ailing in Judaism, and then agree on what are the cures (i.e., the "shifts") which should occur in them, so that they may change into assuming a new, healthy paradigm. This suggested process is not required to be logical (though some logic may have to be employed to refute it!). The real test of the new theory, however, must be in its ability to supply answers to whatever demands it was constructed to fulfill. But, first, it needs to be proposed, and, for that, the new attributes need to be presented as clearly as possible, so that the new paradigm emanating from them will finally emerge.

Let us check out the Jewish attributes we have discovered so far, as appearing in Chapter 16. The list comprises the more ancient ones, first noted at the end of Chapter 2. They were —

1. Loyalty to the nation;
2. Unity at all costs;
3. Contradiction;
4. Obeying all of God's commandments;
5. The notion of a Chosen People (implying separateness).

It is important to note that *Implying separateness*, which I put in parentheses, is a late addition; it looks as if separateness is so typical to Judaism, that, until now, we have not even bothered to mention it as a separate attribute!

In Chapter 16, we extended the list to include the remaining pre-Halachic attributes, which also came up quite early in our discussion —

6. The rule of justice;
7. Being the victim;
8. Wanderers by nature.

Not forgetting the reservations mentioned in the previous chapter — referring to some arbitrariness in the choosing of these attributes — it is quite striking to realize how little they have altered in the duration of thousands of years in exile.

But now, having acquired some taste for new-paradigm thinking, the old list should be extended — primarily, in order to discover the additional qualities which have developed and sustained our nation *in* exile. I will enumerate them in advance — i.e., prior to examining their evolvement; I wish you, the reader, to feel a full partner in the final process of evolving what I have come to consider as the emergence of the new Jewish paradigm.

The added attributes are of a more general nature than the previous ones. They are:

9. Balance;

10. Community life;

11. Creativity;

12. Continuity.

How have I come to single out these new attributes? So far, I have referred to various Jewish traits as qualities, notions, characteristics, and even tenets or principles, without paying much attention to the term I used. It didn't matter much, as long as the meaning was clear. From now on, I will use them in a certain agreed manner. I will refer to two separate classes of attributes: one, the new-paradigm *means* of assessing any phenomenon — like that of regarding the whole first — and the other, a particular quality we have attributed to that phenomenon, which was discovered by those very means. I am suggesting to do so in order to underline the notion that the means by which we study a phenomenon largely determines what we discover. Whenever I use any of the other terms — such as "quality, "trait," etc. — it would indicate the more or less accepted meaning of that "quality" — i.e., *before* it has been accepted by us as representing a new-paradigm attribute of Judaism.

Even though the new paradigm was only suggested at the start, I have been guided by its principles throughout. These principles have been flexible, regarding the "thing itself" as constantly undergoing *some* change — in relation to both our own thinking, and changing conditions, to the extent that even monotheism stopped being regarded as a major Jewish attribute. Other notions, such as *unity, loyalty* and *justice* — in particular *universal* justice — were losing their centrality in Judaism in the course of time. On the other hand, we have found that *contradiction* had managed to sustain its status — indeed, acquired a central position — I dare say, equal to that of separateness.

In sum, in order to allot new attributes to Judaism, it is agreed that some of its old ones will be found to have altered, some discarded, some merged with another attribute, etc. It is my intention to show how contradiction has given rise to another attribute — which may look like its opposite — that of *balance*. In my understanding, this newly-conceived or, rather, newly-detected attribute of balance has sustained our nation through thick and thin, equal to, if not more than, any other quality in Judaism,.

This attribute represents an ability to strike a balance between divisive extremes. It is usually a covert quality, yet at certain historical moments it has surfaced. In the past, due to this ability, when unable to cope with internal extremes, Judaism hastened to part with them whatever the cost, as was the case with Christianity. But, for long periods, this covert attribute has kept its workings solely *within* Judaism. Nowadays, this balancing attribute is solemnly voiced at every soldier's grave in the Aramaic words of the prayer for the deceased, asking God to bring about our age-long dream of peace and tranquility. It is at work at this very moment, when, after a hundred years of siege, the people of Israel have shown an inner capacity for charity towards the State's multitudinous enemies — a widespread mood that has surprised even the most avowed peace-lovers among us. As said, often, this quality is muted. In fact, it is normally stronger *after* a disaster occurs than just before it, when it is most required. But, not ten years ago, it was exemplified *during* a crisis, when Israel, under its right-wing Prime Minister, refrained from striking back during the Gulf War — the only time when missiles, which could carry chemical and nuclear warheads, were ever used worldwide.

Side by side with the separatist tendency, this attribute of balance has never been absent from Judaism. To further support this claim, let me cite an example, pertaining to the most momentous *paradigm shift* in our history since the so-called Sinai Revelation. It was the rise of Spiritual Judaism, close on the heels of the fall of Jerusalem and the destruction of the Second Temple in 70 C.E.

Just before that tragic event, equaled only by the Holocaust, Rabbi Yochanan ben Zakkai was smuggled out of Jerusalem in a coffin into the besieging Roman camp. What he asked for, and eventually received, was the right to establish a non-political, spiritual center for the Jews, outside of Jerusalem. From that moment on, for close to two thousand years, what is termed *spiritual Judaism* has survived along the lines that the rabbi formulated. True, sixty years after ben Zakkai's Center had been established in Yavneh, another Jewish rebellion erupted, led by Bar Kochba, even more futile and lethal than the previous one, and was given the unreserved blessing of some of ben Zakkai's most venerated disciples (see Chapter 12), and yet, spiritual Judaism survived. Many other horrendous trials followed and, still, spiritual Judaism survives. What balanced foresight must have guided those ancestors of ours, and what balanced wisdom must we display today in order to free ourselves from the stranglehold of Halacha, which actually started its ordered existence in Yavneh!

I do not envisage anyone needing to be smuggled out in a coffin in order to start a contemporary new paradigm; the world is a lot more open today. Yet it is the same balanced courage that ben Zakkai displayed then that we are now called upon to muster, in order to bring about an age of peace — namely, a quality of deep and far-sighted balance.

Another attribute to join the list of old Jewish attributes is that of the Jewish persistence in preserving its *communities*. Interesting to note that the Hebrew term for community, *kehillah*, derives from the Semitic root K.H.L., and *kahal*, in the Bible, meant an ethnic-religious congregation of Hebrews. This attribute, like others besides, has it roots in the Jewish ethos from even before normative Judaism.

We have already spent some time on the value Jews set on communal life, in particular on the interrelation between community-life and Jewish religious life (see Chapter 15). I also suggested there that the proponents of the new paradigm — many of whom not being religious — set great store by community-life, viewing it as the nursing ground for spiritual growth and ecological awareness. Community-life is both intimate and uniquely future-oriented. In his book, *Ecology, Community and Lifestyle*, Arne Naess, the founder of Deep Ecology, predicts that, when revived, community life will affect everyone's lifestyle without exception.

This attribute connects to yet another newly-suggested central Jewish attribute: *creativity*. In Judaism, creativity can be seen as both being community-induced and, conversely, born in individuals who were ricocheted from mainstream Judaism. Regarding the former, I would like to weigh its importance against the backdrop of a process which nowadays affects all Western culture and, to a lesser extent, the East, too. I will draw on personal experience.

After a few years in Britain, when I had stopped enjoying the life of a carefree student, I became aware of certain aridity concerning all life around me — in the big cities as well as in the smaller, provincial townships. Authentic culture had been increasingly relegated to the periphery, as, for example, the rich choral traditions of the coal-mining communities of South Wales. The mining communities themselves were rapidly disappearing from the world, because of the race for cheap oil. E.F. Schumacher's "Small is Beautiful" presented a frightening account regarding the counter-ecological and anti-social national and global policies, which did not only decimate traditional communities but, in the long run, proved to be uneconomical as well. Yet, notwithstanding the long process of dilapidation of traditional communities, I noticed that the English notorious inhibitedness was giving way to a kind of hunger for authentic creations within some sort of community revival.

Later, going to the United States, I was surprised to discover how authentic traditional culture still showed an immense renewal potential. The chief authentic cultural wealth of America seemed to come from Black music, preserved and revitalized by descendants of slaves — the very music which had given this otherwise rootless civilization one of its deepest communal anchors. By and by, I came to discover more authentic community-originated cultural pockets. The list seemed quite long, but was getting shorter by the hour, when rooted communities became the playground for adventurous media producers and diligent anthropologists. At the same time, the yearning for roots was becoming stronger. The new awareness that the Western economy, in spite of its current success, was destructive to the world had reactively produced the New Age movement in all its varying facets. All over the world, a growing surge toward authentic self-expression was in evidence, as opposed to the prevalent commercialized mass culture.

How does Judaism come into all this? It has obviously preserved many of its ancient traditions, concurrently with creating new molds to renew those very traditions. We have already mentioned the Hassidic innovativeness in the seventeenth century and, also, how, two hundred years later, our facility for creating new molds for the new Hebrew culture became the backbone of Zionism. However, for those familiar with the present-day anti-cultural religious surge in Israel, it will come as no surprise to learn that this unique outpour of creativity has recently drawn the wrath of our religious authorities, referring to its participants as *mityavenim* (i.e., pagans), God save us, and their squeals do not fail to have an effect.

So, you may ask, where has this creative quality in Judaism gone? According to the description just given, its fruition is rare; and when it does surface, it is likely to be all but totally stemmed within a hundred years of its inception.

Taking a long view, if the fundamentalist backlash, which is on the ascent the world over, is to carry the day, woe is it to *any* new paradigm. Yet, if zealous fundamentalism can be contained, the Jewish erstwhile cultural acumen can still have its day, incorporating its ancient lore, as it has done this previous century. The progressive and the conservative have always clashed; this struggle has now become existential on a global scale. And, since rooted cultural creations obviously play a significant role in the New Age, Judaism could rate quite significantly as a time-hardened partner in this global battle for spiritual renaissance.

Jewish creativity embodies Judaism's talent for perceiving matters *differently* from its surroundings. It produced many outstanding, revolutionary concepts by Jewish individuals — those of Spinoza, Marx and Freud are three among great, great many. It enriched world's culture far beyond the proportionate size of the Jewish nation. I am well aware, of course, that incredible creativity existed elsewhere as well, i.e., among *all* nations. Yet in the alarming reality of Israeli life today, it is essential to stress the perpetual existence of creativity within our ranks. All this is said notwithstanding the fact that this overall *resiliency-cum-creativity* attribute gave rise to the ill-based belief in the Jewish Heaven-ordained preservation (or continuity) — a power attributed by the religious to Israel's Torah.

Last but not least, in the newly-noted Jewish attributes, is *continuity*. This attribute is so elemental to Judaism, that its power is apparent in most of the other Jewish attributes. Yet it should stand on its own, since it is not identical with the others; in fact, it often becomes the power behind them, enabling them to survive.

In reviewing all the above listed twelve Jewish attributes, we should single out the life-oriented among them. I will do it by first displaying the familiar heading, such as unity, loyalty etc.; then will review its living potential as has come to light in our inquiry. I will be aided by Capra's attributes, of course — but, more importantly, will try to discover how these attributes interrelate, merge, or, conversely, fail to answer the deep needs and demands of our times and, hence, have to be discarded. Those that remain may have undergone some shifts, endowing them with heretofore unexpected vitality.

Finally, because of the immense intricacy of our subject, and in order to map out a workable list of new-paradigm blue print for contemporary Judaism, I will try to compress secondary Jewish attributes into smaller number of primary ones. Obviously, not all secondary attributes, however typically Jewish, will be dealt with. Such are the Semitic beginnings of our nation and the non-Semitic nature of some of the languages (or, rather, jargons) that have been used exclusively by Jews in the Diaspora; some are still extant even in Israel. Although they constitute a central feature in the life of several Jewish communities, the multi-linguistic aspect, as well as the full gamut of other, separate attributes, will have to remain subject for an altogether different, extended study.

As a reminder, let me list the attributes of Capra's new scientific paradigm, as they appear in *Belonging to the Universe*, to aid us in the following review of Jewish attributes. They refer to *shifts* —

I.   From part to a whole;

II. From structure to process;

III. From objective to epistemic;

IV. From building to network as a metaphor of knowledge;

V.   From truth to approximation.

1. Loyalty to the nation

Initially, and until quite recently, this attribute was embodied in loyalty to our one God and His Torah. Since the fall of the Second Temple, it all but relinquished its (normal) national element and, instead, centered on Jewish communal life and communal *learning* as the base for perpetuating the Jewish faith. Today, however, most Jews no longer stay within the boundaries of their original communities, any more than Israelis feel bound to stay in Israel. Most Jews increasingly steer away from frozen communal structures in preference to living within frameworks that are more conducive to dynamic life processes. In terms of the new paradigm, the former Jewish attribute of loyalty to the nation has shifted, in accordance with Capra's second attribute. Had it not been for Israel's state of siege, it would have long merged with other attributes and, thus, lost its primary position altogether. Viewing it in the light of this ongoing process, loyalty to the nation will not feature as a primary attribute in new paradigm Judaism.

2. Unity at all costs

This attribute has been constantly beset by contradiction and polarity. Contrary to unity, the leading contemporary concept regarding human societies is that of *pluralism*. Arne Naess goes a step further: he upholds *diversity* (as distinct from mere plurality) as the most cherished quality in life. If unity indicates permanence befitting a building, diversity is amenable to the metaphor of a network. Contemporary Jewish life certainly resembles a network more than it does a permanent building. Unity at all costs no longer holds as a primary attribute in present-day Judaism.

3. Contradiction

Side by side with polarity, and sometimes synonymous with it, contradiction runs throughout Judaism. But, while polarity was acknowledged by Jewish Sages, and was even branded with the objectionable title of "vain hatred," contradiction was all but ignored. And, since it is not possible to shift away from an entity that one is not aware of, the shift suggested here is in the very awareness of its existence — furthermore, of contradiction being a core element in Judaism. But it goes further than that: the awareness suggested here refers to Judaism as existing outside of Halachic boundaries, and thus becomes a major shift in Jewish consciousness. Judaism has ceased to be "objective," becoming increasingly what every individual takes it to be — i.e., a part of every individual's "epistemology." Contradiction, as well as its derivation, polarity, is our first, newly discovered primary attribute of Judaism.

4. Obeying all of God's Commandments

This, containing the notion that we Jews, and only we, were given the benediction at the Mount Sinai Revelation, has for long generations been religious Judaism's chief characterizer. It has undergone shifts — first, with the creation of normative Judaism in the first Return to Zion (see Chapter 7) and, second, with the advent of Enlightenment in Europe in the eighteenth century. Since then, in no way can this attribute reflect the overall existing Jewish paradigm. Rather, it reflects an anachronism — still used insidiously in Israel to wield political power — and, like the next attribute, is to be discarded forthwith as being exclusively past-oriented.

The shift here derives from the fact that this original Jewish attribute negates *all* the new paradigm ones. I have little desire to pursue this matter in great detail; however, for a reader who has such a need, it may present a meaningful experience in new-paradigm discourse. For instance, should one consider each of the so-called Biblical Mizvot in order to reject their relevance to life or, rather, realize that blind obedience is an old-paradigm attribute and, hence, cannot feature in our envisioned new-paradigm Judaism?

5. The Notion of a Chosen People

This attribute behooves eternal separateness and, as such, has no place in the new paradigm. In Brother David's understanding it would have to be totally discarded. As has been abundantly demonstrated, in Halachic Judaism a whole can be nothing but a Jewish whole, yet a certain shift may have occurred here. In Capra's view, the first shift is in conceiving a whole first; and, as far as a nation is concerned, that larger whole should now be taken to be the universal worldview — as has been promulgated by our Ethical Prophets. From this universal perspective, Judaism might now be able to proceed to regard itself as a chosen part in disseminating the universal message. If this shift ever occurs, then, and only then, this projected shift may yet become the most meaningful in new-paradigm Judaism. For the time being, however, being chosen by God — as understood by most Jews — denotes infinite separateness rather then universal consciousness, and is to be shelved..

6. The Rule of Justice

This ancient Hebrew attribute has long metamorphosed — first, by turning separatist and, then, by giving in to Messianism. If we are tempted to re-examine this elevated, originally-Hebrew principle, we need to ask, What in the envisaged new paradigm can be regarded as constituting a legitimate shift away from our Messianic concept? Messianism has been the most protruding lighthouse in the Jewish faith; and it can be said that the passion of the first pioneers was borne, at least in part, on the wings of the Messianic spirit. The Messianic image may, likewise, transform into a dedication toward social and ecological causes. In some way, if the Messianic concept represents an immutable attribute of God's workings — the *truth* — it can be now seen as being metamorphosed — or shifted — into its *approximation*, into the diversified impulse toward ecological and social balance, as portrayed in Isaiah's End of Days vision, thus making a full circle, bringing Judaism back to its erstwhile acumen for justice. As it stands, it cannot rate as a primary attribute of contemporary Judaism.

7. Being the Victim

This is one of the old Jewish paradigm's strangest aberrations. It is self-righteous, blatantly separatist and bodes destruction. Being deeply rooted in history, it promotes fanaticism, very much like its present-day Islamic collateral. It has no support in new paradigm thinking — unless it is miraculously reversed to promote unconditional compassion toward the other. It would take a huge effort to uproot or, alternatively, transform it. The chance of this projected metamorphosis — of being-the-victim-turned-compassionate — is so remote, that it is of little consequence to regard it as constituting a present-day paradigm attribute.

8. Wanderers by Nature

Wandering can result either from choice or, alternatively, from dire necessity. The epithet *Wandering Jew* certainly denotes the latter. Yet we have seen that, more often than not, throughout our history, our brethren have *chosen* to wander — or, at least, stay away — from their Homeland. A future-oriented wandering-out-of-choice may result from plain curiosity and, thus, become a part of the primary attribute of *creativity*, which we will consider later.

9. Balance

This, by its very nature, should be regarded as the most cherished life-preserving attribute. Yet Judaism seldom advocates it as applying either nationally or universally. All the same, it has maintained it *in practice* through most dire experiences. It is an all-embracing attribute, strongly related to Capra's first attribute and should emphatically rate as a primary one in Judaism, too.

10. Community Life

The basic question regarding this attribute is whether it denotes unity or separateness. Jewish communities displayed unique cohesiveness until fairly recently; and, at the same time, community leaders often barred, with all their might, any of their members from joining the "outside world." In Israel, traditional communities often keep their old traditions, brought over from the countries they themselves regard as "exile." New, non-traditional communities are also formed and sometimes thrive in Israel — and, indeed, show every sign of promoting an alternative lifestyle. But this life-exuding practice is not necessarily "Jewish" — unless some Jewish restrictions are imposed on it, such as not playing music or using microphones in public gatherings on the Sabbath. Community life, though vital for spiritual growth, may take some time before it becomes a positive influence in our new national reality. Regarding life in Israel as a whole, the predicted shift in this area is in freeing Jewish community life altogether from the stifling effects of Jewish separateness. This is another case when an ongoing process indicates a shift, enabling us to regard an inconclusive attribute as *potentially* primary.

11. Creativity

Having been fairly thoroughly discussed earlier in this chapter, there is little we should add regarding this primary Jewish attribute. This vital human quality falls well within all of Capra's new attributes. Clearly, it will require a huge *creative* effort to transform what is inimical to life in our national old mentality, and utilize the proverbial Jewish vitality in the spirit of the new perspective.

12. Continuity

This is by far the most life-exuding quality in Judaism. It has deep roots in the Jewish lore and goes all the way back to the first pronouncement in the first Commandment, pointing at the utmost attribute of Judaism as having freed itself from the House of Bondage. In new-paradigm thinking, it should far exceed the call for sectarian justice, denoting universal balance, as was pronounced by Israel's Prophets. As far as Capra's attributes are concerned, it underlines not only the attribute of shifting from structure to process, but extends it far into the future. It strongly supports both creativity and free communal lifestyle. Like all of our primary attributes, it needs to shift away from separatist tendencies. It then would feature prominently in Israel's survival as manifesting deep fraternal disposition. It may help transform also neighboring old paradigms that threaten Israel's existence. (This last point connects with what is usually regarded as a political issue, requiring a political solution. As explained in Chapter 13, our prolonged conflict can be attributed to our own paradigm no less than it is to Islamic fanatic tendencies.)

In summing up the foregoing survey, let me suggest the following: The new paradigm is unconditionally universal. What it behooves on its parts — including all separate national paradigms — is to join the universal march, believing, each and every partner, in the ability of the new perspective to preserve and promote the diversified potential of each part, it being embedded in all living phenomena.

The four *additional* attributes (9-12) — continuity, polarity, balance & creativity — have now surfaced to assume primary positions. They have emerged as such from the whole foregoing discussion and can be said to constitute, each, an organic compound, incorporating other, secondary attributes. Yet, by themselves, they somehow do not seem to paint a satisfying picture of Judaism. There is a simple reason for it: nothing about them is specifically Jewish! This could be remedied, of course, by prefixing them with the title "Jewish," turning them into "Jewish continuity," "Jewish polarity," etc. But this mechanical amendment will not suffice — for there is a deep reason for their estrangement. The chief, primary Jewish attribute — separateness — is missing here. Separateness is an attribute that has never abated in the whole duration of Jewish history. When brought over from the earlier list, separateness should weld all the primary attributes into describing present-day Judaism.

The final list of primary Jewish attributes should now read as follows:

1. Separateness;
2. Continuity;
3. Polarity;
4. Balance'
5. Creativity.

Let us consider a little further the question of the *necessity* of combining separateness with the other primary attributes. Continuity for instance, denotes perpetuity and is connected with community-life. But community, as we have seen, often denoted unity *as well as* separateness. It is therefore necessary to keep in mind, when referring to continuity as embodying a new-paradigm attribute, to always uphold its life-exuding qualities, for, otherwise, what looks continuous or perpetual, may easily turn out to negate life. The human race has *continuously* waged destructive wars, at times destroying whole cultures and races. It has now reached an age when it cannot contain total wars any longer. From now on, those "glorious" wars, which in our schools still rate as the inevitable, permanent cornerstones of human history, cannot be part and parcel of what we consider to be a future-oriented, life-exuding attribute.

The question arising here is: Why do we include separateness at all as a primary attribute of *present*-day Judaism? Have not many Jews moved, to some extent, closer to others in recent centuries? I take this to be a key question in forming our new paradigm.

A new paradigm requires shifts from, *but not total negation of*, the past. If the Jewish new paradigm were to annul separateness altogether, the result would not be exactly Jewish, would it? The new paradigm needs to *contain* extremes; it cannot do away with them altogether. Polarity, for instance, could be taken to negate balance, but this is not at all the case. While total balance may indicate a certain reduction of polarity, it may also denote death rather than life. (This last claim has been put forward by Stefan Harding, the scientist in residence at Schumacher College, based on a mathematical model of the universe he has developed there.)

Separateness, then, needs to be contained by a continuous interplay with Judaism's other attributes — all of them undergoing substantial shifts in the process.

This chapter, though being rather long, should actually encourage the reader to prolong it even further — each within her or his respective field of interest. To exemplify this, I've devised the following exercise, entitled, *Rules of the Five Jewish New Paradigm Primary Attributes.*

Out of the five we have enumerated, the new game relies heavily on the second player, i.e., *Continuity* (sometimes masquerading as *Perpetuity) and* the fourth, i.e., the *Balancing* player. Together, they keep the game going. These two players tend to keep at bay the oldest participant, called *Separateness*, but accept *Polarity*, that ever-contradicting third player (for, even in their playful mood, they realize that it is ever-present in nature as well as in humans!). Polarity must of course be harnessed by the force of Balance — this impartial umpire — without which no good game can be played for long. This tug of war demands perpetual renewal (we're back to the second and the fourth guys), and the diminution of the separatist influence, in spite of it coming from the most experienced player on the field. They all rather like the last, rather enigmatic fellow that keeps popping up. It is called *Creativity*. (In his Book of Rules, called *The Turning Point*, Capra regards life's perpetual re-creation as manifesting an interchange between homeostasis and change. In our terms, they simply don other titles. i.e., the last four on our list.) Back to our game, in our nasty moments, we might nickname *Creativity "Jewish Nosiness;"* but we must admit that nosiness makes for intimacy — something our "civilized" behavior is so sorely in need of! *Over-Aggressiveness* and *Elitism*, those evil partners to *Separateness*, have no place in our playground whatsoever. True, they often seem to be winning in the short run, but, in the final results, they prove to be a major handicap to everyone, not least to themselves.

With this team, it seems that the new primary attributes of Judaism enable it to join hands with the changing world, even make a rich contribution. It is largely a matter of choice — once the conditions are ripe and the choice is clearly outlined. In order to effect such a substantial shift, it needs to be done collectively, but, remembering that collectives are made up of individuals, it is *they* who need to make a choice first. They can do it in small, intimate, separate groups. But would not separateness deter them from working in integrated groups? Well, it seems that in small portions this old fellow does not necessarily have to be negative — after all, a group is always, to some extent, separate from other groups, and needs its own symbols and identifiers. Separateness is, indeed, necessary — so long as it does not curb the forces of continuity, balance and creativity; and as long as it does not select one extreme to totally exclude and/or demonize the other.

This exercise by no means represents a "truth;" rather, it is a vision, an approximation of a probable future situation. More than anything, it articulates my belief that within Judaism there exist rich qualities, which may enhance and nurture the conception of a new national paradigm, enabling all Jews, as Jews, to become active partners in a sustainable, universal new reality.

We are through and through a politically conscious people — which is probably true of other nations bred on strife, like the Irish and present-day Palestinians. It seems therefore of little use to propagate a new concept unless it points at some practical solutions for our pressing situation. Throughout this study, I have maintained that our old paradigm constitutes a buffer against remedying most of what ails us. And yet, the impeding effect of our old paradigm is not necessarily evident in all fields in Israel: our economy, for example, seems to be thriving. But this is a short-term illusion — for, while it is permanently inflated by outside financial support, at the same time, our hi-tech renowned manpower is increasingly deserting this country, due to the state's slipping fast into a fundamental abyss.

Out of Israel's complex situation, we have dealt extensively with Messianism, which has recently proved to be the most threatening element to our democratic fiber. I have suggested it to be viewed in the context of adhering to our ancient Mitzvot and to having lived away from the Land. But, earlier in this study, we found that today's basic issues are all multi- and intra-national, leaving no people or country outside the global processes. So why should living away from one's homeland matter? Has not air travel become so general that the place of residence — be it one's home or a nation's homeland — has lost its importance? And have we not recently heard that the end of history had come, wherein old national values would have little part to play? But all this does not apply, so it seems, to so many members of our wandering nation!

How could this happen at a time when we, being a liberal democracy of sorts, should have long become part of the open global village?

The ideological concentration on the Holy Land of our Messiah's representatives abroad — whose aim is to cleanse it from the soiling presence of non-Jews — needs no illustration. The trouble is that their support for their cause amounts to hundreds of millions of dollars, coming from innumerable ultra-Orthodox centers and individuals, worldwide. This affects Israeli government's decisions as well as non-governmental educational establishments, "settlers'" organizations and more besides. It is clear that, had it not been for Jewish centers *away* from Israel, the Messianic impulse would have precious little to thrive on *within* Israel.

All this happens when much of contemporary Western Jewry couldn't care less about the Messiah! Jews, worldwide, are gradually abandoning Judaism, because the old religion provides them with little spiritual and even less material substance. But there has remained one common area in which polarized old-paradigm Judaism can operate: the State of Israel. To divest Judaism from the Messianic separatist cloak is, therefore, a most urgent task. The irony of it is that this kind of shift could originate only at the receiving end, in Israel, where the harm is most deeply felt, while it is here that new modes of thinking fare so badly.

A paradigm shift cannot come about in a vacuum. It goes contrary to the mechanistic mega-concept that predominates in the West and sweeps over the rest of the world like a blaze across a parched field. It must draw on the best the new concept has to offer. A new worldview, we say, is necessary for survival; its Jewish shoot is still tender, but it may flourish yet — when not strangulated by the ogre of Messianic fanaticism.

Old Judaism keeps its hallowed as well as temporal *reserves* away from the Israel. It is, indeed, anomalous: Judaism thrives globally, but keeps up its endemic separateness *within* the global situation. There is no escaping from the realization that, as long as we do not shift consciously away from this anachronistic arrangement, the old Jewish paradigm will go on successfully impeding the nation of Israel from becoming normal — let alone adopting a new paradigm. This is the main reason which made me entitle this book "Toward a new *Jewish* Paradigm," rather than concerning myself with the rather restricted — however balligerent — *Israeli* paradigm.

It is not really possible to foretell where exactly the shift will manifest itself, and in what manner it will develop here. No one recommends a *state ministry* to issue new-paradigm regulations! One can certainly witness some life- and future-oriented attributes being aired and put into practice in Israel. My hope is that my words are heeded by those new-paradigm practitioners — first and foremost by my children's generation. While increasingly questioning the validity of their Judaism, they are also attracted to New Age discourse and some of its practice. Yet they are often deterred from adopting mew-paradigm attitudes, half-consciously attaching to them the sterility of the West, of which they constitute a part....

Local new consciousness needs to develop through an organic relationship with what goes on in the world. Yet it is also possible for an Israeli to discover universal tenets dormant in *Jewish* values, as long as he/she finds new ways to remold that inheritance to serve the new demands of life.

Let me also suggest: the fact that the Zionist paradigm has been shaken to its foundations should not necessarily discourage anyone from embracing the new paradigm. Zionism resembles the new worldview a lot more than does traditional Judaism. Its relatively short life-span in no way proves a new Jewish paradigm is destined to fail. On the contrary: it should highlight the *possibility* of creating a new Jewish paradigm, when the missing dimension in Zionism is introduced — that of integrating the best in Judaism with the rest of the world.

Finally, I wish to pay special homage to Israel's festivals. For many secular people they constitute their major emotional bond to Judaism. Earlier, when I touched on the holidays, my stress was on what must be excluded from them, viz. the customs, laws and texts that glorify and perpetuate separateness and hatred of the stranger. But I have also suggested the composition of new texts and new rituals. Many people, young and old, teachers, artists and parents, are creating new molds for Israel's festivals and enlarge on the existing ones. Such innovations are introduced in many parts of the world — in fact, I believe, more abroad then here, in Israel, where Halachic instruction is increasingly becoming the law. This is one of my suggestions as to how non-Israeli Jewry can help us here: spiritually! It is a lot more beneficial than financial handouts, which, like power, corrupt.

From the outset I feared that, having expected a detailed plan for action, many readers might be disappointed in not finding one here — one of instant effect. Even before the Hebrew publication of this book, I was asked to supply practical guidance. "What should we *do* right *now*?" many asked, impatiently. What is the point of writing a book of no *practical* value, they seemed to be saying, while many, anyway, do such wonderful new-paradigm work? Isn't that what matters most — even when not called new paradigm? I myself often join "new paradigm" acts — such as assisting nine-year-olds who study traditional agriculture, plowing with a donkey — forgetting all about paradigms. But then the Halachic backlash keeps invading young people's homes and hearts, putting all progressive attitudes on the defensive. This is when I become convinced that clearing the ground in order to enable the new paradigm to take root on Israeli soil must be done, first and foremost, by addressing its *Jewish* aspect, as I have tried to do here.

A paradigm is not a detailed order of the day, but, rather (repeat after me!), "all thoughts, views and values which together form the picture that represents the frame and the direction in which society apprehends and organizes itself." Unfortunately, to create this framework takes time. Even Honi ha-Me'agel — that mystic who questioned the wisdom in planting a tree whose fruit the planter would never live to eat — needed seventy years to learn his lesson. Still, the pace of modern life is much more rapid than it was two thousand years ago. The dangers, too, are faster in coming. An Iraqi missile travels faster than a Roman galley. And if the term paradigm still sounds alien to many, it is not a minute too soon to get closely acquainted with it.

What is there to *do*? My answer is, to discover and encourage every new paradigm thought, act and deed, and internalize the knowledge that we are already in the future, in a new age.

Afterword

Concerning Jewish mysticism, diversity & new-paradigm Islam.

Throughout this study, I have refrained from referring to one particular area of Jewish teaching — that of the Kabbala. On the whole, mysticism has attained eminence in new-paradigm discourse; so, why not mention the leading Jewish mystical school while envisioning a new Jewish paradigm?

I admit personally to having little need for mystical elements in my worldview; but this cannot explain my reluctance to treat the subject fairly. My objection to Kabbala — by far exceeding my hesitation toward some other mystical disciplines — derives from its basic separatist element. Whenever the subject comes up, the Kabbalist will introduce its main feature as the ability to divine untold secrets inherent in the Hebrew letters of the Bible. In my understanding this means that, by definition, those who are unable to read Hebrew will never truly understand the powers of creation.

The Hebrew Bible is translatable, of course. Its translated texts have become cultural cornerstones for great parts of humanity, whatever scripts they are written in. The New Testament, too, reaches most of us through translation: originally, it was written in Greek, while Jesus must have spoken Aramaic, sprinkled with Hebrew quotes from the Bible. Still, I am invited to read it in any language and am not told I must go back to the original in order to understand what Jesus said. But not so with the Kabbala: despite some claims about it being the most Westernized of mystical schools, the said, self-imposed restriction makes most if not all non-Jews unable to share its secrets.

But what about other branches of mysticism? Surely, there are many of us who are no longer satisfied with what rational explanations have to offer. Many physical phenomena — let alone reflections, moods and spiritual yearnings — do not fit into rational explanation. The question can now be extended to apply to paradigm shifts as a whole: do they require — or fit into — any rational explanation? Let us take a bird's eye view of some major transitions in our world and find out whether they constitute any consistent, rational pattern.

Mid-eighth century B.C.E., the universal perspective was pronounced, first in Samaria and then in Jerusalem, by Israel's great *monotheists*. Three and a half centuries later, not a week's sailing trip from Jaffa, the Greek *polytheists* elevated diversity to the heights of human achievement, at the same time heralding individual choice and excellence in a way that could not have been dreamt of by the Hebrews. In Plato's dialogue, Phaedrus, we read:

> "Everyone chooses his love from the universal ranks of beauty, according to his character. Then he molds his choice, makes it his god, falls down before it and worships it. (...) The followers of Zeus desire that their beloved should have a soul like Zeus, and when they have found their lover, they do all they can to confirm such godlike nature in him. (...) Their recollections cling to that image, they become obsessed by it and, finally, they receive from it the very character and disposition they themselves endowed it with."

While this lucid expression of burgeoning *diversity* was written, Judaism had sunk into Halachic sectarianism, wielded by Ezra's *haredim.* But then, four centuries later, a Jew named Jesus turned the tables again, making monotheism the guiding force in Western culture for centuries to come. His followers branded the Greeks pagan, destroyed their art and tore down their magnificent temples. The Renaissance tried to create an amalgam, eventually declaring *science* to be the height of human achievement. But not for long. Three centuries after Newton, Western man has hit a blank wall, when unable to find happiness in his monistic, mechanistic, linear worldview. Now Far-Eastern non-linear and diversified modes of thinking are rushing in for the rescue, supplying new cures for the arid soul of Western man. This new shift is often led by women, bringing to mind Joseph Campbell's strident accusation of the Judeans for having been the first to brand the pre-Biblical reigning she-deity — a monster!

Is polytheism (or its collateral, diversity) the contemporary order of the day? Not so — if judging by monotheistic fundamentalism raging about us. For an Israeli, the question becomes increasingly pressing by the hour: Is there any way one can combat, for one, the Islamic threat to liberal values, rationally? Many of my enlightened friends — including some erudite, open-minded Christians — say outright that fundamentalism is inherent in Muhammad's teaching and personal biography to a degree that puts it beyond repair. My intuition tells me quite another tale.

In communicating on a daily basis with Palestinian friends, I have experienced layers of warmth and emotional intelligence, characteristic to their Islamic upbringing, far beyond the common Western capacity. Such moments made me able to appreciate afresh — what my rational mind had informed me earlier, without success — the gigantic Islamic cultural achievement, without which none of Western civilization could have arisen from the Dark Ages.

Looking at the aforementioned shifts in Western civilization shows that the separatist periodical outbreaks have always given in to a kind of inclusiveness. What is new about the present shift is that it indicates a truly new mode of observation. It is no longer the "correct" cure combating rationally an "incorrect" aberration. Rather, it is the deep-ecological approach of finding in the other the basic elements inherent in all living systems — and, therefore, a one, which should be embraced universally — leading toward containment rather than eternal conflicts of opposites.

I am thoroughly convinced that a new-paradigm-Islam researcher is at work, somewhere, this very moment. I wish we had discovered each other sooner. My request is, please, get in touch.

About the author

As a youth, Mokadi fought in the 1948 war, defending the kibbutz where he was raised. Having completed his military service, he went to London to study drama, and for the greater part of his life, acted and directed in, and wrote for, the theatre, both in Israel and in England (including two coast-to-coast tours of North America). In London, Mokadi won the William Poel Memorial Prize for dramatic rendition, jointly with Judi Dench, and in Israel, his film, "Repeat Dive," won the Best Film Award in 1982.

Mokadi has founded a number of theatres in Israel and England and taught in a variety of colleges, including Tel Aviv and Beer Sheba Universities.

Mokadi is a peace activist of long standing, having recently directed the film "Flowers of Hope," describing nine-year-olds from both Israel and Palestine, spending a year together working the land. About "Flowers of Hope" David Grossman has written: "…the natural warm touch among children and among adults who are enemies for a time… the generous forgiving seed which is still alive…"

Mokadi's recent written works include: A historical fiction — a trilogy — "Life of a Prophet", on the life of the Biblical prophet, Amos (1987-1995); a volume of short stories "My Sister Ileah" (1994); "The Challenge, a New Jewish Paradigm" (Hebrew edition, 1997).

The next novel, "Just living," based on his father's pioneering days in Ottoman Palestine early last century, is nearing completion.

Mokadi lives near Jerusalem, is married and has five children.